Liberating Service Learning
and the Rest of Higher Education
Civic Engagement

Liberating Service Learning and the Rest of Higher Education Civic Engagement

RANDY STOECKER

TEMPLE UNIVERSITY PRESS
Philadelphia • Rome • Tokyo

TEMPLE UNIVERSITY PRESS
Philadelphia, Pennsylvania 19122
www.temple.edu/tempress

Library of Congress Cataloging-in-Publication Data

Names: Stoecker, Randy, 1959– author.
Title: Liberating service learning and the rest of higher education civic engagement / Randy
 Stoecker.
Description: Philadelphia, Pennsylvania : Temple University Press, 2016. | Includes
 bibliographical references and index.
Identifiers: LCCN 2015039523| ISBN 9781439913512 (hardback : alk. paper) | ISBN
 9781439913529 (paperback : alk. paper) | ISBN 9781439913536 (e-book)
Subjects: LCSH: Service learning—United States. | Civics—Study and teaching
 (Higher)—United States. | Community and college—United States. | Education,
 Higher—Aims and objectives—United States. | BISAC: EDUCATION / Higher. |
 EDUCATION / Philosophy & Social Aspects. | SOCIAL SCIENCE / Research.
Classification: LCC LC220.5 .S76 2016 | DDC 361.37—dc23
LC record available at http://lccn.loc.gov/2015039523

Printed in the United States of America

9 8 7 6 5 4 3 2 1

To all those who struggle against oppression, exploitation, and exclusion

Contents

Prelude

Confessions and Acknowledgments

"I think you need to deal with the question up front: 'Do I have a right to write this book?'" So my friend and colleague Larry Stillman challenged me on reading my first draft.

Indeed, do I? This book confronts what I do and the reasons that I do it. It points a spotlight glare on my own contradictions. It pushes past my comfort zone and the comfort zones of colleagues who have read and commented on my early drafts.

Writing a book that confronts the sacred assumptions of the higher education civic engagement establishment feels risky. And perhaps it is. Until early July 2015, I was a tenured full professor, a member of the faculty in one of the top-ranked graduate programs in the United States at one of the top-tier universities in the world. But the Wisconsin state government, controlled entirely by far-right politicians, passed a "revision" to the tenure statutes that for all practical purposes eliminated academic freedom. So I am now forced to consider what in this book might risk my employment or my ability to get a new job in a university where tenure is still protected. Well, I've considered it, and decided that if I can't write the book that I think needs to be written, then I shouldn't write at all. But it now feels a lot more risky than it did when I wrote the first draft.

Even having said that, my salary is now over $100,000 per year—an amount I used to say no one should earn. And even with the hatred of educators and knowledge spreading throughout the state of Wisconsin, I am still among the privileged.

So I am working through my feeling of risk. I am embarrassed by this feeling because my actual risks pale in comparison to the everyday risks of the people "in the community" I purport to use my position to support. None of them have any job protection at all. Many of them don't have jobs. Most of them experience housing and food insecurity on a regular basis. They live in a milieu where chemical dependency, violence, racial profiling, and the health effects of concentrated poverty produce sometimes irreversible damage.

So I write this book partly to honor their everyday risks that now include the risks they take whenever one of us academics or our students appear on their doorstep with an offer of "partnership." I write with the hope that I may help to reduce their risk in doing so. And I am heartened that at least some of my friends who have read my early drafts and heard my talks on this topic think that these things need to be said.

I also write this book out of a need to be honest with myself. Over the year that I spent working on the first draft, what I was learning compelled me to resign from two leadership positions. In one case, I was a trustee for a philanthropic foundation that funded forms of action research, including community-university partnerships. As a board of trustees, we were academics deciding who would be funded and who would not be and paying ourselves an annual honorarium collectively equal to a grant. It eventually became obvious to me how wrong both things were. In the other case, I was on a steering committee for a network trying to focus community-based research on community outcomes. But all funding, public relations, and leadership were controlled through universities, and here again the contradictions eventually became too much for me. So I have seen the oppressor from the inside. Indeed, I have been complicit in the oppression perpetrated by both foundations and universities. Knowing the contorted self-justifying politics of elitist academic control over supposed community-university partnerships from the inside also gives me a standpoint to say something about it because I have been, and to an extent still am, part of the problem.

But I must ask the question from another angle. Do I only think I have a right to write this book because I have the privilege of being critical? Comfortable as I am with my upper middle class job that pays all the bills, I can make unaccountable critiques about what we should and should not do to "help" those who can't pay their bills, all while I am lacking the personal experience of oppression, exploitation, and exclusion (though I will note that growing up rural and working class definitely helped me appreciate the value of a dollar). And my critiques, if taken wrong, could result in those who have less getting even less. Who am I to say what the oppressed, the exploited, and the excluded deserve and when they deserve it?

Here I am heartened that at least I am not pursuing my own critique but attempting to learn from and amplify the critiques of those who directly experience these issues. The book *The Revolution Will Not Be Funded*, for example, was not written solely by academics but substantially by constituency-based activists coming out of activist discussions. And most of my other work is informed by the voices of those struggling directly with a sick social system and/or those actively working to change it.

So I don't know if I have a right to write this book, but I feel compelled to write it. For me, it is a journey of self-discovery. Doing service learning has, from my very first attempts, felt like wearing a hair shirt—a constant state of physical discomfort—though in this case the discomfort comes from inside, from the gut. There is something that feels almost inherently unfair about service learning, like an imposition. And it's not just an imposition on impoverished community members. It's also an imposition on students—an extra set of requirements heaped upon students who are already too busy just fulfilling the basic requirements of reading the books, writing the papers, and taking the tests, along with working as many hours as they can to help pay my salary.

I have been "practicing" forms of community-engaged scholarship including service learning for thirty years now, and in my case practice does not make perfect. In fact, the more I practice, the more imperfect I feel—the more I see the contradictions, the unrealized potential, the unrecognized urgency of the causes. I worry about the amount of time that community organization staff and community members put into partnership projects where the benefits may be indirect and tangential to the community's most pressing needs. I worry about the time that students put into projects they say that they learned little from because I tried to make sure that they had already learned what they needed to know to do the project well. I worry about the grant money that we seek out to do the projects and the compromises and conflicts those funds create among impoverished community residents who want to be paid with that money and then argue over who should be paid. Every project I do only helps me see more problems with how we do this work.

But I worry most about the practice I see all around me. Service learning offices that have reduced themselves to volunteer pipelines rather than thriving intellectual centers for figuring out how to maximize community learning and community outcomes. University administrators who think the goal is to get more service learning rather than better and wouldn't know what "better" was if it came up and hugged them. And my ever stronger feeling that there is something fundamentally wrong with our practice. None of the existing critiques go deep enough; none of the existing alternatives seem alternative enough. I can't find a path in this field that feels truly good both morally and technically.

So the final way I think of Larry's question is whether I have a right to criticize the hard work of so many people in the field. Who am I to stand in judgment of scholars who are at least as educated, practiced, and well meaning as I? Criticism seems to be out of vogue in service learning. On most campuses, service learning is "celebrated" rather than critiqued, with the mantra about the importance of reflection relegated to a twice-a-semester in-class exercise rather than the core of the practice. So I feel very self-conscious offering a critique.

But I can't ignore the depth of my disappointment with what we have not accomplished, and I can't shake my sense of compulsion to try to make it better. So this book is my search to find out why I feel so alienated from a practice that I spend so much time doing, researching, and writing about. Our current practice can't just *feel* wrong, it has to *be* wrong. I am wearing a hair shirt without even understanding what I am penitent for.

Of course, it's actually not true that I have no idea. I do have some. I know that I'm a fish out of water in academia to begin with. I'm first-generation college from a rural working class background one generation off the farm, fitting in neither the conservative circumstances from which I came nor the high-brow culture in which I now exist. And my life-long success in school has meant that I have literally been "in school" since I was five years old—half a century. It's just that in 1988 I started getting paid for it. But for a rural working class kid to be in school invokes a certain sense of uselessness. Real people—in my case real men—do real work. They come home dirty, with calluses on their hands, sore backs, and an in-bred resentment of those who live privileged lives. They learn how to use a pipe wrench by using a pipe wrench, and their results are immediate and visible—the water flows without leaking, the electricity flows without tripping the breaker, the textured paint covers the drywall tape and joint compound that covers the drywall that covers the wall studs.

I was taught, not by school, that accomplishment is about visible results. And I must admit that my greatest satisfaction still comes from doing the hand work of the working class, even though I'm a rank amateur hobbled by a life spent in school, too soft and too old to survive an eight- or ten-hour day doing real work. So I try to turn school into real work through "civic engagement." I am proud of some of the successes I have been a part of (and, to be clear, only a small part): $2 million for neighborhood-based development groups in Toledo, a couple of community development victories in the Cedar-Riverside neighborhood of Minneapolis, better information technology for Australian neighborhood organizations, improved community organizing and lower crime in Toledo's Lagrange neighborhood, a new community center in southwest Madison, and a few others. But none of these have come easy. Many are the equivalent of putting up the wall crooked, tearing it down, putting it up again, and then getting the biggest hammer you have and pounding it until it's plumb and square. And all around me I see others engaged in higher education civic engagement who don't even care if a wall gets built, let alone whether it is quality construction.

So I am writing to figure out whether and how I can feel good about doing this work, and that means I need to figure out whether there are practical ways to do it better. Not a little better. A lot better. Because things are really bad out there. Workers are losing their right to organize, women are losing their right to control their own bodies, the poor and the elderly are losing their right to vote, and those who have endured the legacy of slavery, genocide, and colonization continue to find not just liberty and the pursuit of happiness but life itself to be elusive dreams. And if I can't make a difference—not a maybe-someday-in-the-future-because-some-student-I-taught-maybe-influenced-someone-who-maybe-indirectly-influenced-some-change difference but an immediate and visible direct difference in the ability of a collective of oppressed, exploited, and excluded people to gain and practice power—then I have failed.

I have also failed if I can't help turn out students who can also do this. For a brief shining moment in 2011 and 2012, I saw hope. My graduate students (and I am proud to say that a number of them were *my* graduate students—my advisees) helped lead the occupation of the Wisconsin state capitol against the anti-democratic, anti-worker, anti-justice policies of the right-wing politicians who had taken power. The next time I taught my community organizing course, I realized that nearly everyone in the class had slept in the capitol, had carried a sign, or had otherwise been involved in struggling for justice. But when I most recently taught the course, only a handful of the students had even been to a demonstration. They had no experience to draw on—nothing to make the class material come alive for them. All this service learning and an entire community organizing class of students had no service learning with any *civic* engagement—only *service* engagement.

So I do have to write this book. But only as a way of clarifying my own purpose. I do not attempt to write on behalf of, in place of, or in advocacy for, anyone. And I have not just a right but an obligation to be part of the solution rather than part of the problem.

But I must admit that, while I alone take responsibility for the words on these pages, I alone cannot take credit. It was not just me writing this book; it was me writing through all the experiences and all the voices of all I have encountered. Those who labored through my first draft—Mary Brydon-Miller, Bessa Whitmore, Beth Tryon, Larry Stillman—were especially the kinds of friends I needed. They told me when I was going too far. I admit that I have not heeded all of their advice, but I have listened to it.

I also need to thank what remains of the culture of academia and the University of Wisconsin–Madison's adherence to it. I wrote the very first draft of this book while "on sabbatical"—basically a semester free from my regular job obligations to do projects just like this. Everyone (yes, I mean everyone) should have such benefits, and it is an indicator of our lack of enlightenment as a society that they are not universal.

I sit here writing with Joey, the fifty-pound standard poodle snuggled on top of my right arm. Pretty soon he will hop off the couch and use his combination laser beam stare and bosun's whistle whine to demand a walk. As of this paragraph, he's still a pup at just under two years, and it would be unrealistically anthropomorphic of me to pretend that he thinks I need a break. He simply thinks he needs a walk. But it still serves the purpose of getting me away from the laptop and out into the fresh air (fresh air this time of year being about ten degrees Fahrenheit with the wind blowing the real-feel temperature down to below zero).

Another part of this book was written with another dog and a cat. Koda and Ginger, respectively, were my companions at Heather and Don's place up in central Canada. There is no road where they live, but there is wifi! You either take a boat or hike a mile through the woods to get there. In a house built on a rise up from the lake, their kitchen and living room look out across one of the most peaceful landscapes available to humans in the fall, after all the summer cottagers have evacuated back to the city. Every morning for three days I got to take a walk in the woods with Koda running free around me. Then during the day, with Heather and Don off to work, Ginger would come to visit, curling up on my lap purring (Mary Ann, the other family cat, remained assertively at a distance). The peacefulness brought some calm to my angst, hopefully enhancing my reflexivity.

I always want to acknowledge the perspective I get from the other members of my family: Tammy my life partner, and Haley our daughter. Tammy's patience with my demands for alone time both allows me to write and keeps me reflective. She is, to my amazement, able to juggle sometimes hourly phone interruptions and chefery (she is still the most amazing vegan chef I know) with her own writing, while a single interruption will throw my concentration off for the next hour. And Haley, having just finished her undergraduate degree, has become a mirror for my own intellectualism/activism. A dual African American studies and history major, her hyperbole makes me simultaneously cringe and cheer. It makes me cringe because it sounds just like the academic rants I tend toward. It makes me cheer because, deep down, it's right even when its tone is confrontational.

I have had student role models who have inspired my thinking in the past few years. You will read in these pages about my growing interest in allyship. Dadit Hidayat showed me how this practice works in his relationship with The Natural Step Monona organization, and he brought me in for the excitement of a three-year social change project with the group. Charity Schmidt and Dena Ohlinger showed me what it means to take allyship to its self-sacrificing logical conclusion. Ashleigh Ross, in a dissertation ultimately critiquing her own engagement scholarship work in New Orleans, gave me courage to develop my critique and apply it to my work.

Then there are the community groups. My friends in Peterborough and Minden in Ontario are many, and I particularly want to recognize Todd Barr and Heather Reid. Each facilitated some of my writing retreat, but they did much more—connecting me to groups in Peterborough and Minden doing the work of community organizing and development and giving me opportunities to learn from them. I have also been particularly inspired by the people of southwest Madison, who are tackling some of the most challenging race and class conflicts in the city. They welcomed (and, indeed, increasingly *expected*) my allyship.

I also must thank a variety of brave service learning program directors and community-engaged faculty who in the past few years brought me to their campuses to try out and develop these ideas. I hesitate to name them lest their work be jeopardized through association with the ideas in this book, but they know who they are. And a doff of the hat to my colleagues in the Rural Alliance for Service Learning, who provide the single best collection of practices that approach the way I think our work should be done.

Perhaps most important are the community workers out there whose work is so much more on the ground than mine and from whom I have learned so much about daily perseverance. Jerry Braatz, Steve Chmielewski, Laura Dombrock, Amy Griel, and Ann Weid are all University of Wisconsin Cooperative Extension community educators who have engaged me with their work building neighborhood organizations in Waukesha, Wisconsin. And then there is Kim Neuschel, a public health nurse whose work channeling Lillian Wald—the founder of public health nursing—in southwest Madison has been awe inspiring. It is a great loss to the profession of public health nursing and the city of Madison that new administrators at Public Health Madison Dane County lacked the vision to continue the program supporting her work. Southwest Madison and I miss her fiercely.

Then, of course, someone has to make this work available to you, the reader. My relationship with Temple University Press began back in the 1990s. This is my third book with them, now with Micah Kleit as my editor. Micah was immediately supportive when I approached him with this idea, and he found supportive reviewers who helped identify the weaknesses and confusions in my thinking. Corey Dolgon and José Calderón both later revealed themselves to me. They are two of the best activist scholar role models I know and I'm proud and humbled that Temple would choose them to review this work. Temple's willingness to continue pursuing work that pushes the boundaries of higher education civic engagement is reassuring. Publishing a book is a lot of work, with a lot of moving parts, and Temple University Press organizes those parts as well as I have seen. I also want to thank Fran Andersen, of Newgen North America, for her efficient and skillful handling of both the production process and me. I'm protective of my writing style, probably to my own detriment, and Fran responded with kindness to my protests over copyediting. So I alone am responsible for whatever convoluted prose you find in the coming pages.

Finally, I commend you, dear reader, for taking up the challenge of trying out these ideas. If you are like me, you will alternately feel defensive, amused, and consternated. You might not see a clear path forward, but I hope you find ideas that can help guide the next path. May your journey be fruitful.

Liberating Service Learning
and the Rest of Higher Education
Civic Engagement

I

The Problem and
Its Context

1

Why I Worry

Summer 2013: I just left a student disciplinary hearing.

I was there to testify on the importance of student involvement in civil disobedience. The students being subjected to the university disciplinary process had been involved with a nascent worker organization in a year-long battle trying to get the university to cancel a contract with a pizza company that had thwarted a worker unionization effort and had engaged in questionable labor practices (Konopacki, 2013; Schneider, 2013a). The university chancellor had rebuffed the students' efforts and ignored a recommendation from a university committee to cancel the contract. Feeling that their requests for a dialogue with the chancellor were being ignored, the students resorted to the only tactic they believed would get the chancellor to meet with them—they occupied his office. But instead of dialogue, the administration responded with swift and forceful police action, busting in the door, unceremoniously removing the students, and bringing them up on student conduct charges.

Then, of course, came the disciplinary hearing.

The experience rubbed raw a worry inside me that had been festering for quite some time. What if the students had done this as part of a course? What if it had been an officially designated service learning course? Could I have put together a service learning course proposal for "students to engage with worker unionization efforts, including acts of civil disobedience focused on the university"? If your reaction is cynical laughter, you are not alone. And if your reaction is shock that I would even suggest such a thing, you are also probably not alone.

The occupying students, from my standpoint, were participating in the most honorable form of engaged learning. At great personal risk and sacrifice, they were supporting a community effort getting at one of the root causes of poverty—the poor pay and treatment of food workers. They had done their homework—on civil disobedience, on labor relations law, on the findings of National Labor Relations Board investigations into the vendor, and on workers' experiences in the workplace. In contrast to typical service learners, who put in their twenty hours (or fewer) and are never heard from again, these students had committed mind, soul, and body to a community cause for the duration of the struggle.

I needed to understand why (beyond, of course, the obvious power analysis) such engagement wouldn't be considered legitimate service learning. It was far more intellectual and far more deeply engaged than practically any example of service learning I can think of. If those students had been part of a course that included readings on food systems, food worker exploitation, and social action, their strategy and actions might have been even more thoughtful and more successful. But I have difficulty believing such a course would have been supported by the university as "valid" service learning.

But I also have a more basic concern. I need to understand why, even when it is promoted by the centers of the supposedly greatest and brightest intellects, service learning seems to focus on being the least intellectual practice in higher education. We seem to have shaped our service learning programs to offer the least we can rather than the most. The largest program at the Morgridge Center for Public Service, at my university, is the volunteer program. That program simply provides a pipeline of students to put in hours with service organizations. It connects to the institution's intellectual resources in only token ways. This program, consequently, is the least we can do, not the best.

I write as a service learning practitioner who is dissatisfied with my own practice as well as the practice I see in the literature and at conferences. I want to figure out a service learning practice that doesn't stop at totaling hours from time sheets, "building relationships," and providing a tick box for the university's community engagement Carnegie classification. I want a practice that becomes part of real social change—that helps to end conditions of oppression, exploitation, and exclusion in society.

So *Liberating Service Learning* is a purposeful double entendre—a dual meaning that defines this book.

Perhaps most obviously, *Liberating Service Learning* is about a form of service learning that "liberates" those who participate in it whether they come from the higher education institution or "the community."

My focus is the United States, where the practice and culture of higher education service learning seem to have become the most established, and the most problematic. In contrast to the European Union, where issues like "citizen access to science" and science shop models of research service have gained ascendance, or in Canada, where activists and academics have developed methods of community-based knowledge mobilization (though the pressures to reduce higher education civic engagement to a student education program are increasing in both places), here in the United States we seem to have remained stuck in a higher education–focused model of service learning. There is a long history in the United States, some of which we will explore, of using service learning to impact the thinking and attitudes of, that is, to "liberate," students. In fact, we could say that service learning in its contemporary, institutionalized form was founded on a mission of liberating students. Sometimes service learning advocates have based their work on an explicitly experiential pedagogy and other times on a moralistic student development approach. In either case, the goal has been student development.

There has also been a long-standing debate about the outcomes of these efforts. Lots of research asserts that service learning has the intended liberating effect on students. Analysts have documented desirable outcomes such as civic consciousness, civic engagement, kinder attitudes towards others, and better learning (Celio, Durlak, & Dymnicki, 2011; Eyler & Giles, 1999; Eyler, Giles, Stenson, & Gray, 2001), but these touted outcomes have typically been small (Parker-Gwin & Mabry, 1998; J. L. Warren, 2012) and in some cases absent (Reinke, 2003).

Disturbingly, even though students today are more likely than they have been in decades past to engage in community service, they are less likely to be politically engaged. And service learning doesn't seem to be helping matters (Harker, 2014; Koliba, 2004; Reinke, 2003) . According to a 2013 student survey from the Harvard University Institute of Politics, 53 percent of college students perform community service whereas only 11 percent participate in a government or political organization or issue. And while very little research exists on the learning outcomes of student activism, what we do have points unequivocally in the direction of deep benefits (McAdam, 1988; Rosas, 2010).

We also have research that raises questions about the singularly positive message put forth by proponents about the effects of service learning. That research suggests that service learning can also reinforce stereotypes of the poor, oppressed, and excluded (see E. Medina, 2011; Mitchell, 2010). Many service learning promoters are not worried about these less positive findings; they attribute reinforcement of stereotypes, for example, to bad practice, arguing that it can occur under conditions where the student and the community partner do not have shared goals and motivations (Billig & Eyler, 2003, p. 15).

But there may be more at work. Bad practice, and even what service learning proponents consider good practice, may be rooted in bad theory. Morton (1995) describes continuums of service learning that allow both "charity" and "change" practices to have standing in the academy and in society, as if the two are different only in degree rather than kind. As we will see, the theoretical flaws in such thinking lay bare the fundamental problem with what I call *institutionalized service learning*—that form of service learning that is officially promoted by and supported by higher education institutions.

We get a bit more sense of the fundamental problems with institutionalized service learning when we consider that researchers have studied with any rigor mainly the question of "liberation" through service learning in relation to students. The overwhelming majority of institutionalized service learning advocates consider service learning to be a pedagogy, with the implication that it's only for students. While they assume there are outcomes for individuals in communities from institutionalized service learning activities like tutoring programs, they sorely neglect theorizing and analyzing the process by which such outcomes occur. Studies of the community side of service learning are all but absent in the literature, with only a few studies of actual community outcomes (Reeb & Folger, 2013). Where such studies do exist, they emphasize what students did rather than what community members did (Schmidt & Robby, 2002), focus on individual effects rather than community effects (Schmidt & Robby, 2002), and only document how community members felt about the service rather than what outcomes actually resulted (Reeb & Folger, 2013).

There is also a lack of any larger theoretical approach to institutionalized service learning that can help us think about intended and unintended outcomes, and their causes. Consequently, we lack understanding of, for example, the safety valve function that institutionalized service learning as charity work plays in preventing the exploited, oppressed, and excluded from engaging in all-out revolt (Piven & Cloward, 1993) or the culturally demeaning definitions of the poor that charity promotes (Lupton, 2012). And the reluctance of both higher education institutions and students to support more politicized, activist civic engagement is well documented (Bickford & Reynolds, 2002; Bringle, Hatcher, & MacIntosh, 2006; Kajner, Chovanec, Underwood, & Mian, 2013; Liu & Kelly, 2009; Moely & Miron, 2005; Morton, 1995; Robinson, 2000a, 2000b; see also Chovanec, Kajner, Mian, & Underwood, 2011). Then there is the problem of the "community partner," which is often a service provider that does things for or to a constituency rather than building the collective power of constituency members.

The risk is that we institutionalized service learning practitioners will become complicit in maintaining exclusion, exploitation, and oppression. For what does institutionalized service learning do? It helps children adjust to oppressive and ineffective schools rather than organize them to change their schools. It helps parents cope with the ravages of an exclusionary and exploitive economic system rather than challenge it. It helps people understand and follow the bureaucratic rules rather than organize to change them. It helps people conform to, and fit into, the existing social system that does not allow them to do more than eke out an unrewarding and unfulfilling survival. And even those who may not share this particular interpretation of the ill effects of institutionalized service learning nonetheless have been unable to document any significant social changes accruing from their efforts.

As someone who practices higher education civic engagement, including institutionalized service learning, I stay awake at night worrying about my own practice. Working with a neighborhood group that wanted to turn a vacant duplex into a community center, my students and I helped the group learn city zoning code, housing code, and accessibility law so they could see what they were up against. We helped them learn about what other community centers did. We helped them gather information from their own community so they could say what they wanted to happen in such a center. But we (and I should really say "I") didn't do nearly as well helping the residents learn lobbying, organizing, and change making, so while they actually got the city to purchase the building, its transformation into a community center was tied up for more than two years in all kinds of bureaucratic red tape and residents did not have the organizing capacity to speed things along. These problems are not just about the theories that we institutionalized service learning practitioners carry around in our heads. It is also about the theories that constituency members carry around in their heads and our role in contributing to theory that people can use to make more sense of their world and act in more collectively liberating ways within it by understanding how to transform it.

The questionable practices and results of the first meaning of *liberating service learning* lead us to the other half of the meaning. So the other way that I mean liberating service learning focuses on institutionalized service learning's lack of accomplishment within the framework of the first meaning, and what we need to do to free the practice from its historical baggage so that it can truly achieve the first meaning not just for students but for everyone. Thus, how do we liberate institutionalized service learning itself and what do we liberate it from?

We need to start by laying bare the taken-for-granted assumptions behind the dominant institutionalized service learning practices. We need to uncover both the manifest theories that drive those assumptions and the latent theories they reflect. It is important for me to emphasize that I'm not talking about a theory of how learning occurs or how students develop (although we will address those topics). Institutionalized service learning is rife with such theories, even in published form. They are theories within a theory. The choice of pedagogical theories as the dominant category of theorizing in institutionalized service learning, for example, unwittingly and unreflectively expresses the deeper theoretical/philosophical assumption that institutionalized service learning is about affecting students, not communities, and it privileges formal institutionalized education practice above other forms of acting in society. Thus, we will work our way toward a theory that takes into account the total package of how bigger change occurs and how all the pieces and parties involved in institutionalized service learning fit together in such bigger change.

The lack of an explicit theory guiding service learning practice, I will show, allows it to drift without rudder or paddle on the currents of dominant neoliberal theories about class, race, gender, ability and power in this country. And because the dominant theories are constrained in the narrow swath of liberal-conservative thinking within neoliberalism, the lack of an alternative explicit theory that can provide such direction has led to a consequently system-maintaining practice. Thus, *liberating* service learning is about making its current theory explicit, deconstructing it, and then building a new theory that can lead to new practice to produce better results.

Toward that end, this book has three parts. Part I, where you are now, through Chapter 3, paints a historical and theoretical context for the rest of the book. The real work comes in the next two parts. I organize the rest of the book, Parts II and III, around the four concepts of *learning, service, community*, and *change*. But Parts II and III take very different perspectives on those concepts. Part II—Chapters 4 through 7—focuses on understanding the theoretical and philosophical underpinnings of institutionalized service learning. We explore *learning, service, community*, and *change* in that order because that appears to be the order in which they are emphasized in current institutionalized service learning practice. Each chapter presents and deconstructs the dominant theories explicitly promoted or implicitly expressed by institutionalized service learning. For me, Part II is depressing reading and contrasts starkly with the usual self-celebratory presentation you may be used to.

Part III—Chapters 8 through 11—is, for me, the energizing alternative, where we switch our perspective from the current theories of institutionalized service learning to a different set of theories that provide a foundation for liberating service learning. Once again we explore the four main concepts— learning, service, community, and change. But this time we reverse the order because the first difference between institutionalized service learning and liberating service learning is the relative emphasis the perspectives place on each of the four concepts. In liberating service learning, *change* is the most important, followed by *community*, then *service*, and then *learning*. Chapter 8 thus begins by focusing on change and allowing a theory of change to drive our thinking about the other three concepts. Next we cover community as the main locus of our efforts. That helps us to think about strategies of "service" and in fact entirely rethink the concept of service. We end with learning, and we dramatically shift the target and strategy of learning and reimagine the process through the discussions of change, community, and service. As a consequence, we see just how different our practice can be and how our higher education institutions will have to change to support it. Chapter 12 then explores what the future may hold and what challenges we may face in attempting to create a better future for all.

You might ask at this point whether I really mean this book to be just about "service learning." What about higher education community engagement or higher education civic engagement or community-based research or community-university partnerships? And what about academic service learning or community-engaged learning or . . . or . . . ? We discuss this issue again in Chapters 2 and 3, but I want to make clear that I mean to talk about all of these things. Like our "community partners," I don't see a lot of difference between these labels in practice. And there may not even be much difference in theory. Even Battistoni's (2002) work trying to distinguish higher education civic engagement from service learning ends up defining civic engagement as basically involving community placements, reflections, and reciprocity—just like institutionalized service learning. I am talking about any attempt by any part of any higher education institution to encourage or force students to engage in labor or research with any off-campus constituency or organization.

Finally, here are a few short notes on usage:

- You will notice that I am forgoing the usual accepted practice of using some variation of "he or she" in favor of variations of "they" or "them." As meanings of gender change with lightning speed, "he" and "she" are no longer inclusive of the rainbow of genders out there. And I like the rainbow.
- It seems that every day a new term pops up to describe how higher education people interact with community people. But none of the terms relate to any distinctions in on-the-ground practice. You will sometimes see me using the generic "service learning" or "community engagement" or "civic engagement." I tend to like "civic engagement," but the Carnegie Foundation uses "community engagement" and the variability in practice, for me, makes the labels interchangeable. So whenever I use any of these three terms, it is just as a generic catchall.
- Many people make much of whether and when there should be a hyphen between "service" and "learning." I do not because I do not subscribe to the argument, as you will see, that "service" actually modifies the "learning." In fact, I argue that the focus on *learning* constrains and contorts *service*. To me, service learning is simply a concept, like auto maintenance or dental hygiene. But if you need hyphens, please feel free to add them in on your own personal, hopefully locally owned store-bought copy. :-)

2

A Brief Counterintuitive History
of Service Learning

As with all things, we can begin to understand the dynamics of a present state by looking into its past. So it is with service learning. Becoming conscious of how we got to the present state of practice, and the assumed theories underlying it, is an important task that can help us see not just the need for change but the possibilities for it.

Where does one start a history of service learning? Of course, so many people trace their influences to John Dewey that the early twentieth century seems the logical starting point. But it is also true that a lot has changed in historical circumstances since then. Starting with Dewey also means starting with a definition of institutionalized service learning that privileges higher education–centric models and official service learning systems (like federal programs). As we will see, definitions drawn from Dewey emphasize the *learning* half of the phrase, with requirements for experiential pedagogy, reflection exercises, and the like, and most require students to be in a course, put in hours in some community agency, and write reflection papers. But many community groups find our obsession with defining service learning to be pedantic and distracting. When a student shows up on their doorstep, they often don't know if that student is simply volunteering, getting graded, or fulfilling some less strenuous course requirement (J. A. Ross, 2014). They don't distinguish a student completing an internship from one completing a service requirement for a course except that they know the intern will be there for longer (Garcia, Nehrling, Martin, & SeBlonka, 2009). Furthermore, the strict definitions of institutionalized service learning actually exclude the very activities that may most achieve the goals of effective "service" and deep "learning" that go beyond understanding the placement to developing a theoretical understanding of the underlying social/political/economic issues exhibited by that placement. These definitions also do not include the rise of community-based research, which does everything that institutionalized service learning does plus involves students in actual research that can create new knowledge (Strand, Marullo, Cutforth, Stoecker, & Donohue, 2003; van de Sande & Schwartz, 2011).

So I will not begin with Dewey, in order to make visible other practices from the past that may be less institutionalized and can help move us into the future. Thus I draw my initial inspiration from those who look to late nineteenth- and early twentieth-century settlement houses for perspectives on service learning. Daynes and Longo (2004) focus on Jane Addams and Ellen Gates Starr's Hull House. Stevens (2003) shows how late nineteenth- and early twentieth-century Black scholars and educators working on community issues used a settlement house model.

I also want to start with the settlement house model, but with a slightly different tack and an earlier starting point. This starting point is Christmas Eve of 1884 in East London. On that day Samuel Barnett (and likely unnamed others because nothing like this is ever accomplished alone) opened Toynbee Hall and founded the concept of the settlement house (Till, 2013). Barnett chose the name Toynbee to honor the late Oxford economic historian Arnold Toynbee, who was the engaged scholar role model of his time because of his work with the poor of London's East End (Begum, 2011; Montague, 1888). The purpose was to build on a growing interest among students of Toynbee and others to directly engage with the great social issues of the day and create a more systematic means to connect the privileged with the marginalized. In the prose of the time, "It is the object of the 'Universities Settlement' to link the Universities with East London, and to direct the human sympathies, the energies, and the public spirit of Oxford and Cambridge to the actual conditions of town life" (Gell, 1888, p. 60). Intriguingly, the emphasis was on recruiting college students and graduates for full-time residential involvement in the settlements. The connections between this work and higher education were not clear or formalized in the way that institutionalized service learning is today. The contrast between modern institutionalized service learning and the much greater commitment students made then, for less extrinsic reward, is intriguing.

Toynbee Hall, and many of the settlements that followed it, were intellectual spaces. Graduates taught courses in, for, and with local community members, and these were not just trades and skills courses. Many emphasized theory and philosophy so that community residents could have access to the same intellectual resources as the privileged (Begum, 2011; Gell, 1888; Till, 2013), suggesting a role for the humanities in engaged scholarship today that Sandy (2013) argues for. Ideally, the intellectual influences extended both ways—with neighborhood residents imparting their life skills (often craft skills) and university graduates imparting theory, art, and literature (Daynes & Longo, 2004).

The "university settlement" idea caught on both in the United Kingdom and in the United States. Some settlement houses were sponsored by universities, and others had relationships with university departments and programs, particularly in the emerging field of social work. A national College Settlements Association, incorporated in 1894, linked university-affiliated settlement houses across cities like New York, Boston, Philadelphia, and Chicago (*Vassar Miscellany Weekly*, 1916). The model is intriguing, particularly its residential emphasis. With a resident volunteer staff, the opportunities to create a truly intellectual and collectivist space were enhanced. And their character that eschewed religious indoctrination and simple charity separated them, and sometimes alienated them, from dominant forms of community service of the time (Lasch-Quinn, 1993, p. 53; Till, 2013). Of course, not all settlements focused on building the power of the dispossessed. Some of those most associated with elite universities consciously defined their work as ameliorative and, most important, as defusing class struggle while maintaining class inequality (Mieras, 2008)—an explicit early incarnation of the model of social service as safety valve. And the tensions between developing communities and training students rose up in the settlements before mid-century. Gay Braxton (1949), the director of Neighborhood House in Madison, Wisconsin, said of the students she supervised: "I would challenge . . . that the undergraduate students should be given more responsibility from the beginning. In my 27 years of experience in the student worker field, I am convinced that the success of the group is much more important than the education, at that time of the student leader, who could only blunder at the expense of the group."

Today we have separated out the collective residential character of the settlement house model and segregated it from place-based communities. There is little truly residential-based higher education community engagement. Alternative spring breaks or brief summer immersion programs with a residential aspect happen in Chicago (Snyder & Karlen, 2014; Western Michigan University, 2014), Appalachia (Big Creek People in Action, 2014), and, of course, New Orleans (J. A. Ross, 2014), among many other places, but they are very short and usually exchange students' unskilled physical labor for learning. Even programs like AmeriCorps VISTA typically place students in a larger geographic space like a city or region rather than in a marginalized neighborhood. The current student development trend—the living-learning community—is safely tucked away in university dormitories, well away from whatever the supposed focus of the community is, even when the living-learning community is focused on institutionalized service learning.

The other strength of the settlement house model was its community focus. It was not about meeting curricular or hours requirements. In the best cases, it was about empowering the people of an excluded neighborhood while offering them informally packaged higher education from which they were normally excluded, and educating the privileged in the externalities of their privilege in the hope that all could come to a common understanding of the path to the good society. Of course, this was also the model's weakness. Although settlement houses flourished into the mid-twentieth century fully rooted in a neighborhood community, connected to progressivism and socialism, and led by women (A. F. Davis, 1984; Deegan, 1988), the settlement model was never able to transform higher education.

Perhaps illustrative of the settlement model's marginalization is that most institutionalized service learning proponents start with John Dewey, the American philosopher who is portrayed as the most important justification for service learning. Dewey was a contemporary, and some even say friend, of Jane Addams, the co-founder with Ellen Gates Starr of the famous Chicago settlement called Hull House. But it appears that Dewey is in fact not part of service learning's history at all but simply its philosophical rationalization. He was certainly civically engaged, but his work in the classroom apparently did not include civic engagement. Rather, it was described as sometimes nonlinear lecture and often wide-ranging back-and-forth discussion. And it was always described as happening in a classroom (Martin, 2003, pp. 258–263). Furthermore, the experiential educational philosophy attributed to him focused on children, not adults, and this included the experimental schools he established. Dewey, it seems, had no interest in theorizing about educating the working adult or even the college student, given that he practiced the same lecture-discussion style at Hull House as he did in the university classroom. Although he had a professional relationship with Jane Addams and Hull House, there is no evidence that he engaged his students as service learners in the settlement's work (Campbell, 1995; Casil, 2006; Dalton, 2002; Martin, 2003; Rockefeller, 1991; Westbrook, 1993).

It is odd that institutionalized service learning would claim as its hero someone who did not practice service learning and focused his educational theories on children. At the same time, this explains a lot about institutionalized service learning. Designing an institutionalized service learning model from a source that requires no change in higher education itself also provides no threat to the dominant higher education institutional structure. And with indications that the best of Dewey perhaps resulted from the influence of Jane Addams (Stengel, 2007), rather than vice versa, we are pointed once again to the settlement house model.

The institutional structure of higher education, and especially its role in the education process, was left intact even when its professors became personally civically engaged. Then, with World War II and the postwar right-wing fear-of-everything period of the 1950s distracting people's thoughts, that structure remained entrenched until something finally snapped.

And when it snapped, it snapped big, and we have "the sixties." But the sixties actually began in the fifties. Rosa Parks was arrested on December 1, 1955, and what is important about this event is that it came shortly after she had attended a workshop at the Highlander Folk School in rural Tennessee. Today Highlander is a little known place, but its role in the civil rights movement and movements that followed is huge. We will learn more later, but it is important here to know that Highlander traces at least part of its influence to the settlement house movement in the United States in general and to Jane Addams of Hull House in particular. Parks attended Highlander to learn about how to make the *Brown v. Board of Education* desegregation decision an enforceable reality (Adams, 1975; Ashby, 2008). The school followed a unique education model of bringing community people together to learn from each other rather than only from a group of experts. People went there to learn for the purpose of informing action (Adams, 1975). We will see that Myles Horton's work at Highlander, along with the work of other popular educators like Paulo Freire, are gaining some ascendency in institutionalized service learning, although not in the way they would have intended.

The energy created by the Montgomery bus boycott, among other events, quickly grew into what we know as the civil rights movement. And in 1960 it also grew into a college student movement. When four students from North Carolina Agricultural and Technical University—Joseph McNeil, Franklin McCain, Ezell Blair, Jr., and David Richmond—sat at the whites-only lunch counter in the Greensboro, North Carolina, Woolworth's, they sparked the imaginations of Black students across the South and, indeed, the imaginations of many students across the nation and the racial divide (Morris, 1981). Shaw University was the site of the founding of the resultant Student Nonviolent Coordinating Committee, and the Highlander Folk School was the site of both the planning meeting for the Shaw gathering and its most important subsequent meeting (Adams, 1975). Then there was Freedom Summer, which recruited students from across the nation for voter registration and other movement work in the South. By 1964 it had become clear that not just African American but white college students were risking their very lives by participating in Freedom Summer when James Chaney, Andrew Goodman, and Michael Schwerner were shot dead in Mississippi.

Not only Black college students helped define the 1960s. The famous occupation of Alcatraz Island by Native Americans that began in late 1969 and lasted for nearly a year and a half was organized at least partly by students from San Francisco State University (SFSU) and UCLA. The initial leadership met and organized through their involvement in the brand-new Native American

Studies Program at SFSU, and the majority of the initial occupiers came from UCLA. The subsequent rise of the Red Power movement in the United States has been attributed to the work of these students (Johnson, Champagne, & Nagel, 1997). It was also on California college campuses that another movement, if not birthed, was catalyzed. In April of 1969, Chicano college students came together at the University of California–Santa Barbara to form Movimiento Estudiantil Chicano de Aztlán, or MEChA. MEChA brought together college students and youth activists and then grew throughout college campuses and beyond (Muñoz, 1989).

Action expanded quickly into the anti-war movement and moved onto campus itself. Campus activism produced one of the most intellectually engaged periods in the nation's history. As teach-ins—large gatherings organized by faculty and students for mutual education about the war and its political context—took hold, intellectual work and action consciously merged. It took the killings of students by police and military—at Kent State University, Jackson State University, Orangeburg South Carolina, and other places—for universities to begin to revert to the restricted teaching environments they had been designed as (Hine, 1996). But, even then, changes began to spread through higher education as student groups helped put pressure on mainstream universities that would allow the voices of women and people of color to be better expressed through their own departments and programs (Boxer, 2001; La Belle & Ward, 1996).

So much else happened during that era through professors and students that is undocumented—classes supporting action around poverty, racism, sexism and other exclusions in society. And all of it is completely missing from the official histories of institutionalized service learning. When service learning proponents look back on the 1960s, all they see is "Peace Corps, VISTA, college work-study, and the White House Fellows programs" (Gallagher, Planowski, & Tarbell, n.d.). In other words, only officially sanctioned and apolitical student engagement was counted as institutionalized service learning, regardless of whether other forms of student engagement actually better accomplished the goals of "service" and "learning."

Consider for a moment that perhaps the best higher education service learning done in the history of the United States was done under the label of "student activism." This was service learning that was intellectually rich and explicitly civically engaged—in other words, political and unabashedly focused on social change. And it was massively widespread. By 1968 membership in the student organization perhaps most intensely involved in the integration of activism and intellectualism, Students for a Democratic Society, had reputedly peaked at 100,000 (Hunt, 1999). This engaged learning rarely got credit in the classroom. It wasn't recognized as anything but disruption by the administrators of the colleges and universities where it occurred, but from the viewpoint of history it is called "the movement" (Anderson, 1996). Students were jailed, tear-gassed, beaten, and even killed for their efforts, and their accomplishments were beyond profound. Those involved both in mind and in body across the racial divide with grassroots communities helped produce the Voting Rights Act and the Civil Rights Act in the mid-1960s. They helped end a war. They helped amplify women's voices for control over their own bodies, justice in the workplace, and equality in the polity. They helped transform our thinking about our relationship with the rest of nature.

The contrast, in both learning and service, to today's meek, institution-bound, visionless service learning should be shaming. The most important lessons, the most important actions, the most important methods, were created through student organizing that institutionalized service learning doesn't even recognize. The activist service learning moment has been washed from history. The National Service Learning Clearinghouse (2013) historical timeline, which was the standard bearer for institutionalized service learning before it met its own demise, didn't even mention it.

The sixties, which actually lasted into the seventies, died down. It would take a whole other book to understand why, and that is not our purpose here in any event. However, it is important to note a few important variables implicated in the waning of student protest. One was political. Colleges and universities had their reputations questioned from the left for being too constraining and from the right for being too lenient and liberal (in both the political and the intellectual sense). Another was the changing economy. The economic decline of the 1970s, along with the weakened status of universities, fueled reductions in government funding for higher education and consequently rapidly rising tuitions (Newfield, 2008). As a result, the pressure was on students (and their parents) to see a return on their tuition dollar. And the attack against the 1960s culture of student civic engagement was in full swing, from then governor Ronald Reagan in California, who had promised a "bloodbath" to take over People's Park from Berkeley's youth (Cannon, 2003, p. 339), to then president Richard Nixon in Washington, who was much more strategic in trying to demobilize students (Reeves, 2002). Progressive power building in general was under sophisticated attack as philanthropic foundations shifted their financial support from the more political community organizing to safer, more controlled community development that didn't challenge power (Fisher, 1994; Yin, 1998).

As activism went into abeyance, journalist Tom Wolfe (1976) labeled the 1970s the "me decade," and the label generalized to the youth of the time as the "me generation" (Wolfe, n.d.). Others, such as Christopher Lasch (1979), joined the fray in promoting an image of youth as self-centered. Also, the culture was clearly changing. Popular culture went from sitcoms about conservative parents and liberal children like *All in the Family* to sitcoms about liberal parents and conservative children like *Family Ties*. When those con-servative children started voting, they became swept up in the right-wing tide that elected and re-elected Ronald Reagan to the presidency of the United States (Ullman, 1986).

The 1950s and 1960s activist students, many of whom were professors by now, had to face this new rising right-wing youth culture. I was there as a student in the 1980s. Our professors were disappointed in the dominant student culture, as were those few of us who were activist students. It seems consistent that during this time a practice of institutionalized service learning focused on students would gain ascendency. Outspoken critics of institutionalized service learning such as John Egger (2007, 2008) and Carl Bankston (2011, 2012a, 2012b, 2013) in fact see a vast liberal conspiracy in institutionalized service learning—attempting to shape the minds of youth by confronting them face to face with the results of right-wing fiscal and cultural policy in the person-age of patrons of soup kitchens and homeless shelters, and others living with poverty.

Then the other hero of institutionalized service learning, Ernest Boyer, comes on the scene. Boyer had for a while been calling for community service for both high school and college students (1983, 1987), but it was not until his famous *Scholarship Reconsidered* in 1990 that he exploded onto the scene and became a touchstone for institutionalized service learning. Boyer's influence is important because it cemented the *internal* institutional focus of higher education community engagement. What he called the "scholarship of application" maintained the scholar in charge, and he used the examples of "medical diagnosis, serving clients in psychotherapy, shaping public policy, creating an architectural design, or working with the public schools" (Boyer, 1990, p. 23). Sadly, too many people ignored his final article on the subject, *The Scholarship of Engagement*, which suggested that Boyer himself was taking it to the next level, from academy-directed scholarship to something more active and engaged:

> At one level, the scholarship of engagement means connecting the rich resources of the university to our most pressing social, civic, and ethical problems, to our children, to our schools, to our teachers, and to our cities—just to name the ones I am personally in touch with most frequently; you could name others. Campuses would be viewed by both students and professors not as isolated islands but as staging grounds for action.
>
> But at a deeper level . . . I'm convinced that ultimately, the scholarship of engagement means creating a special climate in which the academic and civic cultures communicate more continuously and more creatively with each other, helping to enlarge what anthropologist

Clifford Geertz describes as the universe of human discourse and en-
riching the quality of life for all of us. (Boyer, 1996, pp. 32–33)

Instead, service learning became institutionalized and "declawed" in the
analysis of Corey Dolgon (2010). One of the first signs of the institutional
colonization of service learning's potential was its establishment as official
policy in the National and Community Service Trust Act, signed into law in
1990 by President George H. W. Bush, which defined institutionalized service
learning as a practice:

(A) under which students or participants learn and develop through
active participation in thoughtfully organized service that—(i) is
conducted in and meets the needs of a community; (ii) is coordinated with an elementary school, secondary school, institution of
higher education, or community service program, and with the
community; (iii) and helps foster civic responsibility; and
(B) that—(i) is integrated into and enhances the academic curriculum
of the students, or the educational components of the community service program in which the participants are enrolled; and
(ii) provides structured time for the students or participants to reflect on the service experience. (National and Community Service
Trust Act of 1990)

Education and *service*, not *change* and *action*, are the terms of emphasis
here. Of course, this is as expected. But it is important that this is in contrast
to the three principles established in 1979 by Robert Sigmon when he was assistant director of a community-based organization:

1. Those being served control the service(s) provided.
2. Those being served become better able to serve and be served by
their own actions.
3. Those who serve also are learners and have significant control over
what is to be learned.

Sigmon's standards are often cited but poorly followed and probably even
more poorly understood. The word *control* points to the weak politics implied
by today's rhetoric of "partnership" and "reciprocity," as we will see. An emphasis on the served also serving points to a capacity-building mission that is
absent in institutionalized service learning today. And when we link the third
standard back to the second, we understand that those being served, because
they serve, are also learners. Back in 1979, Sigmon was disappointed by the
shortcomings he saw in the practice: "Unfortunately, learning objectives may

be superimposed upon, rather than derived from the service task [and] the nature of the service receive[s] limited attention." There is no evidence that Sigmon would be any happier about the situation today, when curricular demands still drive student engagement and there is no empowerment philosophy providing a foundation for it.

The constriction of service learning's potential was further established with the Corporation for National and Community Service (n.d.), created in 1993, which became a major funding source for institutionalized service learning programs. In 1994 the Department of Housing and Urban Development launched the Community Outreach Partnership Center (COPC) grant program to fund higher education community engagement. Both forms of funding further centered the resources for higher education community engagement in higher education institutions themselves. This is in contrast to, for example, the Canadian Community-University Research Alliances program, which also funded community groups—though not in the numbers many would have liked—and more balanced community-university partnerships (Social Sciences and Humanities Research Council, 2013), and at least its spirit, if not its previous funding levels, were continued when it was ended and rolled into other Social Sciences and Humanities Research Council programs.

This latest period also saw an explosion of network organizations designed to further institutionalized service learning and community engagement: Campus Compact, the Engagement Scholarship Consortium, the Campus Outreach Opportunity League, the International Association for Research on Service Learning, just to name a few.

But an institution-centered model of service learning has not been cemented into place yet. Critiques dating back more than a decade from practitioners who worried that institutionalized service learning was neither good learning nor good service (D. Brown, 2000; Eby, 1998; Eyler & Giles, 1999) have led to a disorganization in the field that I welcome. One consequence has been a chaos of labels—"academic service learning," "community-based learning," "engaged [fill in the blank]" or "[fill in the blank] engagement"—as practitioners have either tried to overcome the weaknesses of institutionalized service learning or simply tried to rebrand bad practice. Even students have gotten in the act, no longer willing to simply accept institutionalized service learning and the required volunteerism that comes with it (O. Johnson, 2012; Swanson, 2010). Marquette University's student government, at an institution that prides itself on its institutionalized service learning image, voted against a policy that would have its own members provide five hours of mandatory service (Simonaitis, 2010).

How did we go from higher education community engagement located in and focused on the community to an institutionalized service learning bureaucracy? Why is the official history of institutionalized service learning so at odds with the history of the most important and consequential forms of student engagement? Why is institutionalized service learning so barren of any outcomes of consequence? The answers to those questions require thinking about the theoretical and philosophical justifications for institutionalized service learning itself.

3

Theories (Conscious and Unconscious) of Institutionalized Service Learning

There is both an opportunity and a need to examine the conscious and unconscious theories driving what I will be calling *institutionalized service learning*. As I've mentioned, institutionalized service learning is designed and controlled inside of higher education institutions, and includes any activities where students have contact with groups and individuals off campus for the purpose of serving institution-based educational and/or student development goals. While the practice is usually course-based, it can also involve internships, and even co- or extracurricular service hours required, promoted, or rewarded by the institution with a philosophical justification of the service furthering student development or education.

Such a description flies in the face of most definitions that make fine and nuanced distinctions between service learning, community service, civic engagement, or any number of other labels where the actual practices are so diverse that they undermine the solidity of any label. For the moment, I want to focus not on what may be different but on what is similar across practices. I also want to focus as much on what theories are unreflectively expressed through institutionalized service learning practice as on what theories are explicitly used to justify it.

For the time being, then, I look not at the exceptions but at the typical practices of institutionalized service learning. There are, of course, many exceptions to what I will describe as institutionalized service learning. So if you believe yourself to be practicing one of the exceptions, you may not see your practice reflected in this book until Chapter 8 or later. Some of you may even object to my assertion of the dominance of a single institutionalized service learning form. And, after all, it is fair to say that there is no single *explicit* theory of service learning. Various analysts have tried to divide up the theoretical thinking behind service learning in various ways, but usually resulting in various taxonomies of practice rather than in deep theoretical foundations for various forms of practice.

There are two somewhat deeper attempts at reviewing the theoretical/philosophical approaches to service learning. An edited collection by Speck and Hoppe (2004a) distinguishes philanthropic, civic engagement, and communitarian philosophies of service learning. The philanthropic approach is designed to instill in students an attitude of philanthropy toward the poor. The civic engagement approach is designed to instill in them values of democratic participation and an identity of change agent. Finally, the communitarian approach is designed to produce a sense of commonality and shared experience across social divides. Note that all three approaches center on changing students, but only the third suggests that perhaps someone else is involved in the relationship, and only the second suggests the possibility that change may be part of the equation.

Butin divides the theories behind service learning into technical (pedagogy), cultural (self-knowledge), and political perspectives, and then Butin adds a new anti-foundational perspective (pragmatist). He sees the technical perspective as the most prominent approach (2010, pp. 8–14), but divides actual practice differently, arguing that service learning "is an amalgam of, among other things, experiential education, action research, critical theory, progressive education, adult education, social justice education, constructivism, community-based research, multicultural education, and undergraduate research" (2010, p. 41). I admit that I do not know what Butin means by "other things," but practices to produce community outcomes, such as community organizing and development, are conspicuously absent from this list.

Perhaps the most important division in the world of service learning theory is between the "charity" and "change" approaches. Morton (1995) describes charity and change service learning as on a single continuum, and adds a "project" approach on the continuum between them. It is intriguing that Morton argues against those who see charity and change as separate categories, asserting that they do not have "a way of recognizing service as anything other than a weak form of charity" (p. 23). But that seems exactly the point. As we will see, "service" as it is practiced and promoted in institutionalized service learning does indeed seem to be a weak form of charity. Student-community engagement that emphasizes change in power relationships threatens institutional power, and students who practice such engagement risk facing the wrath of the student code of conduct. Now, to be fair, Morton seems to argue that we should all be moving along the continuum from charity to project to change service learning, but there is a stark absence of evidence that this is occurring or that it could be a gradual linear process.

Among those who maintain categorical distinctions between charity and change approaches, Mooney and Edwards (2001) distinguish six forms of "experiential learning"—out-of-class activities, volunteering, service add-ons, internships, service learning, and service learning advocacy. They find that only service learning advocacy has an action component, but they cannot escape the bias of seeing students, not the community, leading the action. Marullo and Edwards (2000) develop the idea of social justice service learning. Their model contrasts with the charity approach in that it is designed to "empower the recipients" (p. 901). To do so, it requires students to explore the root causes of social problems, see social rather than just individual causes of problems, sustain faculty-student-community collaboration, build community, and promote principles of social justice. Here, too, it is important that much of the intellectual and research focus is still on the students and the higher education institution, with the effects of the service learning on the community reduced to an afterthought and community members labeled as "recipients" even when they are to become "empowered" as a consequence.

There is not much in the way of a fully flowered progressive theory of service learning that moves beyond the academy. There are few Marxist critiques (see, for example, D. Brown, 2000), which seems odd indeed given the presence of poverty and class issues as abstract targets of institutionalized service learning practice. There are also very few feminist critiques (see Gilbert & Masucci, 2004; Walker, 2000), although there is some feminist-influenced practice (Balliet & Heffernan, 2000; Rhoads, 1997; Williams & Ferber, 2008). We are beginning to see some critical race theory critiques informing effective practice (Cahill, 2009; Oden & Casey, 2007; Shabazz & Cooks, 2014; Verjee, 2012) on the margins, but on the margins is still very much where they remain.

From a more conservative standpoint in academia, we see a vocal sideswipe at service learning as a liberal conspiracy, which may be more accurate than we would like to accept. Butin, one of the deepest thinkers about service learning, charges that the practice "embodies a liberal agenda under the guise of a universalistic garb" (2010, p. 35). Egger (2007, 2008), a more conservative critic, makes the same charge from what sounds like a libertarian anti-government standpoint, and Bankston (2011, 2012a, 2012b, 2013) seems to add an anti–political correctness critique. In general, these critics see promoters of institutionalized service learning using it to frame poverty as a result of class, race, and gender discrimination and to reinforce the idea that more government regulation and income redistribution are the solution. They charge that such framing is politically motivated and politically biased.

Of course, the term *liberal* in the United States, just like the word *socialist* (unlike *conservative*, which adherents proudly use to self-label), is an imprecise placeholder with too much political baggage to be of much use. In the hands of U.S. conservatives, *liberal* usually becomes a stand-in for "big government" or "low morality" or both. So does the charge fit? I argue that institutionalized service learning actually embodies a much more conservative politics. One thing we do know is that institutionalized service learning shies away from advocacy in favor of charity work. And that charity work is typically in the nonprofit, not the government, sector. Second, much of the purpose of institutionalized service learning is in propagating deeper moral values in students, especially in faith-based institutions, where service learning is arguably at its most powerful. Now, it may be the case that many faculty and administrative promoters of institutionalized service learning have personally "liberal" politics, but by and large the practice of institutionalized service learning does not reflect such politics.

These critics' confusion, I think, comes from the same source as the other problems with institutionalized service learning. The critics are only focusing on the education of students, not on the role of institutionalized service learning in the society. Thus, they see the institutional requirement, and the content of the service learning, and charge that institutionalized service learning is promoting a viewpoint. Perhaps we can cut them a little slack in that regard, although it is troubling that even they cannot see the extent to which they have bought into the assumptions and biases of the dominant institutionalized service learning model.

When we shift from looking at the pedagogical content of much institutionalized service learning to considering how it operates off campus, I share Kliewer's (2013) concern that, in fact, the practice of institutionalized service learning is much more likely to reflect neoliberalism than liberalism. *Neoliberalism* is also an oft-misunderstood term. It is actually a born-again old economic liberalism. Originally, liberal economic philosophy was about a belief in structuring society to allow maximum economic freedom. For Adam Smith (1776) and his followers, such as Milton Friedman (1962), it meant that the market would take care of itself and government should not intervene. The re-ascendency of that philosophy in the 1980s, perhaps partly a side effect of the social and cultural liberalism of the previous decades, is illustrated in many institutionalized service learning practices. Neoliberalism promotes the responsibility of the individual entrepreneur (whether for-profit or nonprofit) and the primacy of the autonomous individual against collective accountability.

Neoliberalism is applied more and more to describe contemporary higher education institutions that are being transformed by privatization into places of less and less academic freedom and autonomy and more and more concern for "serving customers" such as students and corporations (Canaan & Shumar, 2008; Giroux, 2013; Greenwood, 2012). Universities and colleges name their labs and classrooms after corporate donors, conduct research funded by them and serving their interests, and resist providing the all-important job protection called tenure to faculty like Ignacio Chapela who actively opposed the neoliberal agenda by pitting his research against big agriculture (Washburn, 2005).

How does institutionalized service learning operate in such a neoliberal environment? Because the purpose of government under neoliberalism is to prioritize the demands of business over the needs of people, and even to control dissent so that business can operate in as unfettered a way as possible, it makes sense that institutionalized service learning undertakes safety valve charity rather than capitalist-challenging social justice work, even though Ayers (2005) offers a passing hopeful comment that institutionalized service learning is not consistent with neoliberalism. Keith (2005), in a more developed analysis, pursues the other argument:

> Neoliberalism takes the central tenets of free market economics and makes them into the general principle for creating the good life and good society. This translates into a view of people as rational choosers who seek to maximize their self-interest, and a preference for private property and market competition over the role of the state as protector of the public good. This trend is propelling universities, schools, and communities toward privatization, entrepreneurship, measurable forms of accountability, and new forms of poverty. The preferred approach to service-learning here involves direct service, especially in areas from which the state is withdrawing, rather than the action of engaged citizens acting in common to advocate alternative visions. (p. 6)

Institutionalized service learning expresses neoliberalism by promoting service to individuals rather than to collectives. It promotes individual success within the system rather than collective challenge against it.

Neoliberalism even disrupts how we think about the ethic of service in institutionalized service learning. And it does this especially regarding students. Consider how often we tell students that institutionalized service learning is "good for your resume" and how often we try to justify it by quantified studies of student learning. So far has neoliberalism become embedded in institutionalized service learning, according to Chovanec et al. (2011), that institutionalized service learning placements are now treated as commodities from which students choose placements in order to serve their own individual ends.

Perhaps nowhere has the influence of neoliberalism become more prominent in institutionalized service learning than in social entrepreneurship. The broader concept of entrepreneurship is the ultimate achievement of neoliberalism—the mystifying glorification of individuals mythically succeeding on their own. And social entrepreneurship tries to graft kindness onto this mythical individualism. Service learners are now taught to be social entrepreneurs. In 2014 Belmont University's social entrepreneurship major advertised itself with a photo of a student painting a house (Belmont University, n.d.)—this at an institution that saw one of the most inspiring forms of student social change engagement when a broad swath of students organized successfully against anti-gay university policies (Boettcher, 2011; Tennessee Guerilla Women, 2010). This story is, of course, nowhere to be found in the university's community engagement promotional materials.

The next four chapters explore all of this in more depth. They look at the theoretical ideas that inform, or are exposed by, the core concepts of institutionalized service learning and the broader field of higher education community engagement that derives from it.

What are these core concepts? Clearly, service and learning are the two most important. Since the field's inception, these have been the concepts around which practice has developed. But the word *community* is also used so frequently that we must spend some time understanding how it is used or at least what its use implies. There is one more concept that has been relegated to the margins but is nonetheless held up as a standard of practice—change. Certainly, change is promoted most by those practicing a social justice model of service learning. However, even those who practice the charity model either hope or assume that their after-school programs, their tutoring programs, their English-language learning programs will change individuals.

Here conceptual ordering is important. As we see in Part III, a different ordering provides a foundation for a different practice. If the first priority of service learning is learning, the practice will look very different than if the first priority is change. But the implications go even deeper than this. It is not just that institutionalized service learning prioritizes learning but that it prioritizes a particular pedagogy for a particular audience that then shapes how the practice approaches the other three concepts.

So this begins our exploration of institutionalized service learning. In Part II, we will consider first how institutionalized service learning thinks about learning. Next, we will look at service, then community, and then change.

Interlude

If fire departments were organized like institutionalized service learning:

- The fire department would fight fires only at certain times of the year. Got a fire in July? Tough.

- The firefighters would fight fires only for set hours. If your fire lasted longer, you would just have to try to put out the rest of it yourself.

- The fire department would require everyone to fight fires, even people who were scared of fire or were really bad at it. Or,

- Fighting fires would be optional.

- The firefighters would get to choose whether they wanted to fight your fire or someone else's.

- There wouldn't be any training. In fact the purpose of fighting fires would be to provide training. If your house burned down in the process, it would still be good training.

- The firefighters would only fight fires that fit their internally designed resources. If you had a fire on the twelfth floor and their ladder truck only went to the fifth floor, too bad.

- While your house was burning, you'd be transferred six times and have to leave voice mails trying to find a firefighter who was not too busy.

- You'd have to supply your own water and probably coffee and doughnuts for the firefighters.

- They wouldn't want to fight fires far away from the fire station.

- The fire department would send only one firefighter regardless of the size of the fire or if you even had one.

- The fire captain would never be there to direct the firefighters.

II

Institutionalized
Service Learning

4

What Is Institutionalized Service Learning's Theory of Learning?

> No pedagogy which is truly liberating can remain distant from the oppressed by treating them as unfortunates and by presenting for their emulation models from among the oppressors.
>
> —PAULO FREIRE, *Pedagogy of the Oppressed*

Google the phrase "service learning as pedagogy" and you will get an endless list of exact matches. Overwhelmingly, when people talk about service learning they talk about it as a pedagogy. Yes, there is increasing language about community partnerships, but the focus has always been, and remains, on learning. And not just learning in general, but college student learning. So we start our journey into understanding the theory of institutionalized service learning by understanding pedagogy.

Side Effects of Institutionalized Service Learning as a Pedagogy

The source of the term *pedagogy* is attributed to the Greeks, where it translated to "leading the child" (Hiemstra & Sisco, 1990, p. 231) and primarily referred to a method of teaching children (Hiemstra & Sisco, 1990). But since the Greeks, it seems that we have broadened the term to refer to teaching methods with any group of any age.

The first concern we should have, then, is what problematic assumptions the concept of pedagogy carries with it as we assign institutionalized service learning to the status of a pedagogy. The issue here is that institutionalized service learning has become quite literally a form of teaching. In the ideal institutionalized service learning course, from this standpoint, there is a set of learning objectives and a set of methods designed to achieve them. Never mind for the moment that the gulf between actual institutionalized service learning activities and standard course objectives can be canyon wide and ocean deep. The more important issue is that the institutionalized service learning model is one where the professor first creates learning objectives and then tries to find, craft, shape, manipulate, or design service experiences to achieve those objectives. In the model of institutionalized service learning as a pedagogy, the curriculum holds priority (Butin, 2010, p. 19).

This minimally means that the "community" (don't worry, I will problematize this term later) people and/or its space become part of the subject matter. They become, in a pedagogical sense, *objects* of learning much like a worm is an object of learning in a high school biology lab. There are even those who refer to the community as a "laboratory" (Holland, 1997; Howard, 2003; Jelier & Clarke, 1999; Mihalynuk, Seifer, & Community Campus Partnerships for Health, 2007), implying that the people and their place are things to be experimented on. Others refer to it as a "textbook" (Pawlowski, 2007), implying that it is inert intellectual material to be consumed.

Sometimes we also expect community members to do the actual teaching of our students, without remuneration. The question then becomes what pedagogy community members use, or if they even think in terms of a pedagogy. Now, there are many communities with members highly skilled in various ways of teaching, whether conscious or not. But, aside from the ethical question of whether we should ask those community members to provide educational services at a far reduced price (all the way down to, of course, a loss as they spend more time educating students for free than they receive in service from them), there is the strategic question of whether and how the community pedagogy is linked to the classroom pedagogy.

Experiential Learning as Institutionalized Service Learning Pedagogy

It is often unclear what institutionalized service learning educators are referring to when they apply the word *pedagogy* to institutionalized service learning. Overwhelmingly, however, they seem to be referring to a kind of experiential pedagogy. Institutionalized service learning's early leaders, Barbara Jacoby (1996) and Andrew Furco (1996), among others, all emphasized service learning as an experiential learning pedagogy.

The linkage between the labels "service learning" and "experiential learning" is well established. From coast to coast and north to south, many programs incorporate experiential learning, such as at the University of Central Florida (n.d.), Loyola University Chicago (n.d.), the University of Washington (2015), and Northeastern University (2014) to name a very few. The National Society for Experiential Education (2014) awards are dominated by institutionalized service learning programs and promoters.

The focus on experiential education as the pedagogical foundation for institutionalized service learning traces back to John Dewey, whom we met in

Chapter 2. This may be in part because he wrote about both democracy and education, which seemed the perfect combination for a robust institutionalized service learning theory. But Dewey mostly wrote about these things separately, and he built his classroom pedagogy on a separate theoretical foundation than his philosophy of democracy. His 1916 work, *Democracy and Education*, does link the two, but his focus, though difficult to discern, was on how good education promotes good democracy (in terms of both a healthy polity and more general civic engagement) rather than on how civic participation promotes good education. This is important. If the causal pathway is from education to democracy, then education practice can be developed without necessarily referring to civic life. In contrast, the experiential learning philosophy of institutionalized service learning promotes the causal pathway of civic participation promoting good education.

It is in his 1938 work, *Experience and Education*, that Dewey lays out his thinking about experiential learning, but as an educational rather than political philosophy. All learning comes from experience, he seems to say, so the teacher's job is to organize educative experiences. And some of the most fruitful educative experiences come from interacting with things outside of the classroom. Dewey also seems to propose a form of problem-based learning, where students encounter problems in the world, form ideas about them, test out interventions, and draw conclusions from their experiences.

This is all quite consistent with Dewey's ultimate labeling as an American pragmatist philosopher, and it is important to understand the influence of pragmatism in institutionalized service learning. Pragmatism does not concern itself with deep or holistic theory. In many aspects, it is an anti-theory that disregards attempts to develop lasting principles of knowledge, which can also allow for significant moral relativism. Thus, pragmatism becomes linked with, and a justification for, capitalism (Novack, 1975). We explore the political ramifications of pragmatism more in coming chapters, but here we must consider its influence on how institutionalized service learning addresses what constitutes knowledge.

Notwithstanding the differences among American pragmatists, I concern myself here mostly with Dewey's influence. The overall pragmatist belief in the rule of empirical evidence over theoretical principles is keenly present in institutionalized service learning. Furthermore, according to Dewey's (1938) model, the need for learning should be personal—the learner needs to care about the learning. Then the learner needs to go out and try interventions in the world and collect evidence on their effects. It is quite easy to see how such a philosophy leads faculty to send their students out to find their own institutionalized service learning opportunities and treat communities as "laboratories" where the students try things. Doing so is a quintessentially, if relatively unsophisticated, pragmatist approach. Indeed, from the standpoint of pragmatism, it is difficult for students to have an experiential learning "experience" if they have been taught too much beforehand. Pragmatism instills a belief in individuals that they can know and act on the world from their experience. It's the ultimate DIY (do it yourself) philosophy applied to everything. Now, pragmatists do not encourage people to act in disregard of accumulated empirical evidence (though doing so involves only a minor exaggeration of the philosophy), but they do value experimentation. And the moral relativism of pragmatism allows for evidence-independent experimentation. The unreflective promotion of "entrepreneurship" and its supposedly socially conscious cousin, social entrepreneurship, without theorizing whether an individualist profit-based model is ultimately good for society, is a classic illustration of pragmatism's amoral tendencies. Significantly, Dewey (1930/1984) was probably the strongest exception to pragmatist philosophy as a pragmatist who tried to establish some lasting moral principles, thus providing even more justification for seeing him as the philosophical progenitor of institutionalized service learning.

Of course, experiential learning as a foundational pedagogy is about more than Dewey. People also draw on Kolb's (1984) experiential learning model. Kolb built on Dewey and also Kurt Lewin (1948), the person responsible for the establishment of action research (which, intriguingly, is a researcher-centered engaged research model that contrasts with the more activist and empowering participatory research model; see Brown & Tandon, 1983). Kolb also integrated Piaget's (1970/1983) theory of cognitive development in his work. His resultant model of experiential learning is a cycle that moves through the steps of concrete experience, reflective observation, abstract conceptualization, and active experimentation.

Intriguingly, in the practice of institutionalized service learning, practitioners give little serious attention to the development of specific pedagogical strategies around concrete experience, abstract conceptualization, and active experimentation—arguably the most important parts of the cycle. Instead, they primarily focus on reflection.

Reflection, for institutionalized service learning advocates, is where the learning in service learning comes from (Bringle & Hatcher, 2003; Cone & Harris, 1996; Jacoby, 1996). Just how it should happen, however, is unclear. Bringle and Hatcher (2003) list various forms of writing (journals, experiential research papers, case studies, electronic reflections) and then reading and class presentations (though the latter two seem less strategies of reflection and more modalities that may or may not involve reflection). Rodgers (2002) is a rare voice that is more critical of what she sees as a superficial emphasis on reflection in institutionalized service learning teaching. Going again back to Dewey, Rodgers argues that reflection should be a carefully systematic and developmental process guided by a structure of scientific inquiry, and requiring not so much solitary journaling as regular interaction with others.

Such systematic collective reflection is exceedingly difficult to design and consequently exceedingly rare in the institutionalized service learning literature. But there are deeper problems with the fit between experiential learning and institutionalized service learning than the difficulty of doing good reflection.

Why Experiential Learning Does Not Fit Institutionalized Service Learning

There is a challenge when we use experiential learning with people who lack relevant experiences. We cover andragogy in Chapter 11, but suffice it to say here that it contrasts with pedagogy in its specific focus on the education of adults and organizes teaching differently in part because adults have a stockpile of experience to draw on in their learning (Knowles, 1980). While youth certainly have experiences to draw on, stuffing suddenly foreign experiences into their school days through short-term engagement with people who have a very different lived reality hardly seems to fit the experiential learning model.

As an example, let's say I teach a sociology course on social inequality and use some kind of community setting to give students hands-on experience with one of the effects of social inequality, poverty. The students dish out soup at a soup kitchen, or do overnight volunteer stints at a homeless shelter. The problem is that this is not the kind of experience that experiential learning calls for. In experiential learning, the experience of a concept is supposed to be direct. In institutionalized service learning models, the experience is actually the indirect experience of someone else's experience. That is, the student does something for someone else who is actually experiencing poverty. The student does not directly experience poverty—they[1] only experience what it is like to be a volunteer doing things for someone experiencing poverty. Thus, the best-fit learning goal is not an understanding of poverty but an understanding of poverty service provision. This is perhaps good for social work, but the field of social work already has a long-established system of experiential learning directly and logically tied to its learning objectives.

The process of reflection, then, becomes doubly convoluted. Let's apply Kolb's experiential learning model of concrete experience, reflective observation, abstract conceptualization, and active experimentation to a typical institutionalized service learning setting. The student shows up at an agency to

---

1. You will notice that I avoid the accepted use of "he or she" in favor of "they." Because meanings of gender change with lightning speed, "he" and "she" are no longer inclusive of the rainbow of genders out there. And I like the rainbow.

do English-language learning with an undocumented Spanish speaker who works the night shift in a local restaurant kitchen. The course goals focus on understanding Spanish-speaking cultures. The service learning assignment is supposed to serve those course goals. Through a reflection journal, the student is expected to learn about Spanish-speaking cultures.

What is the student's concrete experience in this scenario? It is the experience of an other in an institutionalized service learning setting where that other is defined as a needy recipient. It is the experience of being a teacher. It is the experience of being powerful in contrast to lacking power. It is *not* about being a member of a Spanish-speaking culture. What, then, can students reflect on from such an experience? They can reflect on teaching those others as they are defined in that setting. They can reflect on their complicity in maintaining the disempowering definition of the other in that setting. But the professor is not teaching the students about teaching or about power in such a context. The students' reflections, consequently, will be convoluted at best and irrelevant at worst, and their abstract conceptualizations will be uninformed or misinformed because they have not studied the content of what the concrete experience actually provides. Then, to the extent to which the professor allows or directs students to engage in "experimentation," their chances of doing harm are greatly enhanced.

In addition, many experiential learning advocates emphasize the importance of carefully structuring and actually designing the experience for students and continually monitoring students as they go through it (Gentry, 1990; Wolfe & Byrne, 1975). Too few faculty who send their students out to do institutionalized service learning make any attempt to carefully design the learning experience or engage in the continuous monitoring that is central to the experiential learning model. Instead, they rely on community organizations to find ways to get students to do service for a couple of hours per week and keep a journal on this service that the instructor reads maybe two or three times over the semester. This doesn't mean, of course, that institutionalized service learning scholars haven't emphasized more systematic and conscious design of institutionalized service learning (see, for example, Hatcher & Bringle, 1997). But even careful design can't overcome the fundamental mismatch between what is being taught in a course and what is being experienced in the field.

Another important characteristic of experiential learning is that it is fundamentally emotional (Gentry, 1990; C. R. Rogers, 1983). Even Dewey (1938) seemed to say that the problem with regular schooling was that the process was dull and controlling—emotional characteristics. And, indeed, when we talk about students experiencing different people and doing "hands-on" service, we are talking about an emotional experience. This is why many institutionalized service learning scholars discuss the "discomfort" that they expect students to feel when they are immersed in community settings unfamiliar to them (Coles, 1999; Kajner et al., 2013; Tilley-Lubbs, 2009). And in the parlance of the learning styles literature, emotional learning is kinesthetic. We have not integrated the larger literature on learning styles (Dunn, Beaudry, & Klavas, 2002) into institutionalized service learning, so this aspect of the institutionalized service learning experience remains a theoretical and practical vacuum.

The upshot is that we put too many students in situations that, at best, do not fit course learning goals and, at worst, are wholly inconsistent with them. Most institutionalized service learning placements are more appropriate to students in professional programs (social work, community development, planning, etc.), where the experience of delivering various services is directly related to course content. But for liberal arts students, such placements provide experience that by and large talks past the course content. This is not to say that experiential learning is bad but only that it gets confused when we try to tack institutionalized service learning onto it. Among the valuable examples of true experiential learning is a program in British Columbia, Canada, where medical students attend an Aboriginal cultural camp and learn alongside tribal youth about the tribal culture from elders. Bizarrely, this is called service learning, and the University of British Columbia, not the Aboriginal community or even the Fraser Valley Aboriginal Children and Family Services Society running the camp, received the McConnell Family Foundation Award for Community Service-Learning. When a university receives an award for being served by a community, and when the community rather than the university provides the service, misunderstandings are rampant (University of British Columbia, 2012a, 2012b).

In fact, it is entirely possible that most of the learning goals that institutionalized service learning erroneously links to can be better achieved by straight experiential learning. If we want students to experience poverty, we should have them spend a week on the streets, eating at soup kitchens, getting clothes at the shelter, walking miles, attending mock intake meetings with social workers. This is a version of what two social service agency directors and a business owner in Madison did when they acted as homeless people. And people still deemed their action as controversial in terms of whether it provided a true picture of homelessness (Schneider, 2013b). And yes, it's still only a weak, temporary experience, but it is much more consistent with the spirit and method of experiential learning. Institutionalized service learning isn't even in the ballpark in comparison.

There may be only one work-around for at least part of the disconnect between institutionalized service learning and experiential learning in the liberal arts, and that is through the practice of community-based research, or CBR. Bracketing for the moment the many different labels applied to the practice (Chandler & Torbert, 2003), Porpora (1999) and Strand et al. (2003) have suggested that CBR is a more effective form of service learning, employing the research skills that all students supposedly learn in higher education. In CBR, the conduct of research is the service that students and faculty provide. Ideally, the community chooses the issue and then, together with the researchers, determines the research question and method through a participatory process (van de Sande & Schwartz, 2011), though it is often the case that a nonprofit or government agency that only marginally represents some community constituency makes those decisions. If the faculty and students decide by themselves, it's not CBR (Stoecker, 2013).

The advantage of CBR as an object of both experiential and service learning is that an instructor can tie the experience directly to common course objectives. Students can reflect on the research process, from choosing the research question through presenting and using the results. Like the social work student who reads about interacting with "clients" and then does so in an internship, liberal arts students read about doing research and then can do so in a CBR project. Biology students can do environmental testing, sociology students can do surveys, and so on.

CBR, however, presents only a partial solution to the problem of connecting service and experiential learning. To do effective CBR, students need to understand much more than just research methods. Because CBR occurs in a community context, without education on how to understand and interact in that community context, students will only have raw experience, rather than the kind of systematic experience called for in the experiential learning models. This would require, for example, biology majors taking a course on how to understand communities before going out to do biology-oriented service learning.

Further, understanding community contexts and the need for research can shift us from charity to change models. One does not do research except in the service of knowledge development, and one does not engage in knowledge development in a community context except as part of a change process. But it is also easy for those goals to be subverted. The more that academics control the decisions across the five steps of research—choosing the question, designing the methods, collecting the data, analyzing the data, and acting and reporting on the results—the more even CBR can be done as charity or, indeed, as typical colonizing research. And the less tied the CBR is to a community-organized explicit social change goal and strategy, as we will see, the less good it will do anyone.

Critical Service Learning and Popular Education Pedagogy

For service learning practitioners attempting to move beyond institutionalized service learning, the goal is to instill in students a sense of social justice

(Mitchell, 2008). The purpose is explicitly and honestly progressive. While a main defining characteristic of critical service learning is its more explicit focus on social change strategy and tactics, it also has a distinctive pedagogy. I discuss the philosophy of service in critical service learning in the next chapter. Here I concern myself with the theory of learning in the model.

There are those such as Butin (2010, p. 3) who see service learning generally as challenging traditional classroom pedagogy, and specifically the "banking model" of lectures and tests that Paulo Freire (1970) criticizes. And while experiential education certainly contrasts with traditional pedagogy, Freire's critique goes beyond simply method to also critique the content of traditional pedagogy. Mitchell (2008), following Rhoads (1998), argues that much of the pedagogy in critical service learning focuses on exposing and understanding the injustices of the world. Critical service learning asks why the rich get richer and the poor get poorer, why white men do better than everyone else, how things got this way, and how to change them. This is what Freire (1970) refers to as the process of conscientization.

In fact, much of critical service learning pedagogy attempts to build on Paulo Freire, especially his famous book *Pedagogy of the Oppressed* (1970), and some also draw on the work of Myles Horton of the Highlander Folk School (Adams, 1975), today called the Highlander Research and Education Center. Both men practiced a method widely known as popular education (Horton & Freire, 1991), which is a participatory pedagogy where the learners lead and the teachers facilitate. Commonly, the learners gather together to think through a common issue. In doing so they share their experiences around that issue, draw on and share outside knowledge about that issue, and support each other in thinking more deeply and strategically about that issue. As a pedagogy, popular education draws on the experiences of the learners and adds the critical thinking questions to get people to move from their experience to deeper theoretical thinking about the causes of their experience and strategies to move toward greater social justice. It is important to note that the pedagogy did not originate in classrooms and was not meant for classrooms. Paulo Freire developed the pedagogy while working with Brazilian peasants. Myles Horton developed it while working with isolated rural Appalachian residents, rank-and-file industrial workers, and civil rights activists. This was a model of education with and for the oppressed and the exploited.

So we see some similarity between popular education and experiential education. Both draw on the learner's experience. But they differ in that, for experiential education, the teacher is responsible for creating the experience. In popular education, the assumption is that the learners already have the needed experience. In addition, while experiential education is imbued with pragmatist philosophy that eschews critical theorizing, popular education explicitly engages participants wholeheartedly in critical theorizing and makes it a political process (Deans, 1999). But the most important difference is that the target group for the process shifts from the higher education student in experiential education to the exploited and the oppressed in popular education. This is where the application of popular education fails in institutionalized service learning.

Adaptations of popular education have become the standard in critical service learning. Mitchell (2007) describes the Citizen Scholars program at the University of Minnesota, where students spend four semesters engaged in institutionalized service learning and go through a critical learning process that includes community members in the classroom as instructors. While the focus is on power, however, the service learning is still selected by individual students and is generally individualized. It is unclear the extent to which conscientization and social change become a collective process. Gillis and Mac Lellan (2013) combine a relatively traditional institutionalized service learning placement where students participate with a professional service provider (in this case, a clinic) to provide cardiac screening services and healthy lifestyle training to community members, and then study health inequities in the classroom. It seems they did not involve community members in the same discussions around understanding power in health care delivery. Similarly, Rosenberger (2000) provides an excellent exposition of Freire's method, but applies it only to students. Kajner et al. (2013; see also Chovanec et al., 2011) combined a Freirian theoretical approach in the classroom with placements of students in activist groups. Their focus, too, was on critical education in the classroom, though they invited activist groups to participate in the class (only one took them up on the offer). They also forced students to accept placements with activist groups, arguing that it positively affected students' political perspectives, though they did not study outcomes for the activist organizations and we know from other research that forced placements do not necessarily result in good outcomes for community groups (Garcia et al., 2009). Daigre's (2000) method may be the most consistent of all of them, as he had his students conduct institutionalized service learning in community literacy programs, using Freire's critical literacy training method in the centers and his critical pedagogy method in his own classroom. But even here it is unclear whether the strategy invokes a collective social change process. Calderón and Cadena (2007) do not extensively discuss the Freirian popular education process they used in their work with day laborers, but their method of bringing students and day laborers together to learn and act in collaboration is the example that is perhaps most consistent with the method.

This brief review shows that the implementation of critical service learning is incomplete at best. For one thing, a critical popular education pedagogy requires careful community placement. Putting students in typical community agencies providing services to the casualties of the current unjust social system can be problematic because it invites critique of the role of such agencies in maintaining that system. It certainly becomes difficult for students to fill their service hours when the pedagogy is teaching them to reject what they are doing. More fitting placements are groups that are actively engaged in challenging the system. There are, of course, political challenges to doing so that we will consider later, but there are also pedagogical challenges that require us to elaborate the pedagogy.

For another thing, the ground shifts problematically when we attempt to apply the conscientization model to young, privileged, college students. And those who espouse and practice critical service learning mean to apply this model specifically to college students. The proponents of this approach are, with few exceptions, agonizingly quiet on any application of a popular education pedagogy to the constituents they place their students with. Time and time again, critical service learning proponents apply the pedagogy only to students as a general principle (Calderón, 2007; Gillis & Mac Lellan, 2013; Mitchell, 2008; Porfilio & Hickman, 2011), though there are some possible exceptions. Brown's (2001) process includes community activists in some amount of critical pedagogy. Daigre's (2000) method suggests an application with people receiving literacy training. Oden and Casey (2007) describe both critical social justice approaches to the student side of institutionalized service learning, and in the community side mentoring programs such as the Children's Defense Fund freedom schools, but do not link the two.

In the end, using critical pedagogy with college students holds the same challenges found in experiential learning. The desired learning requires personal experiences of oppression and exploitation that the vast majority of students lack. Conscientization around an issue requires direct experience with it. Certainly, it is possible to adapt the method so that students can explore unearned privilege (Mitchell, 2008) and learn about oppression and exploitation. But that is different from popular education and does not require a service experience.

Does Institutionalized Service Learning Have a Hidden Curriculum?

So far, it appears, the two main pedagogies that institutionalized service learning is supposed to implement—experiential learning and critical pedagogy—seem to be bad theoretical fits. That doesn't make the pedagogies bad or wrong. It only leads us to consider whether institutionalized service learning is of value in meeting their goals. In fact, looking at critical pedagogy, it is interesting how often institutionalized service learning advocates ask students to develop critiques in relation to the issues in their service sites, but not to their own classrooms. And yet, one of the most powerful critiques offered by critical pedagogues such as Freire (1970), Giroux (2001), and others has been their critiques of the hidden curriculum of the classroom.

So it does make sense to ask whether institutionalized service learning itself has a hidden curriculum. We have already seen that, under at least some circumstances, institutionalized service learning can reinforce victim-blaming stereotypes of the "others" receiving the services. Swaminathan (2007) also shows, in secondary school service learning, agency supervisors may treat students more from a standpoint of socializing the students to be service providers, potentially conflicting with social justice goals.

An emerging exposition of institutionalized service learning's hidden curriculum is focusing on its reinforcement of racism. Like much of higher education, service learning is a white-dominated practice. The difference between it and other forms of pedagogy is that it involves an application to, and sadly often an experimentation on, poor people of color. According to Mitchell, Donohue, and Young-Law (2012), the usually invisible cultural norms of whiteness infect institutionalized service learning's definitions of the very act of service and of the populations being subjected to the service. Forms of student-community collaboration that involve people of color in actively organizing around issues of importance to them can help subvert a racialized curriculum (Cahill, 2009) while students are in the community. But there is still some question of what happens in the classroom. Critical pedagogy (popular education) is an attempt to expose a racialized service learning. But even attempts at critical pedagogy can subtly reinforce forms of domination when they are reserved only for the students in the university or college separated from the communities where the service learning is occurring.

Most troublingly, there are also those who worry about the very concept of institutionalized service learning as sending the wrong message. Rosenberger (2000, p. 24) "began to question whether institutionalized service learning is yet another way that those who have power and privilege, even if only by education, name the problems and the solutions for the less privileged. I became concerned that institutionalized service learning easily carries connotations of 'doing good,' of the 'haves' giving to the 'have-nots,' of 'we' serving 'them'—perspectives that reproduce positions of power." Masucci and Renner (2001) similarly wonder whether simply the naming of those who serve in contrast to those who are served reinforces a power imbalance in society. And when the best practices of institutionalized service learning include the admonition that "academic credit is for learning, not for service" (Howard, 2001, p. 16; see also University of Nebraska–Kearney, 2015), we must wonder about the message that sends regarding the relative importance of the community. But it is not just that community service is not seen as worthy of a grade. The most damning part of the hidden curriculum might be that we don't even teach the actual skills needed to effectively carry out the service in institutionalized service learning.

Perhaps the most interesting hidden curriculum comes from the development of service requirements in colleges and universities. We will discuss the actual design and practice of required service in the next chapter. Here we will consider only its pedagogical features. And its most interesting pedagogical features, from an experiential learning standpoint, are that it requires students to put in a certain number of hours at a certain place and have those hours verified. If we want students to share some of the same life experience as their "clients," many of whom must punch a clock and put in hours rather than be trusted to just do good work, higher education service requirements make as close a connection as we could hope for. Yet, I don't know of any professor who engages students in reflecting on the experience of having to put in and document hours rather than be treated as responsible adults.

Then we have the civic education goals of institutionalized service learning. So much of the effort in institutionalized service learning is to create good citizens. But it appears that much of the structure and practice of institutionalized service learning actually limits students' practice of global citizenship—that form of citizenship that is not about documentation and identification with artificial geopolitical boundaries but about a sense of commitment to people across those boundaries. Westheimer and Kahne (2004) distinguish the personally responsible citizen, the participatory citizen, and the justice-oriented citizen as models that can derive from institutionalized service learning. Koliba (2004) worries that institutionalized service learning limits students to becoming personally responsible, or "private" citizens who engage in civil society only as self-interested actors, and consequently adopt a neoliberal ideology that individuals are solely responsible for their fate.

Finally, we must ask whether the dominant forms of institutionalized service learning, where we send students into communities to act, but then bring them back into the classroom to interpret a disconnected experience, are complicit in colonizing forms of knowledge. The idea of knowledge colonization has been exposed by Linda Tuhiwai Smith in her book *Decolonizing Methodologies* (2012). She begins from an indigenous knowledge perspective to critique western forms of knowledge creation and transmission that extract data from communities and then send it through a re/mis-interpretation process that muffles the voices and power of the community. I know of those who would reject my critique of institutionalized service learning's misuse of experiential learning, arguing that they really just want students to experience being around poor people and learn through observing them. To the extent to which the "learning" method in institutionalized service learning mirrors this data extraction and transfer process, it also teaches the hidden curriculum of knowledge colonization.

The Missing Curriculum: Community Practice?

We have seen unequivocally that institutionalized service learning's theories of learning are all theories of student learning. Nowhere do institutionalized service learning proponents focus on community learning. Instead, even among the most progressive institutionalized service learning practitioners, we get statements like this one by Gillis and Mac Lellan (2013): "To promote social justice by raising student awareness of root causes of inequities in the community and engage action."

Furthermore, the substance of the learning in the liberal arts, with the exception of community-based research, remains limited to conceptual learning, and those concepts are further limited to what would otherwise be found in a textbook. So students would learn about concepts like poverty and social inequality but, instead of experiencing poverty, would be experiencing the work of a service provider by tutoring kids who live in poverty. Aside from the disconnect between experience and learning we've already discussed, there is a complementary disconnect between the learning and its lack of relevance in preparing students for playing their role in the experience, because they would not have received education in teaching practices and child development to inform their tutoring. Thus, the students learn neither what the service is actually teaching nor what the course content should be teaching in institutionalized service learning.

This double disconnect occurs because, when we put students in a situation where we expect them to provide service to some group, we either just throw them off the end of the pier and hope they will swim or we rely on some community agency staffperson to train and supervise them. It is rare indeed, for example, to require students to know educational theories and child development theories before we send them out to the tutoring program. So the students really are as nonprofit staff perceive them—just glorified volunteers—and the expectations of them are consequently low (Garcia et al., 2009).

The exception, of course, is in the professional programs. Students in education, social work, planning, and the myriad other professional programs are being specifically educated to provide specific services. When they are sent into the community, it is to do the things they have been trained to do. Even in some professional programs, however, the pressures to do institutionalized service learning is compelling them to send out their untrained first-year students to do the same things as the liberal arts students with the same double disconnect (Schaffer, Bonniwell, De Haan, Thomas, & Holmquist, 2014). Such experience may be useful for students trying to decide whether to pursue the field, but it invokes all the problems that institutionalized service learning in the liberal arts exhibits in the lack of skilled service that students are able to provide and the consequent burden placed on the community groups and organizations subjected to these practices.

But this second disconnect is more than not training students to carry out specific forms of service. It is also students' lack of education regarding this convoluted idea of community. I deal with the concept itself in two Chapters 6 and 9, but for now we must consider the lack of preparation we give students (and, indeed, faculty) to work with communities. The biologist can send students out to test the water in the neighborhood stream, but what happens when they find out it's full of toxins, the results get in the news, and people's property values plummet? The sociologist can send students out to do a community survey on fear of crime, but what happens when the results are used by police to step up enforcement, arresting neighborhood leaders for minor drug offenses and disrupting the social fabric of the community to such an extent that there is even more crime?

If our students are to do "community engagement," what do they need to learn about how communities work, about community power, about community development? It is no surprise that action had the weakest association with student outcomes in a major large sample test of the institutionalized service learning model (Stokamer, 2013). In institutionalized service learning we don't educate our students in either the skills of the action we are expecting from them or the dynamics of the community context in which they will be acting. And this is not just about what students do, don't, and should learn. It is also about the service they can, can't, should, and shouldn't do in the community.

5

What Is Institutionalized Service Learning's Theory of Service?

> As compassionate people, we have been evaluating our charity by the rewards we receive through service, rather than the benefits received by the served. We have failed to adequately calculate the effects of our service on the lives of those reduced to objects of our pity and patronage.
>
> —ROBERT D. LUPTON, *Toxic Charity*

Although *service* comes first in *service learning*, it is only because *service* supposedly modifies *learning*, and this is the first thing to understand. In institutionalized service learning, what service most serves is learning and who it most serves is students. Concomitantly, students serve first and foremost to learn, but institutionalized service learning proponents have increasingly emphasized and developed the idea of service. This chapter explores their elaborations.

Service in Societal Context

Service has a long and powerful history in the world. It has often been an integral philosophical feature of oppressive contexts. In a surprisingly wide variety of circumstances, *service* means unquestioning obedience. When police "serve and protect," they do so with orders from public officials. And if a public official orders them to arrest and handcuff anyone from youths to elders who are singing songs in the state capitol building that the public official finds politically offensive, as happened in Wisconsin in 2013 (DeFour, 2013; Desautels et al., 2013), then that is what they do. To be "in the service" means to pledge one's unquestioning obedience to dictatorial command structures as a soldier. People act "in the service of" all kinds of rigid, institutionalized religious doctrine.

It is interesting in this regard to think of the servant—whom we often picture as someone with lesser power—doing the undignified bidding of someone with the power to command. Of course, we have also redefined this term in concepts like "public servant" and "servant leader" (Greenleaf, 2002)—the latter an especially Orwellian turn of phrase where someone with enough power to command others engages voluntarily in the act of serving and developing those others. Such servant leaders are, of course, always free to restrain and limit the qualities and quantities of leadership that those others may achieve. Being a servant with privilege is quite different from being a servant without it, and this is important to understand when considering institutionalized service learning.

Service is also used as charity in many different circumstances. In Google's collected definitions of service, the first is "the action of helping or doing work for someone." That "for" part has always troubled me, and I explore it more in later chapters. Charity itself is an interestingly problematic concept. One of the main charity models is noblesse oblige. Noblesse oblige is an interesting model, originally associated with the "obligations" of the "nobility" to their subjects. The interesting question in history, however, is whether the obligation refers to the nobility directly helping their subjects—doing *for* them—or using their wealth and power to create conditions where their subjects will not need their direct help. On this question there is no historical clarity (C. Lehmann, 2011; K. D. McCarthy, 1982), but the distinction is crucial, since the two interpretations lead to very different kinds of actions.

Today, it appears that the concept of noblesse oblige is generalized as an obligation upon all those who have been bestowed with privilege to "give back." This notion of "giving back," so common in institutionalized service learning language, is interesting. Because in order to "give back" you must have also "received from" or perhaps "taken from." This phrase gets us to the crux of the contradictions of service in institutionalized service learning. First of all, it assumes that those who serve are the privileged, leaving marginalized those who do not come from backgrounds of privilege but nonetheless engage in work with communities. Institutionalized service learning, of course, does tend to attract those who are white and privileged (Green, 2003; Lin, Schmidt, Tryon, & Stoecker, 2009), and it also tends to alienate students who do not come from privilege (Seider, Huguley, & Novick, 2013). Though we know little of why, perhaps these notions of "charity" and "giving back" don't square very well with many students of color and working class students (Simmons & Toole, 2003; Weah, Simmons, & Hall, 2000). For those are the people, in many cases, who have suffered from the elites who have taken from them or from their forebears.

Second, institutionalized service learning proponents rarely analyze the idea of "giving back," and thus leave open the question of where privilege comes from. Ironically (or perhaps not), one of the more popular uses of this phrase in connection with institutionalized service learning is expressed through a youth restorative justice program. The program engages young offenders in what they call "community service learning" (Degelman, Doggett, & Medina, 2006). While the organizers never explicitly say why they chose the phrase *giving back*, in the restorative justice world one *gives back* after one has *taken from* as part of the process of restoring justice. So the connection in this program is direct. Applying this concept within institutionalized service learning is dangerous indeed, as it compels us to consider what has been taken from the First Peoples of North America through acts of colonization, from Africans brought to this land through slavery, and from Chicanos whose foreparents lost their land and rights through war and ultimate colonization against Mexico. Charity, which the all-knowing Google defines as "the voluntary giving of help . . . to those in need" is neither a just nor a logical response to the historical consequences of such injustice.

Third, this idea of giving back in the form of charity has been questioned by Rhoads (1997), following Barber (1992), as separating self-interest from service. In the charity model of "giving back," charity becomes a sacrifice that must be endured. Not exactly a selling point. It is easy to see how this interpretation can lead to resentment or disingenuous service. The alternative is viewing service as also providing something to the server. Of course, finding motivation to engage in service because of the benefits one derives from it can lead to the exploitive form of institutionalized service learning we will explore later on, so shifting the standpoint only further deepens the problem. In fact, many university and college service learning centers are role models for charity as self-recognition. The Morgridge Center for Public Service at the University of Wisconsin–Madison is not named after an important academic or an important role model for higher education community engagement. It is named after its funder. The Ginsberg Center for Community Service and Learning at the University of Michigan, the Haas Center for Public Service at Stanford University, the Gelfand Center for Service Learning and Outreach at Carnegie Mellon University, and numerous other university and college service learning shops across the country are all named for members of their funders' families.

Another way to think about the idea of "giving back" is through the concept of "unearned privilege" as used in the critical service learning literature (Hannah, Tinkler, & Miller, 2011; Mitchell, 2007, 2008; Rice & Pollack, 2000), although unearned privilege is not as prominent in institutionalized service learning as Mitchell (2008) argues. Asserting that students have unearned privilege, and enduring the resistance that is bound to crop up from students socialized in right-wing and neoliberal political cultures along with the guilt that arises in students socialized in liberal and progressive political cultures, is one challenge. Then, as with the principle of noblesse oblige, designing "service" activities around a theory of unearned privilege is another challenge.

Ultimately, such a journey through the terms *noblesse oblige*, *giving back*, and *unearned privilege* should lead us to a critique of the political economic structures that propel this nation and, indeed, the world. Discussion of how wealth is extracted from the poor, working, and middle classes requires a deep critique of capitalism and it is rare indeed to find students reading Karl Marx, or even Thomas Piketty (2014), in their service learning classes. It seems that nowhere are the contradictions of capitalism better laundered than in the notion of giving back that makes taking from, in the form of profit, seem OK.

In such a context, where challenging the political economic structure is not acceptable, a great deal of institutionalized service learning consequently defaults to charity forms of service. The top ten "community issues" addressed through institutionalized service learning, according to the annual Campus Compact (2012) survey, are K–12 education, hunger, housing/homelessness, poverty, mentoring, environment/sustainability, tutoring, health care, reading/writing, and multiculturalism/diversity. We do not see the terms social justice, worker power, community organizing or anything that directly implies social change work. Even much, though not all, of the environment/sustainability focus of institutionalized service learning is about cleaning up the messes and promoting individual behavior change like recycling rather than targeting the causes and the policy makers.

Although I do not dive into a comprehensive discussion of political economy here, some basic principles are important to help us understand why it is so difficult to institute forms of higher education civic engagement, such as institutionalized service learning, as a way to promote justice rather than simply mop up after the destruction left by our current system.

The first principle is that, when we talk about a political economy, we are talking about how economics and politics intertwine. So, for example, in a political economy where laws support worker unionization, we see higher wages and more benefits than in a political economy where the laws thwart worker unionization (Stevans, 2009). And such laws are not simply made by the polity but are influenced heavily by economic interests. Businesses that threaten to close, move, or reduce hiring extort government policy more easily than the electorate can use voting to combat such tactics.

The second principle is that a capitalist political economy is organized on the basis of profit, which means that business owners do not pay their workers everything that they earn. This is easiest to understand in a manufacturing scenario. When workers build refrigerators or sew shirts or make whatever, capitalists sell those products to consumers. After all the wages paid to those who actually make the product are added up, the total is less than what consumers pay. That is profit. When competition is added into the mix, the pressure is on owners to continually cut costs to win and safeguard their profits. This sets up a struggle between workers and owners. Owners also get greedy, trying to maximize their profit, and when government policy is in their favor, they succeed at getting richer by reducing what they pay workers relative to what the workers produce. The least morally guided among them also use the various structures of discrimination available in society—race, sex/gender, age, ability—to pit groups against each other and encourage them to compete against each other for jobs rather than organize with each other (Gordon, Edwards, & Reich, 1982; Marx, 1867/1999).

The third principle is that such a system is inherently unstable. With everyone competing against everyone, and the culture of greed that is promoted by the possibility of accumulating ever greater wealth, there is little predictability. And that means that there are regular cycles of collapse (Gordon, Edwards, & Reich, 1982), the latest of which most of us experienced beginning in 2008. This is not just old Marxist doctrine. Thomas Piketty's influential book (2014) documents these and other problems wrought by a capitalist economy.

With a government dependent both politically and economically on the cooperation of corporate owners, at times of economic collapse elected officials use the resources of government more to subsidize the wealthy and powerful than to support the victims of unemployment, mortgage foreclosure, and worse. It is into such an unstable context that charity enters in the form of the 501(c)(3) "not for profit" organization. Compared with all the other developed nations of the world, the United States has a frighteningly weak social safety net. Universal health care (Neel, 2008), paid family leave (Hall & Spurlock, 2013), and a variety of other public goods that are standard in the developed world are absent or severely lacking in this country. Instead, we have one of the world's largest agglomerations of nonprofit organizations (Anheier & Salamon, 2006)—nearly a million total (Chalmers, 2013)—as the preferred stopgap.

It is important to understand that this "*five-oh-one-see-three*" nonprofit organization is a part of our political economy. The designation 501(c)(3) refers to United States Internal Revenue Service code that establishes what such organizations can and cannot do. A main advantage of such an organization is that it can receive donations that the donors can then use as tax deductions. But these nonprofit organizations cannot spend more than a small fraction of their efforts on political lobbying, and they cannot spend any of their effort on actual political campaigns. And since there is significant variability in defining what actually counts as lobbying, a lot of nonprofits are scared away from engagement in anything that even suggests they might be politically involved (Mehta, 2009). Finally, of course, these nonprofits face restrictions in the profit they can make from selling things, and particularly in how they distribute those profits. Universities and colleges, which are mostly either government agencies themselves or nonprofits (though the for-profit higher education sector is growing), face similar restrictions.

It is also important to understand that nonprofits are unlike a for-profit business in a very crucial characteristic. A business funds itself by producing goods and services that it exchanges for money with those who consume what they produce. A nonprofit also produces goods and services, but it often gives them away rather than selling them (or, if it does sell them, it is usually at a loss). Consequently, a nonprofit must get its money from someone other than a consumer. Thus the concept of the donor. Donors give money to nonprofits that then provide goods and services to "consumers" or "recipients" or "clients." The important result is that nonprofits don't necessarily produce what the "consumers"—those who access the nonprofit resources—want, or need, as much as they produce what the donors will fund.

Obviously, it takes a lot of money to fund such organizations. It is important to understand that individuals making small donations will never be able to provide enough money to fully support a nonprofit. And into the breach steps the philanthropic foundation. A philanthropic foundation provides a tax shelter structure for the wealthiest people in the nation. Foundations as well are nonprofit organizations. But in their case they exist to hold the money of the very rich, invest it, and then spend a portion of the funds on charitable activities. In most cases, this means that foundations give grants—multimillion-dollar grants in some cases but usually far less—to other nonprofit organizations that provide goods and services to a clientele. And that funding process plays an important role in imposing neoliberalism on higher education civic engagement (Kliewer, 2013).

This system creates what Incite! Women of Color Against Violence (2007, 2014) call the *nonprofit industrial complex*. This is another system that the very rich control. So even if the government would allow nonprofits to do more activist work, wealthy foundations wield their leverage in the system to control activism (Incite!, 2007, 2014; Yin, 1998). Now, there are exceptions. Organizations can also choose to be a 501(c)(4) or a wide variety of other subcategories of nonprofit organization, or simply act as an informal group without becoming incorporated. Such groups have much more political freedom. But they give up the ability to solicit tax-deductible donations, making them much more economically vulnerable.

It is easy to see, then, how the nonprofit industrial complex could support a neoliberal political economy. When funders decide to promote entrepreneurship and social entrepreneurship to support the fiction of the self-made individual; when they fund education programs focused on training individuals to accommodate themselves to a low-skill low-wage low-benefit low-dignity job market; when they trickle just enough funds to food banks, domestic violence shelters, and homeless services to keep the poor alive but vulnerable; when they dump massive funds into right-wing think tanks to promote neoliberalism (Ahn, 2007); when they don't fund community-based leadership programs

(Jagpal & Schlegel, 2015); and when they don't fund organizations that might build grassroots power (Jagpal & Laskowski, 2013), they are crafting a neoliberal society in their own image.

The 501(c)(3) nonprofits, trying to pay their own bills, end up following the money. And those who control the money say that nonprofits have to start looking and acting like corporations. This push for "professionalization" of nonprofits transforms them from constituency-based organizations to outsider-controlled organizations that turn oppressed, exploited, and excluded people into categories of pathology and "consumers" or "clients" of services rather than *constituencies*—people with common life circumstances that can and should be organized—instead reducing and disempowering grassroots leadership in the process. Nonprofits consequently become part of the neoliberal problem rather than part of the progressive solution (Bierria, 2007; King & Osayande, 2007).

Such a system, because it serves the interests of so few, can't be organized overtly. It needs to be camouflaged, which is the task of hegemony.

Neoliberal Hegemony and the Service in Institutionalized Service Learning

The idea of hegemony is best traced to Antonio Gramsci (1971), who wrote about it while a political prisoner of the pre–World War II fascist government in Italy. However, the clearest definition I have found is Nathan Palmer's (2012): "When socially powerful people use their influence to convince less powerful people it is in their best interest to do what is actually in the most powerful people's best interest, that's hegemony." I have come to see the dominant forms of service in institutionalized service learning as expressions of neoliberal hegemony. The service appears as benign or even "good" but its effects are to preserve a social system where wealth and power are increasingly channeled into the hands of the very few.

Let's apply the circumstances created by the social context outlined above to institutionalized service learning. The notion of service as obedience to authority is perhaps the most interesting part of the setup. To the extent that education exists to socialize and fit people into the existing political economy, the structuring of higher education service supports this process remarkably well. To the extent that higher education is really preparing students to be wage labor professionals, it is preparing them to occupy contradictory class positions (Wright, 1985) where they have significant control over the labor process but are still employees and thus have to submit to arbitrary hierarchical authority structures, whether as upper level management or top executives.

It is interesting to look at the rise of "required" service learning in this light. More and more higher education institutions are requiring their students to put in a certain number of community service hours in order to graduate. Nearly two-thirds of Campus Compact (2012) member institutions have some form of institutionalized service learning requirement. In many other cases, individual courses require students to put in service hours as part of their course requirements.

I explored the pedagogical features of this practice in Chapter 4. But the service aspects of this requirement are also worrisome. Aside from the obvious oxymoronic logic of "required volunteerism," this requirement doesn't seem to accomplish what it is designed for. Required community service students are seen by nonprofits as providing low-quality service (Garcia et al., 2009). Required community service may also reduce an individual's propensity to volunteer later in life, as the required nature of the service transforms it from an intrinsically fulfilling act to an extrinsically rewarded hoop to jump through (Helms, 2013). The less choice students have to select their own volunteer work, the fewer positive effects they experience from it (Parker-Gwin & Mabry, 1998; Stukas, Snyder, & Clary, 1999).

Some of the research itself participates in hegemony. The one study that asserts students actually like having a service requirement never asked them directly whether they supported having a requirement (Moely & Ilustre, 2011). Like military service, the main impact of required service learning may not be better community service in the form of both direct service outcomes and support for life-long service, but socialization of students to the acceptance of, and even support for, arbitrary hierarchical authority. Skelton (2004) even reminds us that mandatory community service is a sentence for criminalized behavior.

A particular feature of both explicitly required community service and quasi-required service (which shows up in courses requiring community service even when the institution does not have such a requirement) is the requirement that students put in a certain number of volunteer hours to complete the requirement. Colleges and universities tout the value of their institutionalized service learning programs by bragging about how many "hours" students put in. Fancy and expensive hours tracking software have become the standard tools for showing the commitment to institutionalized service learning. At the University of Wisconsin, students can't get a course counted as service learning unless they put in at least twenty-five hours. It doesn't matter whether they put in twenty-five hours stuffing envelopes, babysitting children, or cleaning trash out of the river as long as they put in twenty-five hours and the professor rationalizes it in writing as relevant to the course. Nor does it matter whether those envelopes result in only a meager attendance at the community meeting, the children grow up trapped in the criminal justice system, and the river remains an algae-infested dead zone. Twenty-five hours is twenty-five hours. The standard, I am embarrassed to say, was the result of research I led showing the problems of "short-term service learning," which is also the most popular form of institutionalized service learning (Martin, SeBlonka, & Tryon, 2009). The research unwittingly led, at the time, to our unfortunate conclusion that more hours would equal better service.

This "hours model"—where we require students just to show up for a preset number of hours—is in some ways an odd choice for institutionalized service learning. It is not that useful for many nonprofit organizations as they struggle to train students who count the training hours as part of their hours requirement and then put in little actual service. Other nonprofits struggle to find actual work for students who have only the benefit of the nonprofit's training rather than relevant coursework to build on (Martin, SeBlonka, & Tryon, 2009). The hours model is also no longer such a good fit for how people actually volunteer. These days the most common form of volunteer is not the person who makes a long-term commitment but the "episodic volunteer" (Cnaan & Handy, 2005; Macduff, 2004). The episodic volunteer shows up for short periods to do specific tasks on projects that have a clear start and a clear end. But we have not yet fully recognized the episodic volunteer reality in institutionalized service learning and, as a consequence, we are both wasting and ignoring student and community resources.

We then couple this unproductive hours model to one of the standard supposed best practices in institutionalized service learning—the long-term partnership (Curwood, Munger, Mitchell, Mackeigan, & Farrar, 2011). The focus of the long-term partnership is on channeling a predictable pipeline of students in the hours model to a specific organization in perpetuity. One could argue that this is a bulwark against the decline of the long-term volunteer. It is also premised in a belief in the importance of "relationships" that we will explore more fully in the next chapter. But one of its consequences is that certain organizations reap a windfall of nearly guaranteed student labor while others are denied such benefits. I've been to more than one community where the practice has created resentments and even divisions between nonprofits who get a steady supply of students and others who are shut out altogether. And there are concerns about structural discrimination in who gets and who doesn't get service learning. The largest organizations, such as schools, who are large at least partly because they are fully and comfortably integrated into the nonprofit industrial complex, are some of the most common recipients (Campus Compact, 2012), as are those organizations closest to campus (Stoecker & Schmidt, 2008). There is not enough pressure for offering institutionalized service learning students to organizations because of their potential for real accomplishment or the criticality of the organization's issue. In a neoliberal context, it is easy to see how the decimation of publicly supported anything creates a severe gap for even basic services—things that used to be provided by tax dollars now must be provided either by fee for service or by voluntary money and labor. In K–12 schools, service learners are a ready source of "voluntary" labor to replace the loss of paid staff.

Of course, politically "controversial" organizations like Planned Parenthood and more activist organizations of any kind have difficulty getting students from institutionalized service learning programs. Instead, the easy choice is the seemingly apolitical 501(c)(3) service nonprofit. And it is not that such service organizations are not controversial. They are not controversial in a neoliberal context. I remember visiting with students from one prominent university's institutionalized service learning program—college students involved in a program to "help kids stay in school." When I gently asked them whether they had any qualms about trying to socialize kids to fit the school rather than organizing the kids to change the school, they looked at me like I was a Martian, and their professor was offended I wasn't congratulating them on what good service learners they were. My question, rather than their service, was deemed controversial. That is how far neoliberal hegemony has infused our thinking.

It might seem odd that some organizations would be complaining that they are not receiving their fair share of service learners when the research is showing that service learners are not all that useful in terms of capacity enhancement. That same research, however, shows that organizations value having service learners even when they are not that useful, seeing them as at least a source of potential volunteers or, down the road, even potential staff or donors (Bell & Carlson, 2009). They do not see students, however, as we try to present them through the promotion of institutionalized service learning—as people bringing knowledge and skill to organizations. Students are, it appears, simply a convenient volunteer pool and higher education institutionalized service learning offices tout their ability to provide a steady stream of volunteers perhaps more than anything else they do.

The ideal service activity in this volunteer-centric model is individual students working for individual organizations serving individual "clients." Here, too, we see the insidious influence of neoliberalism. The ideology of entrepreneurialism, from the individual student supposedly making a difference to the individual organization going it alone even when there are dozens of other nonprofit organizations working on the same problem in the same place, to the individual recipient who will supposedly be lifted up to succeed as an individual, are all symptomatic of neoliberal hegemony.

And while the mantra is that "the community" (which we will deal with in the next chapter) must decide what the need or problem or whatever is that the service learner works on, the reality is that is hardly ever the case. Grab almost any university or college office's definition of institutionalized service learning off their website and you will, in the best cases, read words like "partnering"

or "doing with" or "empowering." But then go to their page listing their partners and, with rare exceptions, you will find charity organizations—organizations doing things to people or for them, rather than with them. You will
find projects that subject recipients to programs designed, packaged and delivered without any apparent influence by the recipients. Especially given how
much institutionalized service learning focuses on children, through programs
designed by adults "for" the children, what would service learning look like
where the children had power in program design and implementation?

There is something about the service in institutionalized service learning
that is even more troubling because it expresses the fundamental principle of
neoliberalism, which is the acceptance of exploitation. One defining feature of
institutionalized service learning is that there is a service provider and a service
recipient. The student is the service provider and some organization or community member is the recipient. But the other even more central defining feature of institutionalized service learning is for the student to learn something.
Now, the problem with combining these two principles is that really effective
service requires the service provider to be well educated and highly skilled.
But the more educated and skilled the student service learner is, the less likely
it is that they will define the experience as educational. The more I train my
students for their work in the community, the more likely it is they will report
on the course evaluation that they didn't learn very much. So the common
practice, especially in the liberal arts as I have discussed, is for faculty to send
out students without much serious educational preparation and to expect the
community and service organizations to provide what is needed.

Institutionalized service learning proponents even promote resume enhancement as a motivation for community service (see, for example, Byrne,
2013; Keller, 2011; Witkop, 2005). So common is this practice that some
community agency staff see institutionalized service learning as community
organizations serving the educational needs of students, and they don't resent
it (Bell & Carlson, 2009). In the worst cases, students end up in a process
that reduces to poverty tourism and/or resume padding, exploiting community agency staff and community members' time for their own education and
career advancement. In most cases, agency staff and/or community members
volunteer their time to educate students—in the experiential learning model,
essentially doing the paid professor's work—and receive less value in return
than they should.

It is easy to see the power dynamics of such a relationship. In one case an
institutionalized service learning office actually organized a student-run week-
end homeless shelter in its gymnasium. To "protect the students," people seeking shelter had to submit to weapons searches and drug tests—the students did
not. Service learning done in a charity model context risks reinforcing a class
structure that separates the haves and have-nots. It may make the haves a bit

more civic-minded, but is just as likely to reinforce neoliberal ideology in its promotion of students as praiseworthy providers of services to those the ideology defines as having "deficits" (Kretzmann & McKnight, 1993; McKnight, 1995) and being "underserved" rather than oppressed, exploited, and excluded. Institutionalized service learning even unwittingly contributes to the culture of exploitation of the have-nots by the haves as students reframe poorly conceived and poorly designed service in the hours model to expand their resumes and enhance their career prospects without providing a proportional lift in the prospects for the have-nots they "serve."

This engages us in a subtle form of "regulating the poor" whereby charity forms of social service expand as oppression and exploitation expand. Social services absorb the misery of the victims and individualize their suffering, instead of organizing groups who could otherwise engage in collective self-help to meet their immediate needs and also work to change the system that is producing their pain (Piven & Cloward, 1993). In its most oppressive manifestations, the charity approach brings with it a subtle form of victim blaming (Ryan, 1976). So, if the tutee misses the tutoring session, it must be because they aren't motivated rather than because the tutor is unhelpful. And the most common form of institutionalized service learning offers depoliticized and individualized treatments to "fix" individuals rather than to change systems.

None of this, of course, is to say that it is bad to help individuals get food, clothing, and shelter. It is only bad to do that without engaging those individuals in a discussion about the political economic system that creates those needs and without an approach that engages those individuals in organizing themselves for collective action to deal not just with the immediate need but also with its cause. This is important. Charity is about doing things to people and for them, maintaining their dependence on the charity provider. When we are the charity provider, we promote dependence, not empowerment. And I know, it takes time to get rid of root causes and, in the meantime, people will go hungry, cold, homeless, and will die. We can't ignore immediate needs. But we can also meet immediate needs in empowering ways, by organizing people to meet their own needs collectively. The examples of groups that have organized for both collective self-help and social change, from the Back of the Yards Neighborhood Organization (Horwitt, 1992; Slayton, 1986) to the United Farm Workers (Ganz, 2009; Rothman, 1995) to the Black Panther Party (Alkebulan, 2007; Oden & Casey, 2007) belie the argument that we shouldn't criticize charity-only approaches because they are necessary. Charity-only approaches can be replaced by collective self-help approaches that not only meet immediate needs but also build power.

If part of neoliberalism's job is to return us to a Hobbesian state of nature where the most brutal and uncaring accumulate the most power and riches, then institutionalized service learning is playing an effective supporting role.

Creating an attitude where volunteerism is becoming a cynical course assignment, counting hours rather than accomplishments, promoting service for individual advancement, and providing just enough charity to maintain the victims of an unjust social system while doing nothing to change that system, institutionalized service learning helps keep the angers and resentments of the have-nots from boiling over while those with the most power and wealth continue to accrue more than their share of both.

The problems and contradictions of institutionalized service learning are not going unnoticed. There is significant push-back on its most oppressive and exploitive qualities.

The Response to Neoliberalism in Institutionalized Service Learning

As critiques built around the most exploitive practices of institutionalized service learning, the ideas of "reciprocity" and "mutual benefit" became prominent in the rhetoric of the practice. The most basic principle behind reciprocity, or mutual benefit, is that both parties should receive something from the relationship. But it's actually more muddy (Kliewer, Sandmann, Kim, & Omerikwa, 2010) and complicated than that, necessitating that we examine the assumptions behind the ideas of reciprocity and mutual benefit. The concepts are somewhat different in their actual definitions, but given that proponents use the terms as more of a principle than an exact practice, and that variations occur in practice regardless of what someone may say their definition is, we can forgive their interchangeability.

Reciprocity is actually an old idea in service learning. Institutionalized service learning proponents generally apply it to the relationship "between the server and the group or person being served" (Jacoby, 1996, p. 7). Jacoby (1996, pp. 7–8), who traces the idea at least back to Kendall (1990), emphasizes reciprocity as the development of a sense of mutual responsibility between server and served. Both community members and students are supposed to get something out of the relationship in a kind of complementarity of benefits. In practice, however, this principle is rarely realized in this way. Coming together and developing a sense of mutual responsibility occurs within members of a single community, not between a student who maybe spends twenty hours total in a community setting, and community members who live there. In addition, true mutual benefit occurs when multiple parties are working toward a shared goal, not when each is working toward a separate goal, which is what happens in typical institutionalized service learning. Even in otherwise highly participatory community-based research projects, the operationalization of reciprocity guiding the collaboration emphasizes separate, rather than common, interests (Maiter, Simich, Jacobson, & Wise, 2008). What we end up with as a consequence is not reciprocity in the sense of Jacoby's and Kendall's mutuality but an exchange relationship between two parties (Keith, 2005). That exchange relationship is ostensibly and typically not even between a student and a community member but between a student and a nonprofit organization. The student is supposed to give service hours and the organization and/or community is supposed to give learning to the student, in which case we get the very strange situation whereby the service recipient becomes the medium through which the exchange is made. The notion of "mutual benefit" is very narrowly defined in this philosophy. Students must benefit, the college/ university reputation should benefit, the nonprofit service organization should benefit, and individuals in communities should benefit. Benefits, except in the case of the higher education institution, are also direct and short-term. This is not about social justice or long-range societal change.

There are a number of other issues that result from defining the exchange relationship as between students and community organizations. First is the question of whether making the student the main party on the higher education side of the exchange is reasonable. Certainly, if the student is acting solely on their own as an independent volunteer, then the relationship is direct. But, when the student is fulfilling institutional requirements, they are acting as a representative of the institution, and the exchange relationship then is also between the community group or organization and the higher education institution. And here is where the notion of reciprocity becomes even stranger. The requirement that any under-resourced community group should provide a benefit to a multimillion- or multibillion-dollar higher education institution in exchange for receiving services from it is odd indeed. Kliewer and colleagues (2010) offer some thinking about reciprocity in relation to this power imbalance, but don't offer guidance on what to do about it.

The concept of reciprocity/mutual benefit becomes even more interesting when we ask what each side is receiving. The institution is receiving reputational credit it can use to recruit tuition-paying students and procure grant funds. The Carnegie community engagement classification requires institutions to document their community engagement activities, albeit superficially, and institutions use the resultant classification to attract additional funding. The institution is also receiving low-cost or even no-cost educational services from communities. It is unclear what the community or nonprofit organization is receiving. It is receiving a certain number of "hours" from students, but those hours are not substantial after you subtract the time that organization staff put in training and supervising the students. And there is a nagging question about what those hours are actually producing. The dearth of research on the actual impacts of institutionalized service learning (Stoecker, Beckman, & Min, 2010; Stoecker & Tryon, 2009a) leads to the worry that community organizations and communities are not getting much out of the deal, and the little research we do have suggests that community groups are mainly hoping that their service to students will result in getting the word out about their issue and perhaps attract more support from the general public (Garcia et al., 2009).

Concern about the lack of impacts of institutionalized service learning that exposes the inequity of "mutual benefit" rhetoric is also fueling an interest in project-based approaches that contrast with the hours model. In a project-based approach, the community group or organization identifies a project it wants done—a website, an annual meeting, a survey, or anything that has a definitive start and a definitive end (Chamberlain, 2003; Coyle, Jamieson, & Oakes, 2005; Draper, 2004). The advantage of the project model over the hours model in relation to mutual benefit is that it produces identifiable deliverables, making it much easier to know what has been accomplished. Community-based research also fits the project model in designing and carrying out research projects.

However, the project model is just as likely as the hours model to be imposed on communities. While the principle is that the community group should choose the project, the reality in many cases is that academics choose what to provide and community groups and organizations are left deciding whether to accept what is being offered. I've been in the position of offering an institutionalized service learning program that provided student-based information technology services to community groups. Many nonprofits took us up on it, but there were other things they would rather have had. When we realized that we didn't have the capacity to offer the high-end start-from-scratch fancy database and content management websites that they hoped for, we had to limit them to their second-choice information technology projects (Stoecker, Loving, Reddy, & Bollig, 2010). Ashleigh Ross (2014) describes the Bayou Bienvenue restoration project in New Orleans, carried out in the wake of Hurricane Katrina, as an example of academics offering a project to communities. In this case, the academics knew how to restore wetlands but not how to restore housing. As with my project, bayou restoration wasn't community's first choice, but they graciously went along with it. There are many other examples. As long as institutionalized service learning has to answer to curricular and disciplinary commands, community groups and organizations will always have to choose from a menu they had no hand in constructing.

As I've already noted, the most conscious response to the creeping influence of neoliberalism in institutionalized service learning is critical service learning. Mitchell (2008) traces her model of critical service learning to Rhoads's (1997) term "critical community service." For Mitchell (2008, p. 51), "Critical service-learning programs encourage students to see themselves as agents of social change, and use the experience of service to address and respond to injustice in communities." Those who practice critical service learning also emphasize the importance of building relationships beyond roles of "have" and "have-not," or the server and the served (Masucci & Renner, 2001; Mitchell, 2008). Wade (2000, p. 97) suggests an intriguing distinction between "service to an individual" and "service for an ideal," implying a critique of the neoliberal individualism inherent in much institutionalized service learning.

But these authors don't really give us much to go on in terms of their actual practice in communities. Mitchell (2008) offers no thoughts on the actual strategy for achieving social justice beyond critical analysis and even preserves some of the problematic features of the charity model such as the long-term partnership. Her application of the model only focuses on the students and suggests that, while she asked students to engage in more critical reflection, the service sites remained the typical placements that themselves were not focused on social change (Mitchell, 2007). Masucci and Renner (2001) only offer "practical" suggestions for inside the classroom. And Wade (2000) really only offers critique. These problems are similar for nearly all the rest of the literature. There is no developed alternative model of actual practice off campus. So service remains service.

The Lack of Service in Institutionalized Service Learning

While the pedagogical principles in institutionalized service learning are clear, even if problematic, the service principles are muddled at best. By and large, institutionalized service learning blindly follows the flow of the nonprofit industrial complex, providing charity style services treating the victims of an unjust political economic system without critiquing either the system or institutionalized service learning's role in maintaining it. Critical service learning does ask deeper questions on this topic, but provides no real guidance on how to change the actual service part of institutionalized service learning. So in the place of skilled professional services we now have required volunteers with little relevant training.

The dominant models of institutionalized service learning thus serve mostly to maintain a growing neoliberal political economic structure and culture. By focusing on individuals serving individuals—through tutoring programs, ESL programs, after-school programs, shelters, and so on—institutionalized service learning maintains a cultural belief in the singular, unreflective neoliberal myth of the autonomous individual. While there may be focus on a systems analysis, at least in critical service learning, there is not a focus on a systems solution in practice. Furthermore, in contrast to its rhetoric, institutionalized service learning's practice is still primarily about individual college students defined as smart and competent serving people who are defined as, at worst, deficient and lacking or, at best, "underserved." This maintains a separation, rather than a connection, between server and served. At its most cynical, the practice of service becomes reduced to an assignment to be completed and a resume line to be achieved.

The problematic nature of service in institutionalized service learning is not simply a result of neoliberalism's contagious and hegemonic influence. After all, service learning is a practice being conducted through the ivory tower. And while we often use the term *ivory tower* pejoratively, the strength of being in an ivory tower is about being above the fray and seeing things that those without access to the tower cannot. We supposedly have sophisticated methods for doing just that, and the most important of those methods is clear conceptualization. But as we move further through the concepts of institutionalized service learning we will see sloppier and sloppier conceptualization.

The next concept, the idea and ideal on which institutionalized service learning is supposedly constructed—the community—is the sloppiest of them all.

6

What Is Institutionalized Service Learning's Theory of Community?

> Economic division is fractioned even more by the tendency of
> professional people and intellectuals to cohere in widely dispersed
> "networks," often to the virtual exclusion of communities. Many
> people now feel more at home, and more at ease socially, at a profes-
> sional convention than in the streets of their own neighborhood.
>
> —WENDELL BERRY, *The Art of the Commonplace*

The term *community* is ever present in the institutionalized service learning literature. Its use dominates journals, infuses practices such as
community-based research or community-based learning, and injects
phrases such as "in the community" across the field. A search of the *Michigan
Journal of Community Service Learning* for the phrase "the community" turned
up 269 articles using it 2,708 times.

However, there is much less discussion in those articles on who the community actually is. And herein lies the problem. The word *community* means
everything and nothing. "Community" refers to nonprofit service organizations that have nothing in common with their target constituency. It refers to
government agencies that often do harm to many constituencies. It refers to
schools that are often controlled by people who have little to no connection
with the families the school serves. It refers to entire cities. It refers to amor-
phous categorical clumps like "the Black community." It refers to constituencies like "the poor." It refers to a nice feeling people get when they are "in
relationship" with each other.

Following Corlett (1993), Keith (2005, p. 16) explores two sources for the
term *community*. The first "emphasizes shared meanings, bonds, and a sense of
belonging." The second "means 'united through service.' This is a minimalist
community whose members are linked through reciprocal duties and obligations involving services. . . ." Not surprisingly then, institutionalized service
learning shops like the Morgridge Center for Public Service at the University
of Wisconsin (2008) clearly veer to the second definition when they define
the community as organizations such as neighborhood associations, nonprofit

agencies, educational organizations like schools, and nongeographic groups who share cultural or value characteristics—like people who are gay. And myriads of practitioners never define the concept at all, going with an unacknowledged implicit gut level belief that somehow they will just know it when they see it. So bad is the situation that, when Cruz and Giles (2000) explored the absence of careful thought about the community in institutionalized service learning, they actually give up on trying to define *community* even as they continued to use the term throughout their article. The next year, Gelmon, Holland, Driscoll, Spring, and Kerrigan (2001) also said they couldn't define community and then defaulted to looking at nonprofit agencies as the proxy for community and the effect of institutionalized service learning on "clients" as the focus of assessment.

And yet, after *learning* and *service*, no term is more important to the practice than *community*. It is what we yearn for, what the best of our nature strives to achieve, what we say we lack. The zeitgeist of U.S. culture holds the idea of community in the highest esteem, and maintains the mantra that there was always "more" community in the past in apparent hopes of realizing it in the present. "Community" is what my students called themselves as they were engaging in the ultimate act of service learning at the time, occupying the state capitol in Wisconsin in opposition to a right-wing government that was systematically dismantling democracy around us. It's what the residents of rural Haliburton County, in central Ontario where I am currently writing, say they are trying to preserve as they organize to maintain their own community radio station, a co-op that sponsors many of the major community service and arts projects, and a practice of neighboring that welcomes travelers from afar into their homes to eat and sleep.

Why has this idea become so important to us? Why do we use this word so frequently in institutionalized service learning? Understanding these questions can help us in understanding part of how institutionalized service learning has developed.

The Idea of Community in the United States

It is important to consider the extent to which the idea of community that we consciously and unconsciously embed in institutionalized service learning derives from eighteenth-century white, Protestant New England, for it is in eighteenth-century New England that the concepts of civic engagement and the interdependent community were most prominent. With small farms rather than the large plantations common in the southern colonies, New England colonial towns, as described by historians, were tight-knit and interdependent. People produced many goods and services locally and bartered and volunteered skills. Townspeople organized civic life through the famous "town meeting," where they came together to discuss the issues of the day and make collective decisions about them (Hall, 2011).

Of course, this idyllic-sounding, fully engaged, fully integrated community only existed for those of its free citizens who bought into the religious doctrine of early New England Protestantism (Knight, 1994; Melish, 2000). This was not an inclusive democracy of diversity. Still, a sanitized version of community that filters through history from its colonial New England origins nonetheless seems to hold an abstract draw for many institutionalized service learning advocates. And yet so much institutionalized service learning practice also seems to problematically reflect that culture with its emphasis on encouraging our mostly white middle and upper middle class students to become engaged in charity work that neither encourages nor supports people who are on the margins—who are of color, are young, and/or are in poverty—to become civically engaged.

In the mid-nineteenth century, Alexis de Tocqueville, one of institutionalized service learning's heroes (Kenny & Gallagher, 2002), arrived on the scene with his famous book *Democracy in America* (1840/1988). de Tocqueville also cited the New England colonies as the source of civic culture in this land still considered new by Europeans, but also provided a much more comprehensive analysis of U.S. politics. It is interesting that practitioners do not cite de Tocqueville so much for his study of the "association" in U.S. society—a *collective* concept—but as justification to urge the *individual* to become engaged in service (Grimm, Dietz, Foster-Bey, Reingold, & Nesbit, 2006; Kenny & Gallagher, 2002, p. 18; UMKC Service-Learning, 2013a, 2013b), to justify charity work (Pritchard, 2001), or to laud the role of the association but then ignore its implications for practice and simply return to a focus on the individual student (Battistoni, 1997).

And yet we can't escape the focus on the individual when we try to talk about the community. de Tocqueville in fact pointed out that the United States has a peculiar civic culture that defines civic engagement not as a moral obligation but as a self-interested calculation. There is no personal gain in doing good just to do good, but to do good because it advances one's own interests. This self-interested individualism also undergirds the idea of reciprocity discussed in Chapter 5, but it is not de Tocqueville's idea. His thinking was not about the exchange of one thing for another but more about the individual understanding that the individual's self-interest is integrally connected to the broader community's interest—that we all sink or swim together. And such thinking made sense at a time when corporations had not yet deskilled people to the point that they were dependent on money to mediate everything, so they in fact were interdependent as they shared and bartered with their neighbors.

This is plus-sum thinking. In a context of true interdependence, my "sacrifice" of time and effort is actually an "investment" because in benefiting the community I also benefit. In Colonial New England, for example, if I spent time helping to build the town hall I got to use it for community events, meetings, and other activities. But today when I help tutor an inner-city kid in math, the material benefits to me are twistedly indirect. To see how my fate, sad to say, is bound up with that child's fate requires the most abstract of reasoning. Direct interdependence simply doesn't exist in such relationships.

It is much easier, in fact, to see how much we now exist in a zero-sum society. Neoliberal hegemony tells us that protecting the environment will reduce jobs, increasing the minimum wage will reduce jobs, providing health care for all will reduce jobs, providing anything for the collective good will harm all individuals. And, because we now live in a neoliberal society, this rhetoric is contextually correct. Because corporations call the shots, they can choose to recover the costs for anything that reduces their profits, like putting scrubbers in their smokestacks, by reducing the pay to workers or increasing the costs to consumers or both. Thus, protecting the environment will cost jobs because corporate controllers can decide that it will cost jobs. Taken to the extreme, this context even makes it possible to think that tutoring an inner-city kid in math could increase that child's chances of getting a college education and add another able mind to the already overbooked jobs competition. Taking the logic just a small step further, is it really in the college student's neoliberally defined self-interest to provide such service and increase the jobs competition?

Add to this the now famous "bowling alone" problem created by Putnam (1995, 2000) in his now famous book. While the debate raged over whether we really participate less (Ladd, 1996; Lee, Oropesa, Metch, & Guest, 1984; N. Lehmann, 1996; Paxton, 1999) in the civic associations that de Tocqueville saw as so quintessentially defining of the United States, institutionalized service learning proponents saw Putnam as a new raison d'être for their practice. But Putnam's *Bowling Alone* is simply one more catchily titled study in a long line of studies on the "decline of community" starting in the 1950s (Nisbet, 1953; Stein, 1960). Interestingly left off of the list of decline of community theorists by institutionalized service learning practitioners and scholars is George Ritzer (1993), who also had a popular book with a catchy title, *The McDonaldization of Society*. Ritzer's argument is that our society, and its organizations, are becoming hyper-rationalized. The core processes at work are efficiency, calculability, predictability, and control. And they result in the systematic dismantling of community as public-private development partnerships replace neighborhoods with top-down planned housing developments, corporations reduce workers to performing deskilled mind-numbing jobs, and bureaucracies sever relationships between humans and replace them with relationships to machines and especially information and communication technologies.

Hyper-rationalization has been extended to higher education (Hayes & Wynyard, 2002), and it is possible to further extend it to institutionalized service learning. By focusing on establishing requirements, standardizing methods, and calculating "hours" to achieve the strangely coveted Carnegie classification, institutionalized service learning has quickly succumbed to the McDonaldization effect. So institutionalized service learning's response to the decline of community is to adopt the characteristics of the declined community. Most distressingly, in our institutionalized service learning courses, we apparently apply the idea of McDonaldization only to interpret and analyze partner organizations (likely without their participation or accountability to them; see V. Johnson, 2008; Rimmerman, 2011) rather than to institutionalized service learning itself.

So, much like the sociology of community, which has removed the idea of a "place" as a requirement for a community (Fischer, 1982), institutionalized service learning has also allowed the term *community* to become disconnected from any concrete anchor as it drifts increasingly toward an idea of *civic* rather than an idea of *community*. But the term itself is still ubiquitous in the literature, so it must mean something. We can get some clues to the theories of community that institutionalized service learning practitioners prefer by looking at their practice. In doing so, we can get a sense of how well those theories serve us.

Theories of Community Reflected in Institutionalized Service Learning

When we look at the institutionalized service learning literature, there is really little discussion of the theories of community preferred by practitioners, though there are a few philosophical articles that review various definitions (Keith, 2005; Koliba, 2004; Ludlum Foos, 1998; Williams & Ehrlich, 2000) or focus on students as a community (Saltmarsh, 1996). As a consequence, we are reduced to inferring what practitioners' theoretical approaches are from the community-related theoretical perspectives that they seem to imply on a regular basis.

Of the theories and philosophies seemingly reflected in institutionalized service learning, perhaps the most comprehensive of them is communitarianism. A strong communitarian vein seems to reside in at least one wing of the institutionalized service learning literature. There is lots of variation within communitarianism, just like in any philosophy, so I will try to focus on what seems to be most common among the most widely read communitarians and the platform they have developed through the Communitarian Network. Communitarianism, in brief, eschews rights-based definitions of citizenship for a rights and responsibilities approach (Barber & Battistoni, 1993; Etzioni, 1996). Politically, it is a mixture of progressive and conservative politics, supporting both limited government but also "domestic disarmament" of individuals using a form of conservative strict constructionism in interpreting the second amendment of the U.S. constitution as applying only to local militias and not to individuals. Communitarians exalt the family (and don't make a special point of highlighting non-nuclear and non-heterosexual family types under that label) and schools as the most important institutions in society (Communitarian Network, 2010).

Like everyone else, communitarians have difficulty defining the word *community* but they seem to imply some kind of face-to-face quality, with interwoven "affect-laden relationships" and a shared culture (Etzioni, 2003, p. 4). Beyond this abstraction, however, the idea disintegrates. Everything from a writing group to a workplace to who knows what can be a community. Communitarians also dispute the typical conceptualization of an opposition between self and community. Rather than seeing community as constraining the development of individual autonomy, they see it as promoting more reflective, responsible, and fully human individuals (Etzioni, 2003). Moral or values education, consequently, becomes centrally important in communitarianism. Perhaps most importantly, however, the idea of structural oppression doesn't exist in communitarian thought. It's either not there or ignored, and this helps direct communitarian thought away from social change.

How is communitarianism reflected in institutionalized service learning practice? Harry Boyte (2003) goes so far as to attribute the growth of institutionalized service learning directly to the influence of communitarianism, though the lack of explicit linkage between communitarian thought and institutionalized service learning practice in the literature leads me to think the influence is more implicit. Regardless, the influence is there. Communitarians promote mandatory education-based community service. For Barber (1991), requiring community service learning is no more problematic than requiring chemistry or English literature. And the communitarian emphasis on values education is reflected in many forms of institutionalized service learning, particularly those that are prominent in faith-based higher education institutions. Communitarianism also invokes the value of reciprocity. But it is not the simple exchange reciprocity practiced in so much institutionalized service learning. Instead, communitarian reciprocity is a principle where "each member of the community owes something to all the rest, and the community owes something to each of its members" (Communitarian Network, 2010).

Now, such community level reciprocity is particularly difficult in institutionalized service learning when there is no community, when students appear only an hour or two a week in a service organization, and when the service maintains the unequal roles of service provider and service recipient. In institutionalized service learning, the practice of reciprocity is based on alienated exchange relationships between people from separate communities who will go their separate ways once the service relationship is ended, straying from communitarian meanings where the reciprocal relationship is between the individuals and their community. The attempts by institutionalized service learning to instill a sense of citizenship in such circumstances retain and reflect neoliberalism's reduction of the global citizen to a "private" citizen whereby one individual exchanges with another individual rather than becomes engaged in a broader web of generalized reciprocity (Keith, 2005). To a large extent, institutionalized service learning proponents seem to have more clarity on the idea of citizenship, at least as it applies to college students, than to either the idea of community or even the civic engagement of the people off campus "being served by" institutionalized service learning.

The distancing of institutionalized service learning from communitarianism in practice, even when institutionalized service learning echoes communitarian principles in rhetoric, is also symptomatic of a second approach to the idea of community—the idea of social capital. Of all the possible theorists of social capital available to institutionalized service learning advocates, they have by and large chosen Robert Putnam. Putnam's (2000) famous bowling alone thesis—that U.S. society is becoming less of a culture of joiners—is also oft-quoted by communitarians (Etzioni, 2003) and reinforces the relevance of both communitarianism and social capital theory as the philosophical foundation for institutionalized service learning practice. Institutionalized service learning thinkers apply Putnam primarily to students, and rarely use him as more than a token reference to cite the declining involvement of people in public life (see Koliba, 2004). But the common use of Putnam helps us understand how institutionalized service learning treats the idea of community.

For Putnam (1995, 2000), social capital is mainly about networks, norms, and trust. To some extent, these things also define his thinking about community. The idea is teleological—networks build trust that builds networks that depend on norms that arise from networks that build trust, and so on. Regardless, for Putnam a strong community has many cross-cutting networks with norms that stabilize them and trust that characterizes those stable networks.

The question is whether institutionalized service learning does anything to build those networks, norms, and trust. Certainly, we can see Putnam's influence in institutionalized service learning's emphasis on "long-term partnerships." Institutionalized service learning advocates presume that a long-term partnership will create stronger networks and more trust between the higher education institution and the nonprofit agency. Of course, therein lies the problem. Technically the relationship is between two formal organizations, even though, as I have discussed, it is often implemented and maintained by students and specific nonprofit staff. But as agency staff come and go and students come and go, the bureaucratic long-term partnership is not between individuals but between organizations, neither of which may actually be controlled by the people most affected by it. This is not a foundation on which to build community.

Putnam prepares institutionalized service learning proponents to respond to this concern by distinguishing between bonding and bridging social capital—roughly analogous to the strong ties and weak ties analysis developed by Granovetter in 1973. Strong ties are close personal relationships. Weak ties are more limited working relationships. Bridging social capital—weak ties—refers to connections between networks of bonded social capital—strong ties. Strong ties characterize strong communities. But higher education institutions and community agencies are linked by working relationships—weak ties. Keith (2005) cites such bridging social capital as a potential focus for institutionalized service learning to build connections between students and poor people, but doing so requires collaboration between those two parties that transcends students giving services to people with needs. Thus, institutionalized service learning practice, which emphasizes individual students filling hours at nonprofit agencies, still begs the question of whether there are any collectivities of strong ties involved in the process. If neither a higher education institution nor a nonprofit agency can be described as a community of strong ties, then what are the weak ties actually linking?

In addition to communitarianism and social capital theory, a third path toward community that institutionalized service learning practitioners have been trying to make is away from a needs-based model that violates the original conceptualization of reciprocity (because it separates the server and the served) and toward "asset-based" thinking (Garoutte & McCarthy-Gilmore, 2014; Learn and Serve America, n.d.; Shabazz & Cooks, 2014). As the critiques of the charity model of institutionalized service learning grew, a parallel critique of social services in general sprang up and attempted to promote "asset-based" approaches (Kretzmann & McKnight, 1993; McKnight, 1995). The idea is that social services approaches assume that people in poverty have "deficits" or personal deficiencies, and that we should instead look upon those people as having "gifts" or "assets." And there is significant fear that institutionalized service learning has, by virtue of its dominant service-oriented charity approach, by default treated people in poor communities as "deficient" (Daynes & Longo, 2004; McCabe, 2004).

The argument of the asset-based service learning perspective is that simply providing services to people starts from an assumption that they are lacking both the substance of the service and the ability to organize the service themselves. So, for example, we provide an after-school tutoring program in a poor neighborhood, designing it on campus, perhaps with nonprofit agency staff, and then we "give" it to the local youth. Such an approach, an asset-based argument asserts, assumes that the youth are deficient in both the academic skills the tutoring provides and in the ability to get the help they need without outsiders providing it for them. And the result, from an asset-based perspective, is that the process sends the message to youth that they should feel stupid and deficient because they "need" "help" and can't help themselves. Consequently, the service activity risks doing harm. So then advocates like Koliba (2004, p. 64) substitute an assets perspective that they assert can prevent institutionalized service learning from doing harm and provide a foundation that empowers communities to engage in collective self-help.

How do institutionalized service learning designers do this? Hatcher and Erasmus (2008) say that employing an asset-based perspective involves shifting from thinking about community needs to focusing on community goals. As we will see, however, asset-based approaches hardly have a lock on that particular strategy. Others advocate "asset mapping," in which residents are surveyed about their skills and talents and often about what strengths they see in their neighborhoods (Shabazz & Cooks, 2014). Cummings (2000) used an asset-based and relational model in making students temporary neighborhood organizers who tried to help residents find the strengths of their neighborhoods and then do their own neighborhood restoration. Kinnevy and Boddie (2001) also used this model, perhaps in part to help students overcome their stereotypes. Keith (1998, p. 88) discussed a community-engaged process that attempted to use an asset-based approach, arguing that "'partnerships' among unequal participants will shift toward a model of service provision that is one-sided and silence the 'lesser' members." Keith's solution was for the more powerful partners to willingly shift their perspective and agree to see the "lesser" members "as having valued resources to bring to the table."

The jury is out on whether institutionalized service learning actually practices an asset-based approach or just espouses it. The focus is still on the people in poverty—we look for the people that we have defined as having deficits, and our treatment for their deficits is to get them to develop their assets. So we still do tutoring, after-school, ESL, shelter, soup kitchen, food bank, and all the other ameliorative charity services. We just now say that we are doing those things to build poor people's assets. Is that an asset-based approach, or just a needs-based approach wrapped in asset language?

Even more troubling, however, is the question of whether the asset-based perspective is another neoliberal wolf in progressive sheep's clothing. The implication of asset-based thinking is that "the community" already has the assets to solve its own problems. If it can't therefore solve its own problems, then it must be the community's fault, not the fault of oppressive, exploitive, and exclusionary social systems (Miller, 2009).

Finally, while others might try to divide up the communitarian, social capital, and asset-based approaches into separate camps, I believe they are very much reflective of a single set of assumptions. For one thing, none of them use the language of exploitation and oppression as theoretical concepts. Nor do they bring the concept of social structure into their analysis. In communitarianism, the good society is achievable by creating norms and rules that balance everyone's rights with everyone's responsibilities. In the social capital perspective, the good society can be achieved by building up everyone's social networks—something that can be achieved everywhere by everyone. In asset-based approaches, the good society can be achieved by discovering and putting to work everyone's assets or "gifts." In all three cases, the good society can be achieved without conflict, and with hard work from individuals integrating themselves into the existing society. Institutionalized service learning, then, becomes an apolitical and potentially even anti-political form of civic engagement that avoids conflict in the act of building assets and relationships.

Is Institutionalized Service Learning's Theory of the Good Community Good?

It is perhaps no surprise that institutionalized service learning would gravitate toward theoretical perspectives about community that ignored social structure and social conflict. Doing so reflects the self-interest of higher education institutions that are reliant on government and, increasingly, corporate funding and we all know about the risks inherent in "biting the hand that feeds you."

But before we go too far in considering the flaws of a communitarian/social capital/asset-based approach, the first thing we must consider is that, to a large extent, institutionalized service learning often isn't working with community at all. There are partial exceptions. Some universities do focus many of their efforts on adjacent neighborhoods, such as the University of Pennsylvania in Philadelphia, Clark University in Worchester, and The Ohio State University in Columbus (though there is some question, especially in the cases of Philadelphia and Columbus, whether it was mostly to gentrify the "undesirable" people out of the neighborhood so the university could control it) and others. But, by and large, institutionalized service learning provides individual students to nonprofit organizations that provide services to individuals whose only connection to each other is a common need.

The inability and unwillingness of institutionalized service learning advocates to take a stand on an actual effective definition of what a community is allows them to continue using the term *community* for all manner of things, which only adds to the intellectual confusion and, consequently, confused practice. We pat ourselves on the back for "serving the community" when, in reality, we have no idea who or what we are serving. Without a strict theory of community, we can't track the unintended consequences of our practices. As long as institutionalized service learning does not really understand community as a concrete thing but only as a blurry abstract emotional thought-feeling, we will not know where we are headed or what we are accomplishing.

When we get right down to it, the people "in the community" we are working with are typically not "in community," and that is exactly why we are working with them. They are isolated, exploited, excluded, oppressed, in conflict, and beset by all the symptoms that such social stresses cause. The places they live in are disorganized by violence from without and within, a lack of quality-of-life amenities, and a lack of income to attract and sustain such amenities.

The asset-based advocates may criticize the above as deficit language. And, while I share the asset-based critique of individualized service approaches, I part company with asset-based community development proponents when they refuse to acknowledge that people who are exploited, oppressed, and excluded lack the benefits enjoyed by the rest of us *by design* and insist they can pull themselves up by their own personal asset bootstraps. Ultimately, I fear, there is a disingenuousness in the asset-based model. Asset-based advocates talk about how we need to focus on assets, but then they keep talking about needs—they need better schools, they need a playground, they need better housing, they need a safe neighborhood—and insert themselves into the process apparently on the assumption, violating their own argument, that the people they are talking about are too deficient to help themselves. Second, asset-based advocates seemingly assume that, whenever anyone talks about a need they are really talking about a deficiency of an individual that is somehow that individual's fault, rather than considering that the needs are imposed upon people by forms of oppression, exploitation, and exclusion resulting from the brutality of unchecked political economic power in neoliberal society. Third, the asset language, by not analyzing why people have needs, becomes complicit in a subtle form of hegemony that distracts us from even noticing the structural power imbalances in our political economic system (Hyatt, 2008).

In institutionalized service learning, the shift from deficit to asset language attempts to support the priority educational mission of institutionalized service learning by purportedly challenging common student stereotypes of people living in poverty. But it doesn't challenge, and even reinforces, common and taken-for-granted student acceptance of the validity of neoliberalism. It even feeds into neoliberalism by promoting the belief that, since individuals all have assets, all they have to do is mobilize those assets and they will be successful in life. The theory distracts us from focusing on the structural barriers to success for entire segments of the population (Stoecker, 2004). Institutionalized service learning advocates miss this crucial point. Koliba (2004), even while worrying deeply about the neoliberal underpinnings of most institutionalized service learning, nonetheless then advocates for an asset approach to institutionalized service learning that carries the same risk.

The problems are similar, but perhaps even deeper, with the social capital approach. The term *social capital* has become so taken for granted that we can't see how it, too, operates hegemonically as a tool of neoliberalism. First, it is important to understand that, as much as it would seem from the institutionalized service learning literature that Putnam is both the first and final word on the concept of social capital, he is not. Bourdieu's (1986) elaboration of the ideas of social capital and cultural capital, for example, doesn't even appear in the institutionalized service learning literature in relation to communities, but only to students (Yeh, 2010). It may be that these ideas don't appear because Bourdieu uses more of a social structural analysis. People don't have more or less social capital simply because of the networks they choose to build but as a result of the networks they may be restricted to because they live in poverty, have more pigment in their skin, are the wrong age, have a visible disability, are non-heteronormative, and so on. And once we realize that, social capital is not nearly as important as social position. The implication of the Putnam style analysis is that social networks always create social capital. But if a group of farmers have a network, but not a plow between them, what is gained?

And here is where we need to dig more deeply into this idea of social capital. We call it social *capital* for a reason. Just like the old adage that it's not what you know but who you know—implying that you can create relationships not for friendship but for personal advantage—we call it social capital because we think about it in terms of its exchange value. And here we must take a detour into a deeper theoretical analysis. *Capital* is a term used to describe the value of something used in exchange. Thus, social capital is social networks that have value in exchange relationships. A century and a half ago Karl Marx (1859) distinguished use values and exchange values. A use value is something that has value in its immediate use—the veggies you grow in your own garden, the clothes you sew for your own wearing, the furniture you build to set your own coffee mug (that you made on your own potter's wheel) on. When you begin to sell those things to others, you transform them into exchange values. They no longer have value in and of themselves, but as commodities.

Such it is also with relationships. When we value our friendships in and of themselves in a form of generalized reciprocity where we bring our friends together to share of each other, those friendships are use values. When we use them to advance our power and wealth we transform them into exchange values. Social capital advocates like Fukuyama (1999) are not even shy about this, stating bluntly that "the economic function of social capital is to reduce the transaction costs associated with formal coordination mechanisms like contracts, hierarchies, bureaucratic rules, and the like." To build up a group's social capital, then is to build up their capacity to engage in contracts, hierarchies, and bureaucratic rules—to become part of the system.

Relationships then become commodities just like vegetables, clothing, furniture, and coffee mugs. And this is the first step on the road to alienation. Referencing, again, Karl Marx (1844/1932), there are four kinds of alienation. In a hierarchically structured society where everything has become commodified—turned into an exchange value in a marketplace—we first become alienated from the product of our labor. We produce things that we don't care about. Second, we become alienated from the process of our labor. Others determine what labor we will do, how much we will do, and when we will do it, causing the act of working to become meaningless. We also become alienated from ourselves. When our work becomes controlled by others for profit, and we produce only for exchange rather than for our own use, we lose track of the essence of who we are because we are no longer producing as a reflection of own identity. Finally, we become alienated from each other, as all our relationships become exchange value relationships rather than use value relationships.

This is what the social capital perspective, because it lacks any critique of the social structure in which it promotes the development of exchange value relationships, propels us toward. In Keith's (2005, p. 11) terms, "Neoliberalism's emphasis on the commercialization of all spheres of life, which is destructive of all collectivities, . . . leaves the unencumbered citizen-turned-consumer and person-turned-into-capital open to the further encroachment of the system, as the lifeworld is now penetrated at its deepest emotional levels through market persuaders that manufacture reality in the quest for market share."

This is the community that institutionalized service learning, according to the theories it follows, strives for.

But what about communitarianism? It too may be in league with neoliberalism. For Boyte (2003), the emphasis on volunteerism and service in communitarianism, along with its lack of any critique of market politics, reveals its neoliberal underpinnings. The deeply crucial question is whether community and capitalism can exist in the same society. For communitarians, the answer is yes, and this allows institutionalized service learning to operate in a social capital, asset-based framework. But the reality may not be so simple. Concrete communities are fundamentally about use values—open space, public amenities, and collective goods such as safe water, air, and soil. Capitalism is fundamentally about transforming use values into exchange values—privatizing and commodifying everything it can so that air, water, land, and people generate profit (Stoecker, 1998).

If community and capitalism are not compatible, then institutionalized service learning cannot solve the problems of the oppressed and exploited by using a communitarian, social capital, asset-based practice. And in following such theories we become part of the problem more than part of the solution.

Remember, though, that as much as I have made of institutionalized service learning's problematic understanding of community, the most important point is that the practice really has no understanding of community but only an implied association with certain theories. To the extent that badly fitted theories are applied badly, such theories may not be as damaging as I fear. The way out of this conundrum is through the final concept crucial to institutionalized service learning—change. But we will not find the path out until we first pass through the thicket of current definitions and practices around the idea of change.

7

What Is Institutionalized Service Learning's Theory of Change?

> As far as we could determine, white culture, if it existed, depended
> primarily upon the exploitation of land, people, and life itself. It
> relied upon novelties and fads to provide an appearance of change
> but it was basically an economic Darwinism that destroyed rather
> than created. (Deloria, 1969/1988, p. 180)

"I believe in *radical* service learning," bellowed the university administrator in his welcoming remarks to the audience at an institutionalized service learning conference. When I asked him if "radical" meant that he would encourage his faculty and students to engage with the organizations then occupying the streets of the nearby capital city to protest the ravages wrought by global capitalism, he simply said, "I'll take it under advisement." Of course, the answer was really no. All he meant by his hyperbole was that he wanted to make all of the faculty make all of their students do community service. Change was not on his agenda.

Nor is change typically on institutionalized service learning's agenda or even its students' (Bickford & Reynolds, 2002; Bringle, Hatcher, & MacIntosh, 2006; Chovanec et al., 2011; Kajner et al., 2013; Liu & Kelly, 2009; Morton, 1995; Robinson, 2000a, 2000b). I have been struck by the extent to which institutionalized service learning avoids supporting change. While at a service learning awards banquet at one institution, I started up a conversation with the student putting the technology together so I could show the obligatory PowerPoint slides. I'd noticed he was wearing a union T-shirt under a loosely buttoned cover shirt, perhaps strategically, so I asked him about it. I came to find out he and a bunch of his student colleagues had been working to support the campus food service workers' unionization effort. I sat through dinner, and the awards—all given to students participating in safe change-avoiding community service efforts directed at children, elders, and animals—worrying about the omission of this student and his colleagues from the list of honorees.

There is nothing unusual about this situation. At the university of Wisconsin–Madison, an institution constantly proclaiming itself the torch-bearer of "The Wisconsin Idea"—the philosophy that the university exists to support the empowerment and development of all people in the state and perhaps beyond—the students you met briefly in the first chapter, and whom I would put at the top of the list for service learning awards, were instead disciplined for occupying the chancellor's office in an attempt to convince him to respect an official university committee recommendation to sever a contract with a company engaging in labor practices that had evoked broad concern. Similar and even worse things have happened at Macalester College in Minnesota (Greder, 2013), and at California university system schools, including UC-Davis where seated peaceful students protesting massive tuition hikes were point-blank pepper-sprayed by police (Asimov, 2011; J. Medina, 2011).

The question of what constitutes real social change is age old. The chapter epigraph by Deloria (1969/1988) was written to explain why many Native Americans rejected participating in the famous 1963 civil rights march on Washington. For some, the march expressed a demand for assimilation rather than change. The same question faces institutionalized service learning. For it appears that there is no demand for radical social change emanating from the institutionalized service learning literature. Institutionalized service learning's focus on social change is usually stated as something like "solving community problems" and is proclaimed absent of any theoretical foundation. The phrase is used frequently (795 times in 140 articles in the *Michigan Journal of Community Service Learning*), but is barely defined, let alone theorized. Morton (1995) has perhaps come the closest to an actual theory of social change for institutionalized service learning, but he ends up more with preferred principles than a theory of how change actually happens. He follows Griffith's (1984) model of moving from anguish to anger to analysis to action, but Griffith is an historian, not a social change theorist, and her model is one of individual transformation rather than social change. Morton also draws on small-group community organizing and community development principles that promote the idea that the people affected by change should have the power to create it. But he does not help us understand how to make any of that happen. The phrase "social justice" also shows up as an idea in institutionalized service learning literature (Ludlum Foos, 1998; Marullo & Edwards, 2000; Mitchell, 2007, 2010), but again as more of a set of principles than a theory. There are philosophers of democracy in institutionalized service learning (see, for example, Leeds, 1999), but none provide us with strong theoretical guidance on how to change our present course to establish, or reestablish, democracy.

One of the main indicators of institutionalized service learning's weak understanding of social change is its almost extreme lack of interest in community outcomes (Stoecker & Tryon, 2009a; Vernon & Ward, 1999). The superficial satisfaction survey is the preferred evaluation vehicle, and all it does is find out whether some nonprofit staffperson liked having a service learner (Birdsall, 2005; Ferrari & Worrall, 2000; Stoecker, Beckman, & Min, 2010; Vernon & Ward, 1999). How can we possibly be serious about social change if we do not study whether and how it happens?

Another indicator of institutionalized service learning's lack of understanding of social change is the almost total absence of attempts to define "social change." The idea is only defined by those few practitioners who emphasize the community-based research form of institutionalized service learning. And there is an important consistency among us (perhaps because we all wrote together). My own work (Stoecker, 2003a, p. 36) said that social change, "defined conservatively, involves restructuring an organization or creating a new program. But it can also be defined radically, including the use of militant tactics to promote massive changes in the distribution of power and resources through far-reaching changes in government policy, economic practices, or cultural norms." Sam Marullo and colleagues (2003, p. 57) also elaborated types of social change, including "enhancing [the] capacity of individuals or community based organizations . . . increasing goods and services delivered to disadvantaged groups and clients . . . empowering constituencies or communities to advance their social change claims . . . and altering the policies and/or social structures that limit opportunities and life chances for classes of disadvantaged people." Strand et al. (2003) talked about "fundamental social change" that focuses on higher education to make it more relevant to communities, helping marginalized communities build their ability to advocate for themselves, and advancing democracy generally by improving the skills of individual participants. This spread of definitions and change foci shows just how unclear even the staunchest advocates of social change are when it comes to just what counts as social change in institutionalized service learning.

But these discussions of social change are not widely cited in the institutionalized service learning literature. Thus, once again, we are confronted with institutionalized service learning's lack of serious reflection about its own work. Of course, this lack of attention to definitions and theory is also at least partly consistent with the influence of Dewey-styled pragmatism on the practice and is even celebrated by some (Tucker, 1999). Recall that in its crassest interpretation pragmatism is simply about trying things to see what works. In that sense, it is quite consistent with U.S. capitalism, where evidence of how much people try things that do not work is shown by the full dockets of bankruptcy courts and the empty storefronts and houses across the country caused by the recent economic collapse and our inability to overcome its affects. From standpoints other than pragmatism, to spend all that energy on developing a theory of student learning, and none on developing a theory of social change, is unethical, unfair, and irresponsible.

So while institutionalized service learning clearly lacks a coherent definition of social change, let alone a theory, we can uncover implicit theories of social change from looking at existing institutionalized service learning practice and thought and connecting the theories most consistent with them.

Ways of Thinking about Change

No discipline has focused on social change more than sociology. Indeed, sociology is a discipline founded on the purpose of understanding social change. So it makes sense to start our discussion of social change with a discussion of the sociological theories of social change that might fit institutionalized service learning.

Sociologists often refer to the two basic approaches to thinking about social change as functionalist theory and conflict theory. There are, of course, many nuances and debates in these rough categories, but it is the agreed-on assumptions in each, rather than the differences in what is built from them, that concern us here.

For our purposes, we can look at three dimensions of these basic theoretical approaches for comparison. The first is whether we see social change as the accumulated result of individual behavior or as a result of the structural characteristics of social systems themselves. The second is whether social change can be accomplished by people acting collaboratively and cooperatively regardless of their social station or requires conflict between opposing groups. The third is whether social change is gradual or sudden.

Functionalist theory emphasizes the first choice on each of these dimensions: social change results from the accumulation of individual behaviors, is generally the result of cooperative action, and is gradual. For conflict theory, social change is a result of tensions within the structure of the social system itself, requires conflict between groups, and is often relatively sudden and dramatic. These perspectives provide different justifications for different social change strategies. In the environmental movement, for example, recycling is built on functionalist theory assumptions. The belief is that change will result from each of us as individuals changing our behavior; recycling is something that everyone can contribute to as an individual; and over a long period of time the accumulated effects of recycling will help reduce landfill use, garbage in the oceans, and so on. Environmental justice activists think differently. They see how the most oppressed, exploited, and excluded people are limited to living downwind of the refineries, downstream of the toxic polluters, with the most leaded soil, and so on. The only practical strategy is organizing the people subjected to such abuse to fight against the corporate and government policy makers causing the problem. And there is no time to waste because people are literally dying, so the refineries have to be cleaned up now, the toxic polluters have to be stopped now, and the policies have to be changed now.

These two theoretical perspectives make value judgments as well as attempt to explain reality. In functionalist theory, sudden and massive change is actually a bad thing—a breakdown in the social system. Normal change is what occurs through the gradual adoption of new technologies, gradual market shifts, or gradual population growth (Eitzen, Zinn, & Smith, 2012; Morrow, 1978). Those who threaten the social order are "deviants," and an entire field of sociology has sprung up to promote the idea of "deviance" (see, for example, Downes & Rock, 2011). From the standpoint of functionalist theory, my students who occupied the chancellor's office were engaging in deviance and threatening the social order; as a consequence, they needed to be put back in their place as students. This is another crucial quality of functionalist theory—the concept of one's place: the healthy society is one that sifts and sorts and coordinates people into an effectively functioning whole, or a kind of "organic solidarity," in the words of the classic sociologist Emile Durkheim (1893/1997). Thus, the functionalist theory of change reflects the same "invisible hand" thinking that propels capitalist ideology.

Functionalist theory is consistent with the thinking of many of the other core theories in institutionalized service learning. Even Dewey, described by Saltmarsh (1996) as a gradualist in thinking about social change, has some consistencies with functionalist theory. Other functionalists, including Amatai Etzioni the famous communitarian (Sciulli, 2011), are not necessarily happy with the way society has unfolded, but because of their theoretical worldview, cannot imagine a way to a better society outside of small gradual changes that might result from attempts at doing things like trying to create a sense of community in small spaces. From a functionalist perspective, disorder would be worse than the current bad situation (Defilippis, Fisher, & Shragge, 2010). Of course, such theorists are all financially comfortable academics, so it is possible to imagine how that would be the case for them personally.

Functionalist theory fits well with institutionalized service learning. To the extent that the nonprofit industrial complex has risen up to absorb the potential for disorder, and the prison industrial complex (A. Davis, 1998)—what we now refer to as mass incarceration (Hedges, 2012; Rakoff, 2015)—has risen up to control what the nonprofit industrial complex cannot, institutionalized service learning that engages students to provide services to people fits well. Helping poor Black kids get better scores on the math tests helps integrate them into their "place" in functionalist society. Helping Spanish-speaking immigrants learn how to read, write, and speak English helps integrate them into their "place" in functionalist society. This is not to say that we shouldn't be helping people do math or English or whatever. But the way we engage in those efforts looks very different when we do it from a theoretical standpoint

informed by functionalist theory versus conflict theory. The difference between mainstream literacy training and Paulo Freire's literacy training built on
conscientization (Degener, 2001) is as different as functionalist theory night
and conflict theory day.

To elaborate, conflict theory sees the emphasis on order and stability in
functionalist theory as a contributor to a social system that is organized so
that some can oppress and exploit others. Yes, each person is certainly fitted into their place, but by their category rather than their humanity. The
social structure, developed and maintained by the powerful to serve their
own self-interests, sorts and fits people by skin color, class, disability, age,
and a variety of other characteristics. Even when people get sorted by their
supposed "skills" it is without attention to the social structures that restrict
many people's abilities to gain knowledge and skills. From a conflict theory
standpoint, the limits that an unfair social structure places on people cannot
be fixed by focusing on helping individuals, because the society is structured
to require a massive proportion of the population to be fitted into unskilled
jobs, paid low wages, and restricted to a short and brutal life expectancy.
There's no space in the current social structure for everyone to be a professional with a secure income and equal power. Thus, the only option for truly
"serving" those excluded from the benefits of society is changing the social
structure. Doing that requires stopping forms of exploitation, oppression,
and exclusion that currently benefit the richest and most powerful. And, of
course, the richest and most powerful are not going to like such a change.
Even many people who are harmed by the system still support it, believing first in the right-wing hegemonic capitalist rhetoric that there is still a
chance, however slim, that they might someday become among the richest
and most powerful if the system stays the same, and second in the notion
that cultural conservatism is more important than economic fairness (Burawoy, 1979; Frank, 2004; Miedzian, 2010). And that means that all attempts
to change the system will involve conflict.

There is some institutionalized service learning literature that consciously
recognizes the distinction between these two theoretical perspectives, especially among those who write about the community-based research form of
community engagement, beginning with Brown and Tandon's (1983) important article comparing action research and participatory research and following
through with my own work (Stoecker, 2003a). But that literature is miniscule.
It is more accurate to say that most institutionalized service learning doesn't
consciously pay any attention to either conflict or functionalist theories. But
the fact that most practitioners have neither heard of nor think about which
sociological theory they are supporting doesn't prevent them from unconsciously acting them out. My purpose here is simply to understand the relationship of these theories to institutionalized service learning practices. And

most institutionalized service learning practice is decidedly functionalist. To start, institutionalized service learning practitioners adopt an individual level of intervention—the individual kid who will get tutored, the individual immigrant who will learn English. Hayes and Cuban (1997), even when adopting a critical postmodernist theory, apply it to individual change. Ludlum Foos (1998), even when working from a feminist theory, focuses on the self and individual change.

This strain of functionalist reasoning in the literature includes the almost instantly famous *A Crucible Moment* (National Task Force on Civic Learning and Democratic Engagement, 2012), which, with a sense of urgency running from its title through the final sentence, beseeches us to advance "democratic values of liberty, justice, domestic tranquility, and the general welfare of the people and the planet" (p. 69). And while the phrase "social justice" is smattered about the work, the word *conflict* only appears a few times and only as a bad thing. Instead, *civility* has become the important catch phrase in all civic engagement. In this spirit, the National Task Force on Civic Learning and Democratic Engagement (2012) proposes deliberative dialogue and cites the California State University at Chico for their "Town Hall Meeting"—a label taken right from colonial New England—as a model for students. They also promote the idea of "collective civic problem solving" but their examples remain largely trapped on campus, with only add-ons for community engagement. And they tie the practices to old notions, with phrases like "The conventional classroom suddenly has a new wing for integrated learning and applied research" (p. 65). They even use the word "laboratory" (p. 65) to refer to community partnership work. When Baltimore erupted in protesting and rioting, in the wake of yet another killing of another African American person by the police, Campus Compact's (2015) response was not to decry the unabated epidemic of police killings, police militarization, and mass incarceration, but to decry the "polarization of our political discourse and a sharp reduction of thoughtful discussion leading to shared solutions based on the common good." The best they could recommend, from this starting point, were safe, functionalist-rooted responses.

While implicitly functionalist in their approach, these practitioners also don't theorize about the potential cumulative effects of their practice, or the relation of their practice to the broader social system. It was in fact the sociologist Robert Merton (1957), a functionalist theorist, who theorized what he called "manifest" and "latent" functions of social actions. From his standpoint, social actions can produce consequences that further one's wishes and/ or undermine them. For example, institutionalized service learning can, as I have been arguing, both help individuals (serving the function of civility, neighborliness, and social cohesion) and preserve the current unjust system by reducing the motivation for those individuals to organize and change the rules and practices that hold them back. Both functions maintain social order, but one is the intended function and the other is unintended.

None of this is to say that institutionalized service learning is somehow out of step with some broader trend. Quite the contrary. In the past couple of decades, non-conflict forms of community change strategy, including asset-based community development (Asset-Based Community Development Institute, 2009), consensus organizing (Consensus Organizing Center, n.d.a), and collective impact (Kania & Kramer, 2011), have become popularized at universities in an attempt to convince us that "change" can happen without conflict and with the blessing and cooperation of the rich and powerful. Michael Eichler's work in establishing the Consensus Organizing Center, for example, was funded by the right-wing Bradley Foundation (Consensus Organizing Center, n.d.b). The misnamed collective impact approach may be the ultimate neoliberal advance of the nonprofit industrial complex as it combines nonprofits, governments, and corporations in "solving problems." In fact, the approach seems to empower everyone except the people experiencing the problem. Not only do these approaches promote fear of conflict, they promote the fiction that conflict is unnecessary. Of course, because collective impact is controlled by profit-focused, bureaucratically controlled, and fiscally dependent organizations, the only "solutions" they will allow are those that do not threaten their own power. Meanwhile, the rich and powerful become richer and more powerful.

Conflict theory is an uncomfortable fit with institutionalized service learning, because it suggests that the best service learning will work with collectives, not individuals. In addition, it suggests that the focus will be helping those collectives to build their power, not their ability to fit in. So people will learn English in the context of organizing to change policies that discriminate against them, not just to compete for crumbs. Finally, a conflict theory lens shows that most service learning risks propping up an unjust system and helping to maintain oppression, exploitation, and exclusion. I don't know of any institutionalized service learning proponents who would argue that racism, sexism, ageism and forms of exclusion, oppression, and exploitation are good. But I also cannot name many who would send students out to work with organizations that hold a conflict orientation and actively engage in fighting the forces causing those evils.

Part of the discomfort with conflict theory among institutionalized service learning practitioners, I suspect, is a discomfort with the idea of conflict. For too many, conflict and violence are the same thing, and the association prevents understanding the important differences between the two. Conflict is a state of society. Workers and owners have interests that are in conflict, as do men and women, dominant and marginalized races/ethnicities, and so on. It's simply a fact. Those facts do include violence, including the continuing epidemic of Black deaths at the hands of the police; the deaths caused by poverty diseases; the destruction of self-esteem caused by low-paid, low-dignity work; the violence of rape and incest; and we can go on. Calls for deliberative dialogue are a woefully incomplete response. And the alternative is not simply violence, as we will see, but a mix of strategies built on an understanding of how society works informed by conflict theory. Some changes, especially those that stop short of redistributing power and wealth, present only mild conflict. And, of course, such small changes can happen, but the question is whether social change—in the sense of the structural redistribution of power—can happen through such strategies. History is replete with evidence that the threat of large-scale uprising and militant action can produce a context where moderate organizations and strategies can gain headway. Moderate civil rights organizations such as the Southern Christian Leadership Conference (SCLC) were able to gain access to policy makers and funders at least partly because more militant organizations such as the Student Nonviolent Coordinating Committee (SNCC) were engaging in much more confrontational action that drove authorities to listen to the moderates (Carson, 1995; Haines, 1984). Similarly, environmental victories have been won not by single organizations but by combinations of militant and moderate organizations (Cramer, 1998). If institutionalized service learning only supports the moderate groups, we reduce its chances of having an impact. Without a strong theory of social change, institutionalized service learning risks running amok in communities, producing unintended side effects. But it is not just the lack of a clear, broad theoretical purpose that endangers the work. It is also the lack of specific, concrete goals that can guide specific institutionalized service learning activities.

Seeing Change: Outputs, Outcomes, Impacts, and Unintended Consequences

Outside of teaching students, what is institutionalized service learning trying to accomplish? Before we can answer that question, we need to consider how to think about it. What does it mean to "accomplish" something?

For at least a couple of decades now, funders have been pressuring community organizations, especially 501(c)(3) nonprofits, to show both that they intend to produce accomplishments and that they have realized their intentions. Nonprofits have been filling out "logic models" and designing evaluations ever since. As a consequence, they have also been adopting the language of *outputs, outcomes, and impacts* promoted by evaluators. The imposition of these practices, tied as they are to the nonprofit industrial complex, has created much resentment and unhelpful behavior. But if we can strip away the distortions caused by funder-driven evaluation, we get to some basic truths. Those who work in organizations that serve people are trying to accomplish something, and it is a great deal easier to know whether they are accomplishing something when they are clear about what accomplishments they want. And toward that end it is helpful, I think, to adapt and own, rather than simply feel victimized by, some of the ideas that come from evaluators.

Take, for example, the distinction between outputs, outcomes, and impacts. Long maintained by evaluation researchers (Rossi, Lipsey, & Freeman, 2004), this distinction says that it is important not to assume that an action is having the intended effect and especially not to mistake the action for the accomplishment. So one hundred people a week get food at the food bank. Does that mean they are getting better nutrition? This is the difference between outputs and outcomes. If the food bank exists to help people get better nutrition but they are walking out the door with salt-laden canned goods rather than fresh fruits and vegetables, the food bank may not be achieving that outcome (better nutrition) even when it is achieving the output (getting lots of people coming to the food bank).

Thus it is with institutionalized service learning. The obsession with counting students and hours and touting the totals as some kind of achievement is a massive confusion of outputs and outcomes. The question, from our standpoint here of asking about social change, is what all those students putting in all those hours are accomplishing. What are the community outcomes? But here, too, there is mass confusion as institutionalized service learning starts celebrating the number of people "served"—the number of children in the tutoring program, the number of English-language learners in the ESL class, and especially the number of students providing these services. Those are all just outputs and the emphasis on counting the number of students shows that even the outputs are confused by the ultimate goal of using institutionalized service learning to educate students. The question of outcomes is the question of whether the community's children are more successful in school and whether the English-language learners are better able to write, speak, and hear in English.

Then, and perhaps most importantly, when we bring in the idea of impacts things get really deep and complicated. It is pretty easy to connect outcomes to outputs. You tutor kids and then follow their test scores. It's pretty empirical. But impacts require theoretical thinking. Impacts are about collective changes. They are about issues of change and justice at broader, deeper levels. They are about those children being able to live in a society where doing better in school will actually matter. Think of how differently we would characterize impacts from a functionalist standpoint versus a conflict theory standpoint. Functionalists would want those children to individually succeed in the existing system. Conflict theorists would want the social structure around those children to change and allow us to consider different kinds of success as important and worthy. And that would reverberate back into what kinds of outcomes we consider of value and then what kinds of actions we engage in to accomplish those outcomes to produce those impacts.

This is deep stuff—with too many variables, too many moving parts, and too much uncertainty to ever say whether one small intervention alone will accomplish such empirically and theoretically distant impacts. But without this thinking, there is no way to know what is being accomplished and what direction it is heading in.

Such is the state of institutionalized service learning. Some analysts, such as Cruz and Giles (2000), actually argue against us focusing on community outcomes and instead urge us to think mainly about how to maintain "partnerships." Likewise, Gelmon et al. (2001) focus most of their attention on the characteristics of the partnership rather than whether it accomplishes anything. Kinnevy and Boddie (2001) provide an elaborate analysis of the partnership process between the University of Pennsylvania and Black church representatives and youth, but they offer barely a few sentences on outcomes and even those are more assertions than well-documented findings. And in fact there was the potential for outcomes, as other Penn students followed up that initial work. Others severely confuse what is an output, outcome and impact. Often, what are listed as outcomes or impacts are really only outputs, such as Vernon and Foster's (2002) finding that service learners helping agencies expand their services is an "impact." Similar confusion exists in Vernon and Ward's 1999 work. Polanyi and Cockburn (2003) list only output goals in a project with injured workers, but refer to their achievement as outcomes and impacts. Andreasen (2002), in an article titled "Civic Responsibility through Mutual Transformation of Town and Gown," can cite only a tangential outcome in one program supporting single parents to get undergraduate education at the author's university. All of the other "impacts" are changes at the university, including the receipt of grants supporting faculty and students. And everything else, in evaluation speak, is simply outputs—numbers of students putting in numbers of hours, and to what effect we do not know. Other research that tries to get at outcomes really only focuses on community organization staff perceptions of how useful the institutionalized service learning has been to them (Bailis & Ganger, 2006; Basinger & Bartholomew, 2006; Blouin & Perry, 2009; Miron & Moely, 2006; Sandy & Holland, 2006; Stoecker & Tryon, 2009b), though even then the results are often not complementary of our practice.

Those of us who are hoping that institutionalized service learning may eventually become convinced of the importance of outcomes and impacts have searched in vain for a substantial literature to guide us. (Stoecker, Beckman, & Min, 2010). There are very few offerings. Schmidt and Robby (2002) use a standard quasi-experimental design to study whether tutoring affects children's test scores. Johnston, Harkavy, Barg, Gerber, and Rulf (2004) engaged students in attempting to study the outcomes of a school nutrition program. Porter, Summers, Toton, and Aisenstein (2008) documented how institutionalized service learning improves individual access to social safety net benefits, providing a rare focus not just on outcomes for individuals but also on policy changes.

This question of studying individual outcomes versus more collective outcomes is important and again shows the bias of institutionalized service learning toward a functionalist analysis of society. But there is an alternative perspective. Marullo et al. (2003) urge us to think about outcomes not just in terms of increasing efficiency and enhancing capacity of community groups, but also empowering constituencies and influencing policy. And the Bonner Foundation (Hackett, 2013)—a philanthropic foundation with a mission of expanding service learning in higher education—has for years been urging institutionalized service learning programs to develop their capacity to engage in policy analysis. But too few analysts and practitioners of institutionalized service learning have followed up on these urgings. When they have, it has been to emphasize the development of the civic engagement of the students (Battistoni, 2002; Sylvester, 2009) rather than that of the oppressed, the exploited, and the excluded. Northeastern University (2013) touts its Service Learning Advocacy Workshop as teaching students "to develop the same knowledge and skills that a professional lobbyist would bring to an issue." To a large extent, it's not just social change that is absent from the agenda of institutionalized service learning, but any kind of change at all. At best, social change remains an undefined phrase in the journals and books, which leaves begging the answer to the next obvious question.

Does Institutionalized Service Learning Create Social Change?

Of course, the answer to the question of whether institutionalized service learning creates social change depends on how we define social change. When we define it as changes to individuals other than students, we have seen that there is a small bit of evidence that individuals have benefited in specific ways from the work of institutionalized service learning. In some cases, they have felt changed. In other cases we have a bit of quantitative or qualitative evidence of change. Such cases of change can only be defined as social change, however, from a functionalist theoretical viewpoint—that the changes in individuals will accumulate slowly over time and eventually add up to larger changes in the society. The jury is still out on whether the accumulated social change ever actually happens.

When we define social change as more collective change, the challenge is greater. Universities that have targeted entire neighborhoods can certainly point to many physical changes in them. But there is some question whether the university's intervention has moved the needle on improving the collective quality of life of the neighborhoods' people. The old federal Community Outreach Partnership Center program, which was designed to impact entire neighborhoods, sadly focused much more on the development of "partnerships" between universities and community agencies rather than on actual community outcomes (Vidal, Nye, Walker, Manjarrez, & Romanik, 2002). As asset-based approaches became popularized in institutionalized service learning, they provided an interesting bridge between more individual change approaches and collective change because asset assessment can be assessment of either the assets of individuals or the assessment of collective community assets like parks, shops, services, and so on. But asset-based approaches, as we have seen, are still thoroughly entrenched in functionalist theory because they assume that community development can occur without conflict.

Thinking about asset assessment brings up the question of whether the community-based research (CBR) form of institutionalized service learning is better at producing social change. While CBR certainly emphasizes social change (see Strand et al., 2003), it is difficult to see actual social change resulting from it. Much of the emphasis of CBR in practice seems to be on organizational and program development. The CBR itself does not produce social change, but informs groups and organizations about how their organization is functioning, what program options are available, and similar issues. Too often it results in little more than a report (Stoecker, 2009).

Take, for example, the debate between proponents of needs assessments and advocates of asset assessments. For all the emphasis on their differences, what is similar in so many cases is their method (Altschuld, 2014). It is typical, in an institutionalized service learning/CBR context, for students to design a survey—it doesn't matter whether they design it to find out needs or assets—go out and collect the data, write up their report, and hand it off to the community organization that commissioned them. The organization may or may not ever do anything with it. More importantly, the organization may or may not ever use it for any social change work. Most likely, they will use it for social service programming.

In such cases, the research process in CBR is the same as the service process in institutionalized service learning—individualized. With institutionalized service learning, students either directly serve individuals or serve organizations that serve individuals. With most asset and needs assessments, students obtain data from individuals. They never link the individuals to each other and the process does not have as its goal the development of relationships among the people being surveyed.

The question this raises is whether needs or assets are our only choices, or whether they are different choices at all. When we assume both an individual *level* of analysis—focusing on understanding an individual's needs or assets—and an individual *unit* of analysis—collecting data individual by individual—are needs and assets reduced to two concepts that depend on each other to exist, like front and back or black and white?

This brings us back to understanding the nonprofit industrial complex that constrains both community groups and higher education institutions. For both are the most common kinds of nonprofits that are most subject to the rules against being politically engaged (setting aside the for-profit educational institutions whose very structure embodies the causes of the problems). Because of the rules imposed on *both* of them, *neither* is free to fully support the kind of civic engagement that can produce social change.

From this analysis it may appear that institutionalized service learning is boxed in from all sides. The impulses toward creating the progressive society have been captured by neoliberalism and transmuted into system-maintaining activities that reproduce exclusion, exploitation, and oppression. Institutionalized service learning does this by acting as a social safety valve, providing those most abused by the current political economy with just enough therapy, necessities of living, and individualized attention to drain off their energy that could otherwise support organizing for collective action. It also does this by individualizing the concept of civic engagement. In institutionalized service learning, universities and colleges send individual students out to do civic engagement, in a model of individualized social entrepreneurship, often serving individual "clients." And the primary goal, remember, is to turn those individual students into individual civically engaged citizens.

In contrast, think of all the things we are not teaching our students and not doing in our communities. We are not teaching collective action. We are not teaching political economy. We are not teaching community organizing and development. We are not teaching social change, except in rare, isolated cases that are often, even more sadly, disconnected from any kind of community engagement. And consequently we are hard-pressed to produce any evidence that we are making things better for more than a few individuals.

Even attempts to move beyond service learning to community-based research (CBR) models are fraught with a lack of change. Tinkler (2010) explores two attempts at community-based research, adapting my own distinction between mainstream and radical CBR (Stoecker, 2003a) and putting them on a continuum. She finds that the further away from radical CBR a project is, the lower its potential for producing substantial social change. Of course, she also finds that it is more difficult to do more radical CBR in institutional settings. Ashleigh Ross (2014) finds, even more disturbingly, that community residents can hardly distinguish CBR from traditional colonizing research.

Can We Liberate Service Learning?

The situation seems bleak. With a neoliberal political economy dismantling every aspect of the social contract, privatizing everything public, and propelling all of us to even greater isolation and alienation from all aspects of life, finding a way out is indeed challenging. The evidence is stacked against the prospects of overcoming the limitations of institutionalized service learning.

But it's important to remember that I have described institutionalized service learning as a set of *dominant* practices, not totalizing practices. There are exceptions. And somehow those exceptions are able to exist. I have also been able to engage in practices that push against all of these tendencies, and it sometimes saddens me even more deeply to know that if I can do it then others can too. Which means that some of the lack of liberating practice is a result of choice.

As we move into the next chapters, which explain how we can develop a new practice built on an alternative theoretical foundation, we see that some of the required changes will be quite small while others will be deep and broad. Some will be easy and some will be hard. And some—in fact some of the most important ones—will only require us to rethink categories. To prepare you, here is what I believe is the most important rethinking we need in all forms of higher education civic engagement: that the most important community asset is its people's anger.

III

Liberating Service Learning

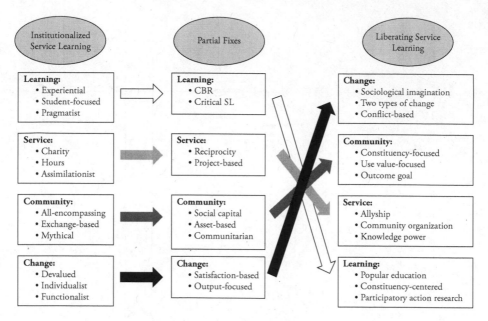

LIBERATING SERVICE LEARNING IN GRAPHIC FORM

Toward a Liberating Theory of Change

In order for us as poor and oppressed people to become part of a society that is meaningful, the system under which we now exist has to be radically changed. This means that we are going to have to learn to think in radical terms. I use the term radical in its original meaning—getting down to and understanding the root cause. It means facing a system that does not lend itself to your needs and devising means by which you change that system.

—ELLA BAKER, 1969 (quoted in B. Ransby, *Ella Baker and the Black Freedom Movement*)

I believe in anger. Not the "hot" irrational anger of violence, vengeance, and virulence but the "cold" rational anger of recognizing injustice and strategizing action that does not produce new injustice. I believe in my anger, but my anger is mostly abstract because I suffer comparatively mildly and mostly indirectly from the injustices wrought by neoliberalism. So I especially believe in the anger of those who do suffer directly and intensely. Their anger too often goes unrecognized or gets diagnosed in various disempowering ways. It gets turned inward into substance abuse and self-abuse and mental illness. It gets turned outward into interpersonal violence and multidirectional hatred. Its expression results in containment by the misnamed "justice system" rather than the achievement of social justice.

The single main task for all of us is to recognize, honor, respect, and help mobilize and organize the expression of this anger. This anger tells us what is really important. It tells us what people most care about. It tells us what is most wrong. It tells us what is most urgent. It tells us our starting point. This is not primarily about recognizing the anger of individuals, though it is that, too. It is about mobilizing collective anger. It is also not about analyzing anger within individuals, though it is that, too. It is about understanding the societal sources of that anger. It is also not about anger with a target, though it is that, too. It is about anger with a goal.

Those of us living in privileged circumstances have a head-in-the-sand approach to most anger. It scares us, intimidates us, leaves us with distaste in the mouth. Alex Gee (2013) tells us that, after giving a presentation on

Wisconsin's status as the number-one incarcerator of Black men in this country, a white woman came up and applauded him for not being one of those "angry Black men." He had to explain to her that in fact he was an angry Black man but was masking his anger for her benefit. As he explained, what person with any moral conscience would not be outraged by the situation? The reaction to his admission led to the Facebook page *Justified Anger: Let's Talk about It* in 2015 and a series of events in two packed rooms leading up to a community-wide event of more than seven hundred people (Gee, 2014; Godar, 2015) committed to a growing organizing effort around racism in Madison.

Institutionalized service learning is the systematic expression of the head-in-the-sand approach. It is why we control the terms of service (to contain the anger), structure it around treatment of individuals (to bleed off the anger), and focus it on resocializing individuals to join the system (to redirect their anger inward). But if we only momentarily attend to our own discomfort with the community's anger, and hopefully our own, we can reflect that our reactions point to how much our current society should scare us, tries to intimidate us, and in fact is itself distasteful. Marilyn Hutchinson, a wise professor who taught me counseling years ago, once advised us students to "start where people are, not where you want them to be." Anger is the starting point. Social change is the purpose.

Those of us who are not angry at the daily injustices that maintain the unearned privilege and power of the very few at the expense of the very many, and even those of us who have only indirect anger, have our own work to do. It's not enough, or even necessarily appropriate, to feel sadness or pity for victims of the system. Sadness and pity are the emotions of charity that only see the injury and not the cause. It's too easy to turn that sadness or pity into blame or anger directed at the victims themselves. But anger based in a systems analysis means one has achieved an analysis that understands the unfairness of the situation.

And so we begin our slow climb out of the valley of institutionalized service learning and toward a practice of higher education community engagement that can liberate us to build a healthy society. And the first thing we have to do differently is change the priority of concepts. Institutionalized service learning starts with student learning, moves through a mostly charity form of service, neglects defining the concept of community that is supposedly its target, and lacks any developed thinking about social change. What I will call, just for convenience, *liberating service learning* needs to begin with elaborating the theory and process of social change that can inform a better understanding of community, providing a new strategy of service and learning that builds communities who can pursue social change.

Cold Anger, the Sociological Imagination, and Knowledge Power

With anger as the starting point and social change as the purpose, it is much easier to understand what social change is. The best social change results in a society where we no longer witness the injuries of injustice because we have removed their causes. So we no longer need to feel anger because we can no longer identify a cause for our anger. To a large extent it means the contradictions that cause conflict in our society no longer exist.

A lot of this is obvious. Homeless people sleeping on the streets in cities replete with abandoned houses. Record profits being extracted in a society with massive unemployment. People dying of preventable and treatable illness in a society with the most advanced health care technology in the world. Such a society is only possible when its members have lost their ability to imagine or desire a better world. I am right now writing in Ontario, Canada. The mayor of Toronto, a crass right-wing politician, has just admitted to smoking crack cocaine and ranting in a drunken rage about killing his enemies after being caught doing both on videos. And the radio is reporting that, since these revelations, his popularity has actually increased. As of this writing, I live in Wisconsin, where another right-wing politician became governor and effectively outlawed public sector labor unions. He won reelection even after a massive recall campaign, with an ability to get one group of workers to redirect their anger at another group of workers. A society where people can only imagine reducing the rights, wages, and security of the majority for the benefit of a tiny minority is a very scary place. In such a context, it's not enough to work problem by problem. We also have to directly support people's ability to think about the system that causes all the problems and imagine new approaches to not just the problems but to the system itself.

We have also been recently witnessing another form of anger—much more rational in its target if not always in its response. When an unarmed young Black man, Michael Brown, was shot dead by a police officer in Ferguson, Missouri, it unleashed the pent-up anger of generations of Black people who had been subjected to increasingly militarized policing increasingly focused on their communities. As killing after killing became more visible through social media and even corporate media, the protests moved from city to city, including here in Madison when the unarmed Tony Robinson was shot dead by a police officer. And those protests, even when they brought significant property destruction and interpersonal violence with them in Ferguson and Baltimore, were remarkably restrained in comparison to the uprisings in the 1960s, or the Rodney King uprising in 1992. The evidence of restraint brought hope that anger could be mobilized for productive social change.

Hence my respect for anger—it can be the cause of both serious irrationality and serious rational action. And that is why it is very important that it be cold anger. Mary Beth Rogers (1990) helped popularize the concept of cold anger from her study of Ernesto Cortes and the Industrial Areas Foundation in Texas. Cortes, like most community organizers, builds grassroots power by helping people identify, share, and link their personal experience with injustice. Sharing and linking the anger that comes with the personal experience of injustice, in this model, creates compassion. That helps turn the anger from the irrational and destructive force that currently exists in Wisconsin and so many other places into constructive energy. It is the fire that keeps people engaged in the struggle for a better society.

But the process of cold anger is not just emotional. It is also intellectual. And in being intellectual it draws on this idea called *the sociological imagination*, coined by C. Wright Mills in 1959 in his famous book of the same name. One of the most important insights in that book was his distinction between personal troubles and public issues. In brief, a personal trouble is something where the cause is located in the individual and the effect is unique to that individual. A public issue is something where the cause is located outside of the individual and the effect is common to many people. Mills used the example of one person being unemployed when everyone else has a job versus when lots of other people are unemployed at the same time. The first can be more easily defined as a personal trouble, but the second is more accurately considered as a public issue. So the two variables at play are where the cause is located (inside or outside the individual) and how widespread the effect is (unique or common).

This way of thinking is not the exclusive invention of C. Wright Mills. Women of the 1960s and 1970s called it *consciousness raising*—linking the personal to the political (Hanisch, 1969, 2006). Mills's contribution was to give the process a systematic theoretical framework.

The sociological imagination is about more than simply an objective reality. It is also about the distinction between perception and reality. When we perceive the cause of someone's pain as their own fault, and when we see their pain as only unique to that individual, we can blame them and isolate them. Doing so also encourages the individual to blame themself and see their pain as unique. The result is that the person turns their anger inward in self-harm or they turn it outward as violence—an individual who at some level knows that their condition is not solely their own fault but has been denied the access to the resources to find and address the actual cause can lash out in unpredictable ways. In contrast, when we perceive the cause of someone's pain as common to many others and the result of social structure, we can help connect people together and have a focus for our efforts. When we see unemployment as the individual's fault, and their unemployment as unique, we recommend job training programs, midlife career change seminars, and employment counseling. When we see unemployment as a public issue, we organize to demand a new economy.

But we often try to have it both ways. We may, for example, claim to understand that an individual's unemployment may not be their own "fault" but then imply, by the kinds of interventions we recommend to them, that it will be their fault if they remain unemployed. If our interventions focus solely on their getting a job and we do not engage them in the civic action needed to analyze and change the political economic system itself, we are undermining the sociological imagination. But when we see the cause of someone's pain as fully a product of a sick social system, and when we support a process whereby that person can work with others in the same situation to figure out what about the system has gone wrong, we are, in C. Wright Mills's words, *transforming personal troubles into public issues*. This provides the opportunity for people to redirect potentially hot irrational anger to become rational productive cold anger.

The work of liberating service learning is to deploy the sociological imagination so that people experiencing the effects of a contorted society can understand how it got this way and imagine and pursue paths to fix it. And it doesn't matter whether the academic substance of the service learning is in the humanities, the natural sciences, the arts, or even the professional disciplines. The sociological imagination is about understanding that the prisoners you are helping to write poetry have a common experience caused by an unfair social system, that the people whose water you are testing for pollution have a common experience caused by an unfair social system, that the people with disabilities you are helping to perform a community theater project have a common experience caused by an unfair social system, and so on. The sociological imagination's process of transforming personal troubles into public issues transforms the way we work with any constituency on any issue.

Another way to think about this is by drawing on Michel Foucault's (1975, 1980) writings on power/knowledge. Foucault's writing is dense, and even more so after translation, so it is difficult to know what he really means by the concept of power/knowledge. The best and most concise interpretation I have seen is Gutting's (2013): "In knowing we control and in controlling we know." In other words, knowledge and power, while separate, are also intertwined. Without knowledge, it is very difficult to gain and wield power and, without power, it is very difficult to gain and wield knowledge.

The translated phrase of power/knowledge is clumsy, so I will instead talk about *knowledge power*. Before going too far down that path, however, it's important to understand that this is not about superficial slogans like "knowledge is power." Knowledge *is not* power. We have the words *knowledge* and *power* because they refer to different things. Power is the truck. Knowledge is the fuel. Fuel itself is not very helpful without a vehicle to put it into motion. And there is an important process that has to happen for the fuel to be useful for the truck, including that you need the truck to get to the fuel. If you know something, but no one believes you know it because you are poor or Black or an immigrant or have an intellectual disability, or, or, or . . . then what you know won't get you power.

Knowledge is also not information. You can't get knowledge from the Internet, you can only get information. Knowledge is what happens when you gather information, sift and winnow it, and produce understanding that helps in effectively interacting with the world. You can't give people knowledge. You can only facilitate a process of people gathering information and turning it into knowledge. When you give someone knowledge you have transformed it back into information. Because your knowledge may not apply everywhere. Even "knowledge" as simple as what snow is will be very different when it falls in a state like Wisconsin where the snowplows are plentiful and ready versus Georgia where snow removal equipment is scarce and the method unpracticed.

This, of course, is the problem with much institutionalized service learning and most forms of higher education community engagement. By assuming that knowledge automatically creates power we can be sloppy with the ways that we develop and transmit knowledge. Thus we come up with concepts like "knowledge transfer," "knowledge mobilization," and "translational research," none of which connect themselves to the sociological imagination.

In the knowledge transfer model, knowledge is created in one place (normally the university) and then transferred to some constituency to get them to do something differently. This process has been systematized globally in agricultural extension, where university researchers create knowledge on new ways to grow food and then try to package that knowledge in ways that will influence actual growers (Ison, 2000; Russell & Ison, 2000). So they transfer the end result of the knowledge process and turn it into information. Translational research, a term being popularized in the field of medicine, is even more removed from knowledge development, as it concentrates on translating basic science into medical practice rather than more directly to communities, though there is some expectation that the "type 2" translational research will provide research findings to practitioners who will then in turn provide it to their patients or the public more generally (Woolf, 2008). In all cases, these practices maintain knowledge power in the hands of the experts, and transform knowledge into information in their efforts to "transfer" or "translate" it to the public. The Canadians have been developing the concept of knowledge mobilization (Social Sciences and Humanities Research Council, 2009–2011), which seems to allow for engaging grassroots constituencies in the co-creation of knowledge. But the co-creation aspect of knowledge mobilization remains woefully under-theorized in favor of a focus on "application."

So knowledge power is about being able to build power and build knowledge in a mutually reinforcing way. And the missing theoretical piece of the puzzle, at least from my reading of Foucault, is action. Foucault's work is full of examples of action, but I don't get the sense that he theorizes action itself. And it is through action that we accomplish social change. If we talk about knowledge and power and action (Stoecker, 2013), we get a fuller sense of what a social change process might look like. Effective action has to be strategic. And that means it needs to be informed by knowledge, which can best be obtained by power. Power, in this model, is the ability to act in ways that produce outcomes. The simple act of making a phone call to a local political representative is an action. But if a person in poverty makes that phone call, their chances of influencing the representative are much slimmer than if a lobbyist backed up by wealthy donors makes that phone call. On the other hand, if the lobbyist lacks knowledge of what moves that politician then even the lobbyist might not succeed at influencing the politician. And a thousand coordinated phone calls from a thousand people in poverty, all of whom have built up knowledge on what moves that local politician, brings together knowledge, power, and action.

For the thousand people living in poverty to do that, however, they all need to develop a sociological imagination, collectively transforming personal troubles into public issues. Combined, the sociological imagination and knowledge power provide a foundational theory of social change for liberating service learning and create a framework by which that poverty constituency and outsider allies liberate their own thinking. And those outsider allies, such as those of us in academia, need to develop that sociological imagination in collaboration with constituency members in order to not fall into the institutionalized service learning, knowledge transfer, translational research trap. As we develop our own sociological imagination, we can engage with constituency members in two forms of social change.

The Two Forms of Social Change

Much of the discussion up to this point may have seemed unduly abstract. But it has all been for a good cause. For our higher education civic engagement, in order to escape the trap of institutionalized service learning that emphasizes system-maintaining student-centered charity approaches, cannot focus only on "solving" specific problems. It must focus simultaneously on a second type of change—change in the social relations of knowledge production (Gaventa, 1993; Stoecker, 2012).

The only way for people excluded from knowledge power to gain it is for them to learn and engage in the process of knowledge production themselves. When we engage with those people to build knowledge power in general, we are engaging in a broader form of social change because we are helping to expand who has power to create knowledge.

This idea of the social relations of knowledge production has been developed by those engaged in the more radical form of community-based research historically referred to as participatory research (Brown & Tandon, 1983). For John Gaventa (1993), there is a social relations of knowledge production just like there is a social relations of material production that was identified by Karl Marx. That means that there is a system of ownership and control over the production process. In the typical material production process, corporate owners control the means of production and, consequently, what is produced, when, and how much. Wage workers, who are also the largest consumer base, then do the actual work that transforms raw materials and raw skills into goods and services. Of course, there are many complications added to the overall production process, but this main distinction will do for now.

In 1991 Rahman argued that the gap between those who had access to the means of knowledge production and those who did not was as large as the gap between those who did and did not have access to the means of material production. But there are some crucial differences between material production and knowledge production, especially now, more than two decades after the introduction of this theory. First, while the gap between those who do and do not have access to the means of knowledge production may be similar to that for material production, the actual means of knowledge production is much easier to access. It takes a lot of machinery and a lot of knowledge to build a refrigerator. It takes far less physical means to learn, and help others develop knowledge about, how the refrigerator works. Wealth is not nearly the barrier to knowledge production that it is to material production. Websites are cheap and the chances of going viral seem so far to be available to anyone with an Internet connection.

On the other hand, the division between knowledge producers and knowledge "consumers" is much greater than it is for material production. The wage labor force of capitalism is also the bulk of the population who consumes what is produced. The people who make and sell the hamburgers and the other things that are still made in this country are also the consumers of those things. But those of us who produce knowledge are actually a very tiny group who has kept the knowledge production process relatively secret by using exclusionary language, restricted professional associations, and off-putting disciplinary cultures. So while it is much cheaper to produce a book (especially an e-book) than a car, the average person lacks the ability to do either. The problem is that it's a lot easier to pretend to know how to produce a book than a car. Anyone can have a blog and say whatever nonsense they want on it. And a blog that is written from systematically developed knowledge can look exactly like one that is filled with nonsense.

Social change, in this context, is building up the capacity of as many people as possible to be able to systematically produce knowledge, not simply receive its translation into mere information. It is about changing the social relations of knowledge production so that those who have been historically excluded from knowledge production can now produce knowledge and have that knowledge heard and respected. If we can engage people together in a collective process of knowledge production, that is even better. It's not about learning math in a tutoring program. It's about learning how to design and then carrying out a math tutoring program. It's about learning the facts of a specific situation while learning about how to uncover the facts of *any* situation. It's about understanding the commonness of one's pain and its social structural source—developing the sociological imagination—and then speaking that knowledge in a collectively amplified voice.

And this moves us to the other form of social change. If the more abstract form of social change is building up people's capacity to produce knowledge to develop their sociological imagination and their knowledge power, thereby transforming the social relations of knowledge production, then the more concrete form of social change is putting those abilities to use by creating change around specific issues. And that involves understanding the community organizing process and how knowledge can support that process.

The term *community organizing* has sadly become nearly as superficially popularized as the term *community*. Put a bunch of people in a room who care about making change and ask how many of them are community organizers and nearly every hand in the room will go up. Ask how many of them have read even a single book on community organizing written by community organizers, or been trained by the national community organizing networks or centers—National People's Action, People Improving Communities through Organizing, the Direct Action and Research Training Center, the Gamaliel Foundation, the Industrial Areas Foundation, Midwest Academy, the People's Institute for Survival and Beyond, the Center for Third World Organizing, Project South—and you'll get mostly blank stares. The ignorance of what it takes to do real community organizing is profound. So it is useful to provide some background.

Community organizing has a long and distinguished history in the United States—some would say all the way back to the revolutionary war. I believe there are at least three names in the field of community organizing that every professor and student (and activist!) must know before attempting to engage in liberating service learning. The first, of course, is Saul Alinsky, with whom the phrase community organizing is inextricably associated. Alinsky's fame is cemented as much by the right-wing activists who profess to hate him even when they use his methods as it is by the myriad of activists with wide-ranging political leanings who have taken his work in directions that would probably have Alinsky turning in his grave. Alinsky established the method of community organizing from the neighborhood up, starting in Back of the Yards in 1930s Chicago and expanding across the country until his death in 1973 (Horwitt, 1992), and wrote two books about it—*Reveille for Radicals* (1969) and *Rules for Radicals* (1971). Alinsky's importance is easy to establish.

The others are more difficult to discuss because they did not write their own books about their work, but their influence has been equally profound. Ella Baker was a civil rights movement organizer, but her practice was quintessentially grassroots community organizing. In contrast to the clergy-centered leadership of the famous Southern Christian Leadership Conference, Baker *allied* (and I use that term quite specifically) herself with the Black youth and the Black working class of the time. She helped organize the Student Nonviolent Coordinating Committee—SNCC—as a participatory democratic group. She helped organize the southern Freedom Schools. And she helped build a grassroots network into the Mississippi Freedom Democratic Party. Miss Baker was adamant in her belief that "strong people don't need strong leaders" (Ransby, 2003).

Then there is Dolores Huerta, the least well known of the three. It has long been the lore in community organizing that Cesar Chavez, whose activist lineage can be traced back to Saul Alinsky through Fred Ross, one of Alinsky's field organizers (F. Ross, 1989), fundamentally transformed Alinsky's community organizing model. Alinsky separated the role of the local leader who chose issues and rallied the people from the role of the community organizer who provided the technical expertise on how to rally the people to win on the issues. Chavez, many believed, collapsed those two roles together into himself as a leader-organizer in the United Farm Workers. The UFW was unique in its early days—part grassroots community organization, part community development organization, and part labor union. But unknown to most of us, myself included, was Dolores Huerta. And she is not known for some of the same reasons that Ella Baker is not known, for she acted as the classic community organizer, pulling people together into groups and actions and keeping herself in the background while supporting the leaders to lead. She was also unique in refusing to submit to nuclear family structures, instead relying on a network of people to collectively raise her children, which was not seen positively by those promoting traditional family values (Chávez, 2005; Garcia, 1993). There are important similarities between the movement roles of Dr. Martin Luther King, Jr. and Ella Baker, and those of Cesar Chavez and Dolores Huerta.

None of this is to deny the importance of activists everywhere who have moved social, cultural, and political mountains. In particular circumstances, there are certainly others to learn about, but Alinsky, Baker, and Huerta provide the most important historical lessons for building communities while building power, something that becomes especially important in the next chapter.

The hallmark of community organizing is that it brings together grassroots people in a local area to identify issues and then organize themselves for self-help to create change around those issues. Ideally, the process also organizes those people into a self-sustaining organization that can take on other issues. Many of those issues, of course, are political, and community organizing is thus also about organizing people into organizations that are strong enough to wield political influence. The principle is that grassroots people, organized together, can provide a political counterweight to the power of money in policy making. In many cases, the role of the community organizer is quite specific and is separate from the community leader. Community leaders must be from the community and be legitimated as leaders by community members. Leaders, ideally, lead a process of collectively making the decisions on what the organization stands for and what it works on. Community organizers may be from outside the organization and are experts on how to structure an organization and choose strategies to achieve the organization's goals. Community organizing also has a sophisticated process that includes methods on how groups can choose issues to work on, recruit participants to work on those issues, and design and carry out strategies that will win those issues (see Kuyek, 2011; Minieri & Getsos, 2007; Sen, 2003; Staples, 2004; Vancouver Citizens Committee, 2014).

Knowledge of community organizing is essential to all higher education civic engagement. Outside interventions can just as easily weaken a community as strengthen it. So every outsider who wants to "help" needs to be skilled in understanding how even interventions with individuals can have rippling impacts across a local community. There is, in fact, no such thing as treating the individual because that individual has relationships with others in the local community and changing the individual will impact their relationships.

It is not possible to cover any adequate amount of community organizing practice here that will prepare students and faculty for community engagement. Students and faculty will need to read the books to have even a chance at developing their own understanding of the practice. But there are some important foundational ideas of social change in a community organizing process. First, there are structural divisions in society, whether it be by social class, race, sex/gender/sexuality, ability, age, or other criteria. And those who currently have the advantage in each of those divisions will not give it up willingly. There is no win-win or plus-sum possibility. Because we are not talking about who gets the goodies. We are talking about who gets the power. Power is not an infinitely expandable commodity. When power is about who gets to decide the structure of the society, everyone can't have expanded power to decide. Anytime someone gets more power to decide, others have to get less power to decide. And that's the second important idea. The fundamental issue is about power. Organizers don't organize people just so they can win on a few issues. They organize people to re-balance power relations and promote participatory democracy. Community organizing is about making every institution, including education, more democratic and participatory. And those of us in higher education need to remember that, when we say we want the people to have more power, we also must include power over even our own work.

Then there are the frameworks for community organizing. For long-time organizer Dave Beckwith (1997), there are four crucial frameworks that define community organizing's theory of change.

The first framework is self-interest. All other things being equal (and it's important to remember that all other things are not always equal), people will follow their perceived self-interest. Self-interest is not selfishness. It is understanding that, if you are a student putting in volunteer hours at the homeless shelter the night before the exam, rather than studying, you risk doing badly on the exam. It's in your self-interest to study instead. Everyone's propensity to engage in any collective effort is always tempered by competing self-interest. So the less that people on the receiving end of institutionalized service learning see it as serving their self-interest (and this can also be collective self-interest), the less they will care about it and participate with it in any more than a token way.

The second framework is that community organizing is a dynamic process that happens over an extended period of time. There are victories and setbacks along the way, even when a group is working on a particular issue. Sometimes the group needs to change strategies, targets, and even issues midstream. And that means those of us who support them with our knowledge work need to shift with them.

The third framework is that conflict and confrontation are integral parts of the process. Because power is a zero-sum concept, a group with less power that is organizing to get more is necessarily going to invoke conflict with those who have too much. You may have heard the famous words of African American Abolitionist Frederick Douglass (1857): "Power concedes nothing without a demand. It never did and it never will." It is worth considering the passage that leads up to that quote:

> If there is no struggle there is no progress. Those who profess to favor freedom and yet deprecate agitation are men who want crops without plowing up the ground; they want rain without thunder and lightning. They want the ocean without the awful roar of its many waters. This struggle may be a moral one, or it may be a physical one, and it may be both moral and physical, but it must be a struggle.

This does not mean bricks and bullets. In fact confrontation can be quite peaceful, but it is nevertheless rooted in an understanding that there is a conflict. And those of us in higher education need to go into every service learning relationship understanding what the conflicts are and how we might deal with them. Community organizers in particular don't trust people who don't take sides. So if we are going to do real community engagement, we need to be prepared to take sides.

The final framework is about choosing or "cutting" issues and developing goals. All groups need to be very strategic about what they try to accomplish. Take on something too big and you risk failing and the group becoming demoralized and falling apart. Choose something that too few people care about and you risk no one showing up to get it. Choose something too vague and you risk factions within the group as different people define the issue differently and then disagree about what to do.

Change is not linear in community organizing—it is not a result of someone coming up with a new idea that gradually finds its way into the culture of society. Change is the clash of opposites, of contradictions. It is the working out of the structural tensions in society between workers and owners, men and women, institutionalized white privilege and diverse others, those who do and do not fit dominant definitions of ability, young and old. The only way to successfully work out those tensions is for power to be balanced among the oppositions. And the only way for power to be balanced is for those with less power in every opposition to organize.

These are the frameworks for the local work that most of us will connect with. We also need to understand that social change isn't just about doing community organizing and it isn't just about working locally. Community organizing is about a group getting power. There are two kinds of power—money and people. Those with money may have more power in the political economy, but those with more people have more power in many other ways such as the diversity of ideas they can generate, and their ability to disrupt business as usual by withholding their willingness to just go along.

But having obtained power, a group needs to do something with it. Having power means being better able to influence the creation of jobs, businesses, housing, and services. That usually means they then need to involve themselves in that creation process—doing community development. Callahan, Mayer, Palmer, and Ferlazzo (1999) use the metaphor of rowing with two oars to make sure that groups neglect neither the power dimension nor the development dimension of community change. And in a neoliberal context, it is usually the power dimension that is neglected. The rise of increasingly popular asset-based community development, consensus organizing, and other conflict-avoiding community change strategies are limited by accommodating neoliberalism to the point where they can only achieve goals that existing power holders will allow to be met (Defilippis, Fisher, & Shragge, 2010). Straight-up community development—the production of businesses and housing in local areas—suffers from similar constriction. Community development organizations are only able to do the kinds of development that funders will fund and governments will approve, unless the community constituency has shown that it can also engage in confrontational power organizing that both funders and governments see as enough of a threat that they stretch to support things they would other have been disinclined toward (Stoecker, 1994, 2003b).

Then we must move beyond the local. Defilippis, Fisher, and Shragge (2010) have documented the limits of local community organizing. Real social change requires linking local actions to a broader movement. This was the brilliance of the civil rights movement as well as the campaign that won the Community Reinvestment Act, which made it more difficult for banks to "redline" entire communities, thereby denying loans in those areas (Squires, 2003). Community organizing networks, perhaps most notably People Improving Communities through Organizing (PICO) have used their local prowess to take on national issues such as health care, immigration, and home finance reform. One thing academics are exceptionally good at is creating very broad geographical networks, and our ability to provide infrastructure to multilocal networks can be a crucial part of both local and broader change.

Social Change and Higher Education Community Engagement

The social change process outlined above is the one that informs liberating service learning. Our engagement with groups and organizations needs to be based in the principles of increasing their knowledge power and enhancing their capacity to achieve the changes they want. It's not about providing charity service and it's not about doing research. It's about supporting both direct action for change on immediate public issues that begin with the local and connect to the global, and broader change in the social relations of knowledge production. And conflict is a necessary part of any change that is actually a change. Helping the poor parent get a job, or tutoring their child to get better grades, is not a change. It is simply temporarily, and probably marginally, integrating them into the existing neoliberal political economy. Change is about transforming the structure of the political economy to distribute wealth to the people who actually earn it, rather than to the owner class. Of course, that doesn't mean that there shouldn't be groups helping people get jobs or education or any of the other necessities of life. But, as we have seen, they can do it by organizing people for collective self-help rather than turning them into individualized and consequently disempowered clients.

We are more prepared for some parts of this change process than others. Supporting changes in the social relations of knowledge production is closest to what we do in higher education normally. The concept of citizen science is rapidly expanding (Silvertown, 2009). Much citizen science involves grassroots people learning how to measure or document phenomena such as airborne pesticides (Harrison, 2011), engage in environmental monitoring (Silvertown, 2009), and a wide variety of other things (*Scientific American*, n.d.). In addition, forms of community-based research and its related practices, *when they involve people not just as free labor in data collection but in every aspect of research from choosing the question and designing the methodology on the front end to doing the analysis and using the results on the back end*, also transform the social relations of knowledge production. Public or citizen journalism is another means of amplifying the voices of community knowledge production (Friedland, 2003). These are all things that many of us are already supporting grassroots people to learn and do.

The problem may be that those of us in academia are too good at teaching knowledge production. The assumption seems to be that simply producing knowledge will produce change, that writing up the research results and "disseminating" them will somehow allow everyone to see the light and change their ways. But that's not even the way it works in the academy, let alone in the real world. The capacity of the public and the powerful to ignore, reject, and even fear knowledge is unbounded. So being able to produce and speak knowledge to power is but one piece of the puzzle.

The other, and in some ways more important, piece is the community organizing action required beyond producing knowledge to create social change. And that demands both knowledge and skills that only a miniscule fraction of the professoriate has even an inkling of. Concepts of community organizing exist in only the most marginal corners of higher education—the rare course in sociology, social work, or political science, or the even rarer community development program. Political science or sociology may offer the occasional social movements course. Organizational development may show up as an elective in sociology, public policy, or business. The process of making social change is usually only a week's worth of content in introductory sociology courses, even when sociologists insist that their entire course is about social change. This means that we are sending students into community contexts to provide untrained forced volunteer "service" with little to no knowledge of either the skills required to do the service or of the indirect effects of their involvement. Even worse, the faculty who send the students out are equally lacking in knowledge of community organizing and social change.

That is not a fatal flaw in creating social change so long as those of us in the academy recognize our own limitations and make sure the people we are working with have access to community organizing knowledge and skills. To a large extent, having a skilled community organizer in place can compensate for this lack of knowledge because the community organizer can educate both community constituency members and outsiders on how social change works in their context. And that then allows us academics to still do what we do best—knowledge production. What community organizers and constituency-based organizations can most gain from higher education community engagement is the knowledge that academics co-produce with groups to help those groups make more informed choices about strategy and tactics to produce social change.

There are a variety of topics about which community organizing groups need to do research to build knowledge. Will Collette (2004) believes that research can help in the following ways: identifying neighborhoods where organizing will be most effective, determining effective strategies, finding resources, developing policy options, documenting an issue for the public, identifying potential allies, exposing a target's weaknesses, and countering the target's definitions. A variety of other research activities can support community organizing in general, including researching community power structures (often called *power mapping* by community organizers) to find out who may be lined up either in favor of or against a group's issue (Hugh, 2011; MoveOn.org, n.d.), researching organizational governance models to find a best fit for a new group, and locating expert resources relevant to the group's issue.

Then there are many specific forms of knowledge production that students and faculty from a wide variety of disciplines can engage in with community groups. These range from supporting a group's efforts to build its power to supporting direct development. Public health students can conduct health impact assessments with community groups to counter corporate and government attempts to control the assessment process. Natural science students can perform soil, air, water, and other kinds of testing. Political science and public policy students can carry out policy research. Humanities students can work with groups on recovering and preserving their history through writing or community theater or art. Engineering students can work with groups on everything from building their information technology capacities to affordably rehabbing buildings. Community and technical college students are educated in so many directly practical forms of work—from medical technology programs to building construction programs—that can contribute to community groups' efforts to build up and repair everything from people to planet.

One of the best examples of integrating community organizing and knowledge development comes from the Morris Justice Project, which organized in response to New York City's "stop and frisk" policy begun in the 1990s. The project began through research conducted by the Public Science Project at the Graduate Center of the City University of New York. Mothers in the

South Bronx neighborhood around Morris Avenue who were also concerned about the often daily police harassment of their sons got connected with this research. Their involvement led to a full-fledged participatory action research process documenting the use and effects of stop and frisk in the neighborhood. As the process evolved, resident researchers took to the streets not only documenting police actions but also engaging their fellow residents in analyzing their data and discussing what makes a safe neighborhood. Their "sidewalk science" organizing efforts expanded to include other higher education support, engagement in the broader struggle to change New York City policing, and expansion into other issues affecting their neighborhood. Stops are now down by 75 percent and one resident who moved her family out of the neighborhood in fear of their safety from the police then moved back (Morris Justice Project, n.d.; Torre et al., 2014).

What is important in all these activities is understanding the broader change processes: changing the social relations of knowledge production and building broad social movements by linking multiple efforts to organize for change in different local settings so that more people can build connections with each other and experience more collective self-determination. The most important challenge to higher education making a contribution to this process, however, is the lack of organizing among constituencies of oppressed, exploited, and excluded peoples. It behooves every college and every university that wants to pay more than lip service to community engagement to establish an endowment to fund full-time community organizers—endowments that can't be taken back when the organizing results in a group that confronts the university or college for its failings. This may seem patently unrealistic. And yet, the University of Toledo for a while employed Dave Beckwith as a community organizer on the staff of its Urban Affairs Center. My work with the Southwest Madison Community Organizers helped obtain a grant from the University of Wisconsin to fund a youth organizer. Pitzer College has supported a community organizer in its institutionalized service learning program (Peterson, Dolan, & Hanft, 2010).

We also need to shift our focus from 501(c)(3) nonprofit organizations to 501(c)(4) social action organizations and even unofficial constituency-controlled community groups as a means of liberating ourselves from the corruption of the nonprofit industrial complex. In Madison and other places where I have traveled, activist groups often feel excluded from access to university and college resources. We can't support social change if we don't ally ourselves with the groups working to achieve it.

We also need to educate faculty and students on community organizing and social change to make them aware of how their engagement influences community dynamics. We have institutional review boards, or ethics boards, that restrict our ability to do research. Because those bodies do such a poor job, by and large, at being able to understand any kind of knowledge production that is community-based, I am loath to suggest expanding their powers. But there is an increasing number of community-based ethics boards springing up in First People's communities and elsewhere (Assembly of First Nations, 2009; Seifer et al., 2009; Silka, Cleghorn, Grullon, & Tellez, 2008). One of the most interesting examples is the Community Research Ethics Office at the Center for Community-Based Research (CREO) in Kitchener-Waterloo, Canada. Based in an independent nonprofit organization, the CREO is independent from higher education institutional agendas, so it can think about community engagement ethics from a community perspective. From this standpoint, ethics can be about not just the effect of data extraction on the individual from whom data is extracted, which is the focus of most ethics reviews today, but about the effect of the overall research process on the community in which it is occurring. The goal, from this standpoint, is to no longer need even alternative ethics review processes because all research will be organized through community groups and there will be no more research exploiting community members. We can get there through community organizing when organized groups hold higher education institutions accountable for engaging in communities in ways that support their collective self-determination.

So our work needs to focus on building up grassroots people's knowledge power and supporting their social change efforts around specific issues. It can feel scary to think about conflict and struggle. But there is no escaping that. There is already conflict and struggle. We need to draw on its energy to transform it into progressive social change. And we have to overcome neoliberal hegemony to do it. We have to liberate ourselves from the thinking that traditional tutoring programs build knowledge power. By focusing on individuals they preserve the competition between people that separates them rather than connects them. Knowledge power is a collective, not an individual, capacity. And we must liberate ourselves from the thinking that food banks create social change. They actually are more likely to prevent social change by feeding people just enough, and defining them as needy enough, to prevent them from organizing. We need tutoring, and we need food banks. But we need them mostly because we are putting more energy into those charity activities than we are into social change.

However, that does not mean that tutoring programs and food banks can't be sites for social change. In an attempt to build a practice of service sociology, Treviño and McCormack (2014) draw on charity sociology, which emphasized the development of neighborhood communities that could, through neighboring, provide for the needs of residents. But beyond service sociology, any place where oppressed, exploited, and excluded people are gathered because they need to get basic needs met is a place where they can engage in a collective process with each other to build knowledge power, work toward community, work together to meet their own needs, and organize for social change. So we move next to the theory of community, and higher education's role in it, because it contains the broad bucket of strategy for the change we want to make.

9

Toward a Liberating Theory of Community

> Dominator culture has tried to keep us all afraid, to make us choose
> safety instead of risk, sameness instead of diversity. Moving through
> that fear, finding out what connects us, reveling in our differences;
> this is the process that brings us closer, that gives us a world of
> shared values, of meaningful community.
>
> —BELL HOOKS, *Teaching Community*

If we are going to say that we work with communities, then we need to know what we mean. We need to restore the word *community* in our culture to mean something rather than everything. To date too many institutionalized service learning analysts only perpetuate the problem of definition by tying themselves up in intellectual knots. Gelmon et al. (2001) cannot overcome the complexity of the context in trying to define community. Bridger and Alter (2006) intellectually stymie themselves in a definitional attempt, concluding that "community boundaries are not clear, extralocal forces often dominate aspects of community life, collective actions often express private rather than public interests, and identities are often tied more to special interests than to the local community" (p. 167).

This is not helpful. Yes, defining community is hard. But that is because we are trying to develop a definition from things that are not communities at all. We actually have a large and historically rich literature in sociology (Goe & Noonan, 2006) that places the definition in a theoretical context, allowing us to discriminate between things that are and are not communities. This is the path I pursue. Thus, my definition of *community* is this: a face-to-face collectivity characterized by a multiplicity of interconnecting and overlapping roles that mutually enhance the sustainability of the collectivity and all of its constituents.

This definition needs some unpacking. *Face to face* means that people interact with each other face to face in a physical place. And this place-based emphasis is much more comfortable for those who start from a community development perspective, such as Robinson and Green (2011a). Collectivities that exist only through distance communication may be extremely valuable to their participants, but they are not communities. *A multiplicity of interconnecting and overlapping roles* refers to people who interact with each other as parents, children, club members, workers, consumers, and a variety of other roles in a single place. Bridger and Alter (2006), much as they seem to have difficulty defining community, nonetheless talk about communities as fields of social interaction in a local place. In such circumstances, people come to know each other in a multiplicity of ways. They come to know their diverse backgrounds, diverse skills and talents, and diverse interests. Thus, a group of people who interact only through a single role, as club members, for example, only see sameness. They are not a community. *Enhance the sustainability of the collectivity and all of its constituents* means that people's interactions make life better for everyone. Collectivities where one powerful group interacts in ways to limit or restrict those with less power are not communities. The opposite is required—interaction in ways that maximize the sustainability of diversity.

It is important to note that I use the word *people* in my elaboration, but I do not use it in the definition itself. That is because I am also honoring Aldo Leopold's 1949 definition of *community* that includes all living things. Such an addition is exceedingly important and invokes the reality that sustainability cannot be achieved by focusing only on the interaction of humans. Plants and animals and microbes are also community constituents in this definition. Ideal communities take into account the interests of all living things because their members understand the web of life.

Mine is an ideal-type definition both in the terms established by Max Weber (1904/1949) and in the sense of "idealistic." For Weber, an ideal-type definition includes all of the features of the hypothetical perfect or complete case of the concept. Most, if not all, actual cases are missing some features. The purpose of an ideal type is to allow us to see the incompleteness and variation of each actual case. For all those groups and networks that are temporary, one-dimensional, and superficial that people want to call a community, I object. Value those things, get involved in them, but don't try to call them communities. And don't use the argument that any "virtual" group or network feels warmer and closer than any place-based group. The absence of strong place-based communities shouldn't reduce us to calling single-interest cyber networks communities. And yes, I know that the places of the ideal-type definition exist only in 1950s TV shows and our imagination. This is where we also consider the definition as idealistic. And idealism is important. In an era where the TV shows don't even promote higher ideals, we reduce our vision to simple and superficial goals. We want too little, and we consequently achieve too little. Perhaps one reason we define everything as community is because we do not have any actual community to experience and raise the standards.

The Struggle for Community: A Theory

We must understand why we don't have such communities. Let's return to the discussion of use values and exchange values in Chapter 6. If we define a community as a face-to-face collectivity characterized by a multiplicity of interconnecting and overlapping roles that mutually enhance the sustainability of the collectivity and all its constituents, we are defining it as a location for the production of use values. In this type of community, no one is homeless, hungry, or scared because everyone is looking out for and supporting each other and is producing for the collective, not the corporate, good. This type of community is focused on the production of use values. People produce for collective benefit rather than for personal gain (which, of course, also enhances personal quality of life). They organize the physical spaces of the community to support the production of use values—gardens, parks, and collective indoor spaces. To the extent that people produce things for others, they do so in direct relationship with those others and in a form of generalized reciprocity—paying it forward—rather than direct exchange. The carpenter builds the toy for the child of the chef across the street. The chef cooks dinner for the neighbor recovering from surgery (don't scoff—this was the neighborhood I lived in as a child—my father was the carpenter and my mother was the tailor). The sustainability of such communities rests on admitting to and acting on, the reality of interdependence. Among the results is a culture that resists Marx's four forms of alienation—people feel a sense of ownership for what they produce (including their relationships); they are in touch with the entire process of their production (I have a dried-flower holder that my father made from an actual tree that grew in our yard); they have genuine sharing relationships with their neighbors; and they understand their role in the interconnected web of all things.

There are still vestiges of such communities in various places, but they have been under attack for as long as we have had capitalism. The drive for profit in a capitalist economy requires that people be alienated. If people know how to produce things on their own, they can produce independently from capitalists. If they have strong relationships with others, they can organize against capitalists. If they can make choices of what to produce based on values rather than economic needs, they can resist capitalist commodification. For these reasons, the self-interest of capitalists is to deskill us, separate us, and stupefy us. In doing so, they drive down wages to drive up profits and weaken our ability to resist. As our wages decline and our skills atrophy, we are forced to work more hours and buy more of what we could otherwise produce for ourselves. And as the things we used to provide for ourselves and our neighbors directly through our own labor become commodified, we become more and more alienated.

Capitalists do this to the physical space of community as well. They buy up farmland to build big-box stores on the outskirts of town, forcing us into our cars where we become further isolated from and distrustful of each other as we jockey for the perfect parking space so we can walk even less. They turn existing physical space—housing or commercial—into rental relationships, alienating both owner and renter from care for the space. The result is decimated downtowns—previously walkable spaces where people could mingle face to face rather than car to car. Public spaces are privatized as neglected parks become dangerous drug emporiums and the public feels chased inside to malls with mall cops. Under neoliberalism, we treat local taxes as an affront to personal liberty rather than as part of our contribution to collective sustainability. Without collective funding, our schools, libraries, parks, and other community collective goods wither away (Stoecker, 1998).

So it is not that community is in decline because we are all making bad choices, as the social capital/communitarian/asset-based theorists would have us believe. Community is *under attack* and has been since at least the nineteenth century (Durkheim, 1893/1997; Simmel, 1905/1956; Toennies, 1887/1963). We cannot "rebuild" community under such circumstances. The social capital/communitarian/asset-based emphasis on rebuilding community by rebuilding "relationships" is patently unrealistic in a context where more people work more hours, after driving longer distances to and from work, and lack any direct material interdependence. Putnam (2000), in *Bowling Alone*, misinterpreted his data. It's not that we're bowling alone. We're not bowling at all. We simply have no time left over (Schor, 1993). The only way to rebuild community is to struggle to push back the attack on it under what Riane Eisler (1988) and then bell hooks (2003) termed *dominator culture*—the culture of competition, hierarchy, and domination that separates us. Along with the obvious efficiency of building community while engaging in struggle, there is also the reality that there can be no community without eliminating the barriers to it.

But where to start? You may have noticed that I seem to be talking about people who have full-time jobs and cars and homes. I have not been talking about the homeless, the destitute, the violently abused (though, for sure, I am talking about the "one paycheck away" demographic). When institutionalized service learning students and, with any luck, their professors reach out into the most beaten-down "communities" in this country, they are reaching into the consequences of dominator culture, which for me is a neoliberal capitalist political economy complicated by the race, sex/gender, ability, age, and other oppressions with which it intertwines. But what institutionalized service learning teaches students to see are individuals who seem to be inarticulate, drug dependent, violent, unskilled, unmotivated, and exhibiting a variety of other undesirable behaviors. The practice doesn't help them see people who have the potential for engaging in the struggle to create community; see the need for struggle; and see our consequent complicity in maintaining dominator culture. We need to change that by first changing our thinking about community and the causes of its demise.

The consequences of defining community as an ideal type, and sticking to it, are quite profound. If there are really no collectivities that even approach the ideal-type definition of community, then there is no such thing as "community-based" anything. There is no such thing as "working with the community." At that point, all the language (not to mention the practice) of institutionalized service learning goes out the window. Instead, there is only working *toward* community. And that requires a shift in language and strategy.

From Community to Constituency and Back Again

If we switch from "working with" or "working in" to "working toward" community, and if we understand that working toward community will meet with resistance from those who buy into the neoliberal capitalist political economy, an entire new world opens up in front of us.

The first thing that this switch offers us is a new clarity in whom we actually work with. You may have noticed my gradually bringing the word *constituency* into the discussion until I made it a core feature of my definition of community in this chapter. In the past, I associated the term *community* with "the people with the problem" (Stoecker, 2003a, p. 41), and I wasn't the only one to be caught up in such confusion. Fourie (2006) defines community as "specific interest groups informally constituted, delineated or defined by their sharing of, and search for solutions to, one or more related development problems/challenges." I now realize that such a group of people is not a community but a constituency. Chapter 8 began talking about the constituency as the starting point for social change. Here the idea becomes the starting point for working toward community and for the basis of diversity in it, so I am going to switch to *constituency* from *community*. That doesn't mean that I'm coining a new term called *constituency-based service learning*. Labels do more to confuse than to clarify, and they all eventually become wrecked by those who attach them sloppily. It is the theory and the practice that matter.)

Constituencies are not communities. At times they are not even collectivities. In the most beat-up places, they are simply groups of people who share such similar circumstances that, if they organized, they could fight back against the forces of oppression, exploitation, and exclusion that block their individual and collective self-sustainability. People in an apartment building who are suffering from poor maintenance and high rents are a constituency. People in a neighborhood who are suffering fear of crime and fear of police are a constituency. Children who are suffering poor education in their school are a constituency. And, yes, it is possible that constituencies can extend far beyond the local—even to the global. For our purposes, however, I focus on constituencies that can become communities—only face-to-face constituencies have such potential.

We are used to hearing about constituencies in relation to electoral politics, and it's not so far off to think about them that way. We define various electoral constituencies like this because of the common policy interests that exist in one constituency and their divergence from those of others. But there can also be diverse constituencies even within a single, common social change effort. The AFL-CIO (2013), for example, has organized constituencies around racial/ethnic interests, veterans' interests, women's interests, and others. In a single neighborhood, then, there may be both a neighborhood constituency and narrower constituencies defined by race/ethnicity, age, or other characteristics. It is important, however, to link the notion of constituency to common circumstances that have a social structural source. While there are probably circumstances where it makes sense to talk about people who like to play chess as a constituency, that is not as powerful as people in a neighborhood who lack decent housing because landlords refuse to care for their apartment buildings.

How do we work with constituencies in ways that work toward community? Here we re-invoke the principles of community organizing introduced in Chapter 8. But we must be careful. As neoliberalism's influence has also invaded community organizing, too much of the practice has focused only on "building community" rather than confronting the barriers to community (Defilippis, Fisher, & Shragge, 2010). In particular "relational organizing" (Gecan, 2002) or "consensus organizing" (Eichler, 2007) seems to eschew political analysis in favor of building relationships. A more sophisticated approach comes from People Improving Communities through Organizing—PICO— who talk about *public relationships*. PICO's emphasis on building public relationships is about developing effective working relationships among people to support action on issues. The PICO relational strategy, then, is explicitly about organizing constituencies into functioning power organizations more than it is about simply rebuilding the bonds of community (Christens, 2010).

It is in struggling against the barriers to community—first perhaps as a single constituency, then in collaboration with other constituencies, and then perhaps with outsider allies—that we work toward community. This highlights the problem with the charity-oriented service provider model. While service organizations often focus on a specific constituency—people who are homeless, or hungry, or jobless—they treat them as, and maintain them as, isolated individuals rather than as constituencies in accordance with the dictates of the nonprofit industrial complex. This makes no progress whatsoever toward community and even helps preserve the absence of community experienced by those constituency members and, indeed, the rest of us. And when those of us from higher education participate in that process, we become complicit in maintaining the absence of community.

What do we do instead? Here is where we move into community organizing and development methods.

Community Organizing Plus

Working toward community, and against the barriers preventing it, involves transforming personal troubles into public issues and practicing community organizing, as discussed in Chapter 8. One of the ways that constituency members are separated from each other is through the neoliberal-imposed definition of their suffering as their own fault, and it doesn't help to counter that with language about how everyone has assets—it's still the same individualization of experience that disconnects rather than connects. We need to engage constituency members in discussing what they have in common. And we can even talk about "needs." Needs, in contrast to the oddly unreflective position of asset-based analysts, do not automatically imply some personal deficiency, and identifying common needs in fact can help make more clear what oppressive social structures outside the individual are creating the needs (Mitchell, 2008). Identifying common needs is the first step in transforming personal troubles—needs defined as personal deficiencies—into public issues. It is also an essential step in working toward community.

The process of transforming personal troubles into public issues through liberating service learning draws on a few crucial principles from community organizing and community development that are necessary to produce real victories and move us closer toward community. These go far beyond the usual vague exhortations to "involve the community" or "meet community-defined needs." They owe much to the principles of good practice from the Community Development Society (CDS; 2013) and to the community organizers I have worked with over the years. I adapt these CDS principles here:

1. Build the leadership of the people struggling against domination, exploitation, and oppression. This means continually finding ways for constituency members to understand the process and the bigger picture, to learn how to take charge of the change process, to exert influence over it, and to spread that influence to as many constituency members as possible.

2. Build the participation of constituency members. Community organizers call this "turnout." This is on the way to building leadership, but understanding the reality that some people will only become involved sometimes. It is about understanding people's self-interest—most people won't get involved in collective struggle unless they see it

as in their self-interest. It is also important that participation be real. This is not about the occasional consultation, but about seeking to involve as many people as possible as often as possible. An organization that has only a few leadership slots will not be as effective in organizing a community as one with many leadership possibilities (Stoecker, 2003b), including alternative collective models such as group-centered leadership (Stall & Stoecker, 1998).

3. Build the organization of constituency members. It's not enough to just get people involved in working on a single issue or a single project. Part of the imbalance of power in this country comes from the fact that capital is organized while those dealing with its externalities are by and large not organized. Being organized means being engaged in an enduring, sustained, systematic way through an organization that can struggle against all of the injustices that present themselves.

4. Build people's capacity to grow collective leadership, expand participation, and build organization to create goal-oriented social change. This is a massive community education process, which I cover in Chapter 11. It focuses on learning how to choose or "cut" an issue—picking a winnable chunk of a big issue. It focuses on how to do turnout, how to build leadership, how to pick winning strategies. There are many wonderful, accessible books and websites that provide more depth on these things (Kuyek, 2011; Minieri & Getsos, 2007; Sen, 2003; Staples, 2004; Vancouver Citizens Committee, 2014).

The process always starts and focuses locally, but the ideal is to grow beyond the local. Many national community organizing networks try to work from local neighborhood organizations to city-wide networks and then to regional and even statewide power bases. The Texas IAF grew from the work of the Industrial Areas Foundation—the national community organizing network founded by Saul Alinsky—and became successful at taking on statewide policy issues (M. Warren, 2001). ACORN—the Association of Community Organizations for Reform Now—before its untimely and tragic demise, took on some of the baddest bad guys on the national scene such as predatory lenders (Atlas, 2010). PICO, as I mentioned, tries to take their community organizing work to a variety of national level issues.

The crucial point here is that we are not simply trying to work toward a white-picket-fence community where everyone is kind and all the children are above average. Not yet at least. We first need to work toward communities of resistance that can remove the barriers to the possibility of the self-determining community. We are, in this intermediate step, working toward social movement communities. Steve Buechler (1990) started us thinking about *social movement communities* as networks of activists that helped maintain social movements. As others worked with the idea, it became more personalized and localized to include strategies for sustaining face-to-face groups who identified with a social change movement even when the movement itself was in abeyance (Taylor, 1989). Thus community becomes the foundation on which the movement depends. Activism that most challenges the most entrenched power can be risky, dangerous, and costly. It requires not just time and commitment but an amazing amount of what is called *social reproduction* (Stoecker, 1992). Activists need to eat, clothe, and shelter themselves. They need to care for their children. They need to keep their spirits up in the midst of defeat and repression. The best way to do this is by forming a community that is not simply "being the change you wish to see in the world" but is also supporting the activism required to achieve that change.

These communities also must start, and must maintain themselves, locally. Because they are composed of constituency members who range from simply being excluded from full participation in society up to being under attack by active discrimination, racial profiling, and criminalization of their behavior, they also need *free spaces* to build community. Free spaces, as defined by Evans and Boyte (1992), are "'schools for democracy,' owned by participants themselves" (p. ix). They are geographically bounded physical spaces that have a quasi-public character. As schools for democracy, they are spaces where constituency members can gather outside of the pressures and surveillance of the oppressor to debate, learn, strategize, theorize, and organize. The freedom school in the southern civil rights era was the quintessential free space (Perlstein, 1990). The social center movement in Europe is perhaps the most contemporary implementation of the idea. Often organized by communal anarchists, social centers are spaces for alternative education and culture where people learn forms of participatory democracy (UK Social Centres Network, n.d.).

Until we have a society where all constituencies can achieve a sustainable good life with integrity, the community we work toward will be one that engages in change making rather than simply place making. This distinction can be found in the community development literature. Bridger and Alter (2006) and Robinson and Green (2011a) follow Summers (1986) in distinguishing between development *in* the community and development *of* the community. Development *in* the community is a product approach—creating jobs, businesses, housing, services, and so on. Development *of* the community is building the power of community members by helping them organize and build their collective capacity. These analysts argue that higher education community engagement—what I called institutionalized service learning—has mainly focused on development *in* the community. The point is not that we shouldn't support jobs, business, housing, and service development. It is that we should support the development of the people's power so they can get these things for themselves and change the conditions of power that prevented them from getting those things in the first place. What oppressed, exploited, and excluded people most need is collective power, because when they have power they can get jobs, housing, and services, and other things. The Community Development Society's (2013) principles of good practice, adapted above, also lay out a "development *of* the community" approach.

I know how tempting it is to go right for the services—right for the production. But we must be careful when we begin talking about development *in* the community because it is so easy to slide into practices that reinforce the nonprofit industrial complex and the neoliberal capitalist political economy it props up. Some of the writings that purport to be about community development, for example, are really about government and social service development (Muirhead & Woolcock, 2008). Others talk only about changes in individuals rather than in their relationships to communities (Mulligan, Scanlon, & Welch, 2008). In other cases, the term is left so undefined to include almost anything (Dubb, 2007). Internationally the situation is similar (see, for example, Crabtree, 2008).

Liberating Service Learning, Community Organizing, and Community Development

None of this is to say that professors and students need to become community organizers. When they do have the skills they can bring together knowledge and power for some impressive victories as Trish O'Kane (2015) has shown in her own work combining action research and community organizing. All but a very few have the skills or the resources to do community organizing. But we must understand that any time we engage with constituency members we are ultimately going to be influencing all of their relationships as well. When we support a job training program, and the most talented people get good jobs through that program, and they move out of the neighborhood, we may have helped the individual but we have worked against, rather than toward, community. When we test the town's soil and it turns up lead contamination from all the leaded gas burned for all those years in the cars traversing the main highly right through the center of town, and the news media learns about it, and property values fall and the town's tax base declines, we have worked against, rather than toward, community. In all of these cases, when we don't understand the community dynamics, and don't make sure that the community is organized to handle the side effects of our engagement, we risk doing more harm than good.

I learned this lesson in my very first attempt as a new assistant professor at community engagement. I was commissioned to conduct a study of all the grassroots community development organizations in the city of Toledo,

Ohio. I dutifully did my interviews, reviewed the documents, gathered the output and outcome data, and wrote the report. It was a dangerously negative report, showing how little the organizations accomplished and how lacking in capacity they were. Released simply as an academic report, it could have led to the demise of the entire grassroots community development sector in Toledo, as funders concluded they were wasting their money and community supporters decided they were wasting their time. But my work was guided throughout by a community organizer, Dave Beckwith, who knew from the beginning how to use my research. He convened a day-long conference around it, organizing a wide-ranging coalition of supporters who got me to do another study on community development funding that the coalition used to bring $2 million in *new* funding for grassroots community development groups (Stoecker & Beckwith, 1992). And while that may be the most extreme example in my career, it is certainly not the only one. All of my most successful community engagement forays have included a collaboration with a community organizer.

Here again is why it is so important to have community organizers and why every college and university should put their money where their mouth is by funding an independently managed pool of money to pay for community organizers. Our grant proposals to do community engagement of any kind should also include funding for community organizers. Ultimately, any scholarship of engagement must include someone highly skilled in understanding the dynamics of community.

When we have such talent on our team, us academics can then play our role of building constituency knowledge power that is consistent with the principles of good community organizing outlined earlier:

1. When we engage with constituencies, our goal is to build constituency leadership over whatever we are doing. If it's a tutoring program, we find ways to support constituency members in leading the process of its design and its execution so that the program doesn't just help individuals but simultaneously builds collective power and collective action. So we don't just shut up and do what they want. Instead we connect our expertise in tutoring programs with their expertise in their community so they can lead wisely in designing their own tutoring program and taking collective control over it.

2. We also need to build the participation of constituency members. We don't just work with a service organization to do things to or for a constituency. We find ways for a growing number of constituency members to participate in influencing the service organization itself. We also don't work solely with just a small group of constituency members who only want power for themselves.

3. It may be most important to attend to building organization in our work. Even if we as professors make an enduring commitment to a cause, our students will generally not. And that means that many of the things that we do with constituencies will necessarily be short-lived. And none of them will matter if there is no enduring constituency-led organization to continue the program, or use the research. Quite honestly, it may be better to do nothing than to ask people to put time into something that comes to a dead stop when the class ends. Because what will be left behind in such cases is not good will and optimism but what community organizers call "burned turf"—resentment and hopelessness that yet another outsider was only involved for their own purposes and abandoned the cause as soon as they got what they wanted. It makes it all the harder for anyone else who wants to act more ethically.

4. Building people's capacity to create social change is the most unrealistic thing for us to do. That is truly the job of the community organizer. But we can build people's knowledge power to use in the struggle. When the group is going up against city hall and needs policy options, we can work with them to research policy options. When a group of youths is trying to change their school, we can work with them to more easily locate information on how other groups of youths changed their schools. We can play our role.

The warning bells that we are doing probably useless and potentially harmful institutionalized service learning should go off when none of these things are happening. If our strategy does not include, or at least link to, developing leadership, organizing constituency members, building constituency-led organizations, and engaging in social change tactics and action, then institutionalized service learning and the nonprofit industrial complex are holding sway.

But meeting the demands of these principles seems like a huge task for academics. Can we really do it? Is any of this even realistic?

The failure to understand what must be done is illustrated by a blog post from Keri Facer, Professor of Educational and Social Futures at the University of Bristol in the UK. After arguing forcefully for "co-production" of research, she counts up the number of UK academics (a bit over 181,000) and then the UK population (about 63 million) and concludes that "given these numbers, even the wholescale transition of university research to co-produced methods would lead to only a limited number of people in the population actually being involved in setting research agendas, defining research questions and shaping research projects." But when you do the math, that's only about 350 people per academic. If we are going to limit seeing ourselves as only engaged in research projects, then we will necessarily limit who gets access to knowledge. But when we see ourselves as contributing to a process of organizing constituencies for power, 350 people per academic is a pretty low goal.

Some universities have attempted to work with collectivities in the form of neighborhoods, though even the best attempts are left wanting. Gilderbloom and Mullins (2005) discuss the engagement of the University of Louisville with the severely disinvested Russell neighborhood in Louisville. But the story, told from the standpoint of academics, privileges university and other already powerful actors in describing what begins to appear as a development *in* the community approach. Similarly, Rodin's (2007) book on the University of Pennsylvania's development work in West Philadelphia is a tale of development *in* the community. The main "community partner" was a Penn faculty and staff organization. Rodin proudly describes how the university *led* the redevelopment in the neighborhood, and justifies the university leadership on the basis of advice from the leader of a development corporation (p. 48), making it sound like just the type of deficiency approach the asset-based advocates so rightly decry.

In contrast, what does it look like for an academic to be part of a development *of* the community process? For me it starts with meeting a community organizer working in a neighborhood—someone who has already been able to bring hundreds of people out for meetings in collaboration with neighborhood leaders. It shifts into me facilitating small research projects to help a newly forming group representing people from multiple neighborhoods do planning. It then results in a variety of meetings involving a few dozen people that leads to a grant that leads to an action research project connecting with over a hundred other neighborhood people leading to the construction of a new community center which will connect with hundreds more neighborhood people—especially youth—all of which is led by neighborhood residents. The process begins to build a stable leadership group and more regular participants. My contribution to this effort was mostly research and planning facilitation, but it was inseparable from the organizing and development work, and that is how we need to think about this work and design it.

We can also see the contrast in narrower projects. Williams (2002), for example, describes a collaboration between a community college and a university to do a community leadership program. However, this effort focused on building the leadership skills of individuals, not on development *of* the community. In contrast, Ken Reardon's work in many places, but perhaps most consistently in East St. Louis, created an ongoing involvement of students with community organizing and development in that city. Their efforts led most notably to a farmers market and many other community improvements, and created the one-of-a-kind East St. Louis Action Research Project (Reardon, 1999) which still exists today. Lambert-Pennington, Reardon, and Robinson (2011) describe a partnership between university staff and a community development corporation that used a community planning and organizing process to build local leadership that focused on development *of* the community toward development *in* the community.

Robinson and Green's (2011b) edited collection perhaps comes the closest to showing some of the models through which institutionalized service learning can become integrated with community development. Their authors explore various approaches to community development, such as technical assistance, self-help, and an interactional method. They discuss sites of community development from urban neighborhoods to rural areas. They cover capacity issues involved in community development, such as action research and leadership development. And they look at community development foci such as health, youth, and schools. It is not always clear how or if the service learning practices supported community development, but they at least provide a framework we can use to judge for ourselves.

There are also some very select examples of attempts to put community organizing and development principles into practice. University Neighborhood Partners, a project of the University of Utah, occupies an actual house in an actual neighborhood on Salt Lake City's west side. They are quite explicit in their attempts to work toward community:

> In all of our work, we do not do, create, or direct programs. We bring people together, from the University and from west side neighborhoods, who share similar goals and who themselves do the work of the partnership. Our work is to support those partnerships by encouraging active communication and information- and resource-sharing among partners, developing personal relationships, and developing a broad knowledge of community and University priorities. (University Neighborhood Partners, 2013)

In one of the very few cases that focus explicitly on integrating community development and service learning for social change, Salant and Laumatia (2011) describe how the University of Idaho, University of Idaho Extension, and the Coeur d'Alene Reservation came together to work toward community. Over a period of years, reservation leadership identified issues they wanted to take on and worked with an Extension educator to build their own capacity to access university resources. But the focus was not just on addressing local issues. It was also about building leadership to better take on issues—working toward community with students and faculty supporting the effort.

In short, liberating service learning works toward community and engages with the practices of community organizing and community development. But how, exactly, do we do that? This is the question we take up next.

10

Toward a Liberating Theory of Service

> When I give food to the poor, they call me a saint. When I ask why they are poor, they call me a communist. (Dom Hélder Câmara, quoted in Camara & McDonagh, 2009, p. 11)

This oft-cited quote is from a Brazilian priest whose outspokenness often got him in trouble with both the Vatican and Brazilian authorities. Paulo Freire, the famous Brazilian educator, credited Câmara with popularization of the term *conscientization* (Freire & Vittoria, 2007, p. 112) that Freire used to such great impact and about which we learn more in the next chapter.

Câmara takes us on the first step toward a liberating theory of service for liberating service learning by focusing on the knowledge question: Why are they poor? For him, and for me, there is no question about where to start looking for the cause. Remember back to the sociological imagination. If there's one poor person in an otherwise wealthy community, we can reasonably begin by asking what is wrong with that person. But when 15 percent of the United States population—*46.5 million people*—live in poverty (U.S. Census, 2013) we have a *public issue* of such disturbing proportions that it is impossible to look anywhere but to the structure of our society itself.

Our "service" then, as participants in higher education, is not about feeding the poor (though we should contribute to that simply as good global citizens) but about contributing to the development of knowledge power that supports the poor in building their collective power to end the causes of poverty. How do we do that?

Allyship

Another increasingly famous quote attributed, through a colonizing knowledge lens, to Australian Aboriginal elder Lilla Watson is "If you have come here to help me, you are wasting your time. But if you have come because your liberation is bound up with mine, then let us work together."

The quote itself, and Watson's reattribution of its source as "Aboriginal activists group, Queensland, 1970s" invites us to rethink our work. As told by Mz. Many Names (2008), the statement was the result of collective discussion among Aboriginal activists. However, the colonizing knowledge process of western thought does not know how to attribute ideas to a collective, so it instead transforms collective knowledge into individual knowledge (L. T. Smith, 2012). And the statement itself recognizes this. The starting point for the critique is "you" and "me," expressing the idea of two individuals. The words "bound up with," "us," and "together" express the contrasting idea of a collective. This is not a minor adjustment. One person who provides resources to another—whether it is food, shelter, math skills, or whatever—exemplifies western individualist thinking. We've already covered the problems with this practice.

But what does it mean for my liberation to be bound up with another's, and especially what does it mean to work together? Here is where we invoke the idea of allyship, which has appeared perhaps most frequently in relation to people who identify as LGBTQ (lesbian, gay, bisexual, transgender, queer; see LGBTQ Allyship, 2013) but has also been developed by indigenous people (Gehl, n.d.) and for more general application (People's Grocery, n.d.). The concept exploded onto the scene in the wake of the police killing of Michael Brown and the consequent uprising in Ferguson, as white people looked for ways to express a shared outrage (Woods, 2014). The idea of allyship explicitly acknowledges that there is a profound difference between those who have a common social structural experience and those who lack the experience. It also acknowledges that there is a place for those who don't share the social structural experience and want to support those who do.

Probably the first principle of allyship is that the people with a common experience determine the other principles of allyship. If I, as an academic, approach some constituency to work with them, my first obligation is to learn how to communicate with them respectfully. Especially among people who are LGBTQ, many allyship guides start by emphasizing principles of language and communication (Adam, n.d.). Others emphasize allies engaging in a process of understanding themselves and broader structural oppression to prepare themselves for allyship (Gehl, n.d.). Anne Bishop (2002) focuses on the importance of understanding not just one oppression but how different oppressions reinforce one another, and working to develop one's own consciousness and liberation on the path to allyship. Many guides also make the point that allyship is not something you practice just when you are with the group but also when you are out in the rest of society (Gender Equity Resource Center, n.d.). Thus, allyship also does not mean that you become an ally to a specific organization, but to a cause and its constituency, and you engage in allyship as part of daily life. Most allyship guides also stress listening more than speaking, and this is something that we academics can be especially good at if we remember that we are learners first. In addition, allies do not speak for or on behalf of a constituency because that would take power from its members; instead, they speak for their own values that are allied with the constituency's values.

It is easy to think of allyship as those with privilege allying themselves with those struggling against oppression. Certainly I occupy a category of privilege in every sense except that I'm not a member of the capitalist class (I'm a white, able-bodied, middle-aged, heterosexual male, and even though not a member of the capitalist class, I still earn an upper middle class income), and I feel compelled to think of myself as an ally in social justice work. But it is important to also consider how people who may experience some oppressions and not others can ally with those who experience those other oppressions. Patel (2011) argues against a "binary model of allyship" that restricts itself to those who have more allying with those who have less, consequently reinforcing notions of top-down relationships. She also explores how privilege imposes costs on those who have it, making it in their interest to fight oppression. Elaborating further, she explores what she calls "horizontal oppression" between groups experiencing oppression but from different structural sources (such as two racial/ethnic groups or a racial group and a gender identity group). All this is to say that allies can come from all kinds of places, and all of the principles of allyship apply except that the ally is from a privileged group. Thus, for example, African American students from a working class background can be allies to people who are middle class, white, and lesbian, and vice versa. In such cases, the discussion of privilege becomes much more complicated and requires an integrated discussion of difference and diversity.

As allyship has gained center stage in the discussion of how white people of privilege can support Black people in the struggle against the once again all too obvious and brutal manifestations of racism, it has further deepened. Petersen-Smith and Bean (2014) worry that allyship can promote passivity—either white people become passive supporters of whatever Black people want or Black people become passive recipients of whatever opportunities white people of privilege make available. Thus, it can maintain the distinction, and distance, between "supporter and supported," and can be a barrier to achieving the next step of solidarity. Petersen-Smith and Bean draw from, among others, Indigenous Action Media (2014) which puts the issue even more starkly, charging that an "ally industrial complex" has arisen that in fact uses the concept to shift focus and power to white people themselves. The organization uses the term *accomplice* instead. The message I take from all of this is that the importance of allyship is in action more than in thought, and that brings us back to the ideas of reciprocity and mutual benefit.

How does allyship fit with the notions of reciprocity and mutual benefit covered in Chapter 3? Keith (2005) gets us part of the way there:

> This discussion brings home the fact that the principle of reciprocity is meant to be counternormative and even, potentially, counterhegemonic, as it proposes alternative ways of being and working with those who are, and are constructed as, underresourced with respect to oneself, which are meant to redress these asymmetries and foster more equitable exchanges, relationships, and communities—including the exchange of knowledge. The issue is how to surface, make visible, further develop, and equitably reassess the value of the resources of these "lesser" groups. (p. 15)

Keith acknowledges the counter-hegemonic potential of working in allyship with people suffering from the damage wrought by our society. But he remains caught in the concept of exchange, and especially in assigning "value" to "resources" for an exchange—a thoroughly western, individualized notion that maintains separation and consequently helps preserve power imbalances. When I have more, and I "exchange" with someone who has less, I still have more.

According to the principle of my liberation being bound up with another's, and the practice of allyship, my benefit does not come from a direct exchange with others, but from my own improved self-understanding, understanding of oppression, and participation in ending oppressive social structures that harm me as well. And that does not come from others taking extra time to teach me, or provide me with research data, but from my participation as an ally in the joint struggle for social justice. This shifts the idea of "mutual benefit" from "you get yours and I get mine" to the idea of producing broader collective social change that liberates everyone by creating a better society. At that point, we recognize our common interests rather than only our separate interests.

Such a stance invokes what is coming to be known as covenantal ethics. In covenantal ethics, we do not become involved with a group to meet our own needs or fulfill some kind of formal agreement, but because we enter into a covenant with a group (Hilsen, 2006). Following Hilsen, Brydon-Miller (2009) describes covenantal ethics in action research as "the acknowledgement of human interdependency, the cogeneration of knowledge, and the development of fairer power relations" (p. 247), "with a common commitment to addressing pressing social, economic, and political issues" (Brydon-Miller & Stoecker, 2010, p. 1). Covenantal ethics shares much with feminist care ethics, while retaining a focus on social justice and avoiding the entanglement of care with institutionalized service learning charity models that Ludlum Foos (1998) gets caught up in. In allyship, the common cause is fairer power relations, which is partly achieved through the process of cogenerating knowledge, and which depends on our acknowledging that we need each other to do both of those things.

Being an ally is not easy. You can't just show up and announce yourself as an ally. I remember working with one group, when I was paid by a philanthropic foundation to document the group's progress. I certainly considered myself an ally, and the foundation thought of itself as an ally. But the group, who was receiving money from the foundation, didn't trust any of us and felt like I had been foisted upon them. I spent a year and a half listening and only asking questions unless I was asked to say something until one day they invited me to facilitate one of their meetings. With other groups the process has gone faster, but it has rarely been smooth. Sooner or later, with every group, I have an experience of being "called out"—basically being confronted with something in my actions or my speech that the group finds inconsistent with my claim of allyship. Sometimes that confrontation is gentle, and sometimes it is quite direct. But, for me, it is always a defining moment as I take it as a sign that someone thinks I am actually worth the trouble of educating and building a public relationship with.

Moving one's allyship to this level takes a serious commitment that moves beyond just putting in time as a professional. Since most students will never fully engage long term in a constituency's struggle, we should not send them out alone to find groups to work with. Instead, we should only engage them with the groups we as faculty are working with as allies. Part of my allyship, then, is connecting students to the constituency's struggle, and taking responsibility for coordinating those students so that the constituency doesn't have to spend their scarce time resources on managing them.

It is through understanding myself as an ally, and helping my students understand how to act as allies, that I move beyond institutionalized service learning to liberating service learning, where we learn *with* others by acting together (something I discuss further in Chapter 11). Being an ally also requires me to no longer think about class projects, or even professional consultation, but about real allyship. Allies are not allies because they are paid or receive course credit to be allies. It is a commitment that reaches into the soul—yet more evidence that required service learning undermines fundamental values of social justice and community. You can't *require* commitment to a cause or to a people. And subjecting people to students who are not committed to their cause only serves your purposes, not theirs.

Liberating service learning means practicing allyship. And practicing allyship is part of the work *toward* community. When I intertwine my liberation with a constituency's, we achieve a common cause and at the same time begin to realize our mutual dependence. Institutionalized service learning only gets as far as attempting to achieve separate benefits—the education of the student and the completion of some task for some group or organization off campus. That maintains separation rather than working toward community.

If we are able to achieve allyship—meaning that we are able to achieve it inside ourselves and in relationship with others—is that enough? Will that move us toward community? The answer is no. In a context where the odds are stacked against creating community, we also need to struggle against the barriers, not just build toward the ideal. And the process of pursuing common cause, and working toward community, is extremely sophisticated, complex, and unpredictable.

Working with Constituencies

As a professor in a higher education institution, I strive as an ally to be a facilitator of knowledge power—working with constituencies so they can build their knowledge to enhance their action. And I take my cues from the principles of allyship and community organizing. Remember that allyship is focused on a constituency, even if it is a disorganized constituency. It is not focused solely on an organization, though it often extends to that. The constituencies with whom I feel the strongest sense of allyship, and to whom I have been referring throughout this book, are those who are oppressed, exploited, and excluded.

Those who are oppressed are the worst off. Because of race/ethnicity, age, disability, and other ascribed characteristics, the structure of our society and those who maintain it deny these people the opportunity even to be exploited—they silence their voices, deny them the use and expression of their skills, and curtail their access to resources. In Dom Hélder Câmara's words, this is "Violence No. 1" (1971), and it results in more violence. The personal troubles of these constituencies are many—drug abuse, gun violence, family abuse, poverty, illness. Transforming these personal troubles into public issues faces the challenges of the oppression itself because part of the oppression involves the denial of ways to access, develop, and act upon knowledge. Working with such groups takes the most skilled community organizers and the most skilled knowledge facilitators. The members of oppressed constituencies are highly mobile—criminalized behavior, housing insecurity, and fear of safety keep these people on the move. So, just when you think you have an organized group, half of them leave the neighborhood and you must start all over again.

Next are the exploited—everyone who works for a profit-extracting organization and does not themselves pocket the profit is exploited. Some, of course, are more exploited than others. Since, as we've discussed, many of the exploited actually support the practice of exploitation, they can be very difficult to work with through allyship. Especially members of the working class often support oppression and exclusion. Like the oppressed, the exploited also suffer a denial of access to knowledge production and skill expression, and even end up voting for those who maintain oppression, exploitation, and exclusion (Frank, 2004). Not only do they find it difficult to transform personal troubles into public issues, they resist it. But while many of them support the capitalist extraction of profit, most don't support the unfettered extraction of profit. And there are occasional historical sparks that lead the exploited to organize and welcome knowledge power. This is the kind of constituency that the University of Wisconsin disciplined students for supporting.

Then there are the excluded. The excluded are often also oppressed or exploited, but are singled out for even worse treatment by members of those constituencies as well as by the exploiters/oppressors. Today the most obvious excluded are those who are LGBTQ, though the situation is changing rapidly except for trans people, who are still left out of many of the changes, and women, who experience continual exclusion on the basis of biology. These are in some cases people with middle class incomes and even relatively powerful political positions who are nonetheless denied basic human rights—marriage, parenthood, comfort of the sick and dying, and control over their own bodies. But the excluded also are the people who speak ideas that challenge the status quo—environmentalists, atheists, feminists. It becomes a bit difficult to talk about these groups as constituencies because they lack the obvious social structural standing of the others. At the same time, we can see some of the structural underpinnings of their exclusion. The lack of reliable and convenient public transportation, the support for unsustainable consumption, the wanton pollution of air, land, and water as a way to boost profit margins, a toxic industrial food system, and so many other things institutionalized by law and maintained by political economic power illustrate the structural underpinnings that exclude environmentalists and show them to be a constituency. Because the excluded are more likely to have access to some power, they are most likely to experience at least some success in their struggles for justice, as we can see from recent gains in the struggle to legalize gay marriage.

The three constituency formations frame my entry points as an academic acting "in service." I work in allyship with those experiencing oppression, exploitation, and exclusion toward ending those conditions and building community. And no, not every group that doesn't get what it wants is oppressed, exploited, or excluded. The simple test is whether what the group wants is to maintain or increase the oppression, exploitation, or exclusion of another group. And again no, stopping one group from oppressing another group is not oppressing the first group.

Knowing something about the possible constituencies is an important first step in deciding how to be an ally. The next step is figuring out how to work with those constituencies. When I work as an ally, I bring skills and resources, not just time. It's not about simple volunteerism, though it can certainly include that. Simple volunteerism is a few hours here and there for things that need to be done, and are doable by nearly anyone. Simple volunteerism, while at the core of global citizenship, is certainly not higher education. And when we make it part of institutionalized service learning we become complicit in restricting constituency access to the riches of higher education institutions by offering only unskilled, unknowledgeable labor. We need to be offering what we're good at, not what we're not good at. In liberating service learning, we need to figure out just what the professor and students are able to bring in terms of skills and resources to specific social change campaigns led by constituency members, and then supply those things.

There are a number of wrong ways to do this, all of which we use with abandon. The first wrong way is to send out our individual students to find their own "partners." The second way is to approach groups with our specific offer (bad) or our specific ask (worse). The third is to make the actual community work an unrelated, ungraded, tangential add-on to a course. There is another way. If a professor is not yet in a situation where constituency groups are inviting them to contribute to the cause, then the professor needs to show up and offer themself as a global citizen and be willing to do anything. My first experience as an academic offering myself to a constituency group resulted in being given the task of cleaning a hallway storage area. It earned me goodwill and respect and—known to the organization staff but not to me—introduced me to the organization's knowledge archives.

One way to begin practice as an ally is to just show up. All effective constituency groups have events of various kinds. Many of those events are open to friends and allies. It is possible to discern the really effective groups because they use such events to educate and recruit. With the less effective groups, of which there are many, the professor will need to approach the leaders during or after the event and offer to contribute. It's also possible to cold-call a group, but less effective. Asking an overworked community group representative to give a professor an exclusive audience already invokes inequality of privilege. Showing up, and thus showing that the professor can contribute as a global citizen, rather than only as a professor who expects research data for an article or course material for students, is the first step in implementing allyship with a specific group.

The next step is determining what the professor, and their students, can offer a group in allyship. This step engages a dialogue process that requires both the professor and the group to understand community organizing and social change.

Knowledge Power, Community Organizing, and Social Change

Putting liberating service learning into a community organizing and development context is so unfamiliar to academia. But if we want our work to matter, we must be able to recognize when a constituency is effectively organized, has clear goals, and is pursuing an effective strategy. We also need a method for learning about the group's knowledge gaps in relation to those capacities. We can't do this without knowing community organizing. At the risk of repeating myself, I have to say that knowing the entire field of community organizing is too much for a single chapter in a book on higher education community engagement. However, I want to build more on what we have been discussing, in this case from our perspective in the academy, looking at the knowledge production perspective.

How do we tell if a group is effectively organized, has clear goals, and is pursuing an effective strategy? One might think that longevity would be an indicator of effective organization, but it can also be an indicator of capture by the nonprofit industrial complex—what social movement theorists might call becalming or cooptation (Zald & Ash, 1966). My first indicator is instead whether the organization is led by its constituency. And I don't mean that it is led by a couple of members who have run the group forever and have no accountability. I mean that there is a regularized process of democracy, engaging the broadest possible base of the constituency, that chooses and reviews the organization's goals, strategies, and leadership. In many cases, this shows up as a massive annual meeting that brings out a large swath of the constituency (in the hundreds or more) to elect leaders and choose priorities for the coming year. In other cases, it may be a smaller group but still a fully horizontal participatory organization without formal leaders but with formalized consensus decision making and clear strategies for getting work done.

What do clear goals look like? Here again, clear goals can be as much an indicator of capture by the nonprofit industrial complex as an indicator of organizational effectiveness. For me, the goals need to be focused on issues, not on logic models and management structures. Clear goals are social changes the group wants to achieve. And the clearest of those goals are things that, when constituency members imagine their achievement, they will be able to see, hear, feel, taste, and smell.

Finally, an effective strategy is one that gets the group closer to achieving the goals. Some groups have a track record of making social changes, and can say how and why they achieved those changes. Beware the group who only protests, or only holds meetings, or only produces policy briefs, or only does any one thing (though there are good groups who only do one thing but are allies of groups who do more). Making social change requires a combination of strategies that need to change over time as the issue and its context changes.

It is in the processes of organizational development, goal development, and strategy development that knowledge gaps may exist. And that is where academic allies can be the most effective. Looking at the knowledge capacities related to organizational development, goal development, and strategy development through an academic lens invokes the social change cycle that I developed in a previous book (Stoecker, 2013). The social change cycle goes through four steps: diagnosis, prescription, implementation, and evaluation. This may sound like the medical model, and it is, with the crucial difference that the constituency, not an outside expert, is in charge of the process. Another way of saying this is that groups need to figure out what they want, they need to figure out how to get it, they need to go after it, and they need to know when they've gotten it. Since I've specified the model in detail elsewhere (Stoecker, 2013), here I want to extend it to show how it intersects with the community organizing challenges of organizational, goal, and strategy development.

The first step, diagnosis, or figuring out what they want, is about the constituency understanding itself and its issues. If a constituency is concerned about crime, the knowledge process involves learning what, where, when, why, and how often the crimes occur and who they affect. If they are concerned about the quality of their water, it is about understanding what is in their water and where it comes from. If the constituency is youth who are concerned about their own academic achievement, diagnosis is about understanding how school works, what they are achieving, and the barriers to achieving more. And, just as a reminder, if it is adults concerned about youth, then the main constituency is the kids, not the grownups.

Understanding an issue in detail allows the constituency group to then "cut the issue," which we've mentioned earlier. Few community groups can take on "crime" in a generalized sense, but they can choose a *specific* kind of crime that *many people care about* and that they believe they *have a realistic chance of impacting*. Most community organizers use a verbal formula for this. I like "POW!" (say it with emphasis!), which stands for *precise, organizable, winnable*. Precise means it is very specific—you know when you are accomplishing it. Organizable means that enough people care enough about it to actually contribute time and resources to it. Winnable means having a realistic chance of achieving it.

It is pretty clear to see what the knowledge needs are in cutting the issue. More important are the community organizing needs. For the constituency to gain knowledge power, the knowledge development process needs to follow the community organizing process. How do we facilitate the knowledge process in a way that also makes it a community organizing process? In theory, it's easy—just follow the community organizing principles. In other words, the process of gathering knowledge should increase the number of constituency members coming together to take on the issue, it should increase their control over the knowledge process, and it should increase their effectiveness at successfully taking on the issue. If professors and students are going to "serve" constituencies, then they need to support the knowledge process to serve these multiple purposes.

There are some basic ways to do this, following magicians Penn and Teller, whose fame comes partially from their willingness to reveal the secrets behind their magic (Teller, 2012). The performing and the revealing are an inseparable duo in knowledge production. Too often, in the CBR (community-based research) form of institutionalized service learning, students are given the research assignment by an organization staffperson and then go away and return with what they assume is a finished product at the end of the semester. There is no "reveal" in such a process. It is only via engaging constituency members at every stage of the research process—forming the question, designing the methods, collecting the data, analyzing the data, and acting on the results (by writing or protesting or whatever)—that the "magic" is revealed as a set of practical procedures that everyone can learn. Going a step further, a real collaboration is not about just revealing secrets to an otherwise passive audience but engaging the audience as full collaborators in creating the magic.

How do we use knowledge processes as community organizing? The starting point is often finding out what people care about. It's not a needs assessment or an asset assessment, but an *issue identification* process that we use. Good community organizers will now be rolling their eyes—they call it door knocking. In door knocking the organizer goes door to door asking people how they feel about their neighborhood, what they like and dislike about it. As the organizer makes their way through the neighborhood, they start hearing themes. In sociology, we would talk about this as interview research and response coding. The difference is that the organizer is also taking names and contact information (an ethics review nightmare at the university, I know). For the organizer, the process is about finding out what issues in the neighborhood people are passionate enough about to involve themselves in. So the organizer starts to hear that some people are concerned about safety, and others are concerned about abandoned houses (and if you're thinking like an organizer you may be wondering if those things are linked). The organizer then recruits people to a meeting to start talking about these issues. What is it about abandoned houses that concern people? If they are homeowners, it might be property values. Or it might be fear of drug dealers using them or kids playing in them or any number of other things. And how do people feel unsafe? Is it that half the streetlights are not working? Is it because there was an especially violent crime recently? Is it because people are dealing drugs out of abandoned houses?

Let's say that the issue is drugs being dealt out of abandoned houses, bringing the two subissues together. The organizer's next task is to take the group through the POW! process. Do they focus on getting rid of all the abandoned houses, or just demand more responsive law enforcement, or just focus on one house, or what? In developing a goal that is precise, organizable, and winnable, the group will need more knowledge. What are the city's policies regarding abandoned housing? Are they being followed? How hard is it to get the police to be more responsive to residents?

In the process of cutting the issue, or shortly after, the group needs to figure out *how* to get what it wants; this is the prescription step. Sometimes this *how* question yields no practical paths, so the group cuts a different issue. So having really good knowledge on *how* is essential to a successful strategy. Building knowledge of *how* to get what the constituency wants can also be part of social movement building because it can link up one local group with other groups who are working on similar issues, increasing their chances of working together for broader social changes. But the group needs to find those other groups, needs to decide what the crucial questions are to ask them, and needs to have enough people to ask all those questions to all those other groups. Once again, professors and students can provide capacity in helping develop the list of questions and the list of other groups to ask those questions of. They might even be able to help with the asking, being wary, however, that doing so might inhibit the ties that could otherwise form between groups if the students are intermediaries.

The question we must always ask ourselves as allies is whether our contribution is enhancing the capacity of the constituency, furthering social change, and working toward community. When we talk about reflection in institutionalized service learning, this is what we should be reflecting on. In liberating service learning, the guiding reflection question is whether our service learning is liberating. So it behooves us to spend a bit of time discussing the topic of capacity building. The idea of capacity building has, like most things, also taken on a neoliberal patina recently. Sucked into the vortex of the nonprofit industrial complex, capacity building can mean structuring otherwise activist community groups to look like and act like corporations, thus controlling them and neutralizing their social change potential (Ife, 2010). When I talk about capacity, I am talking about the group's ability to, in fact, resist those pressures in order to sustain their ability to engage in social change work. It may, for example, mean not having a traditional board of directors, not having a hierarchical staffing structure, and potentially not even having an officially sanctioned nonprofit organization status. And when we are working toward community, we are also talking about building broader capacity among the participants in the effort to sustain a community (Keith, 1998).

When the group has decided what it wants, and how to get it, the next step is to go get it—the implementation step. It may have been clear up to this point that the major contribution professors and students can make to figuring out what the group wants, and how to get it, is the CBR form of institutionalized service learning. This is why Strand et al. (2003) refer to CBR as a higher form of institutionalized service learning. But CBR is not a higher form of anything by itself. It is *only* when we do it in the service of a focused social change campaign that CBR is of any value at all. And even then it's not a panacea. This also doesn't mean that more traditional-appearing service activities are always useless or harmful, and they may in fact be most useful at this stage of the process. Just like CBR, other service learning forms are useless when they are not part of a focused social change campaign. At the implementation stage it may be desirable to do more traditional-appearing service learning. The implementation could be development *in* the community. Computer science departments could be involved in information technology projects. The many programs of technical colleges have amazing knowledge and skills to offer in a very wide range of community development projects, from housing and commercial building redevelopment to health care. The performing arts programs can support community theater, art, and music. The humanities can perform public writings and readings.

It is absolutely essential to understand, however, that we can't do any of these things in a community vacuum. It is not the professor's or the students' place to decide that any group needs a house or a store or a play or an essay. The "what" has to be determined through the first two steps, diagnosis and prescription, and those steps need to be organized to grow the constituency to take the lead in making the "what" happen. Otherwise there is a house or a store or a play or an essay without any goal or any organized constituency, and the "what" becomes simply another in a long list of meaningless "whats" foisted on constituencies by outsiders.

Finally, the group needs a way to know if it has actually gotten what it wants—this is the evaluation step. Sometimes it is easy. If the goal is to build ten affordable houses and those ten houses are now sitting on lots, the evaluation is initially simple. But the goal, for everyone, should be to get constituency members thinking more deeply about their goals and how to evaluate their achievement. Because no group should want simply to build ten houses. They should want to build ten houses because they have ten homeless families or they have ten condemnable buildings occupied by drug dealers, and they want to know what happens to those families or those drug dealers. Here, once again, we can contribute community-based research support.

Liberating Service Learning and Service as Social Change

In liberating service learning, our service becomes our participation in social change. And remember that there are two forms of social change in liberating service learning. The first is the social change that the constituency chooses. The second is the transformation of the social relations of knowledge production. Liberating service learning is about furthering both forms, and here is where Morton's (1995) charity/project/change continuum doesn't work. First, charity and change are not on a continuum. As we have seen, they have different assumptions and different worldviews, not different degrees of the same assumptions and worldviews. Thus, they are categories, not a continuum. More important, putting "project" and "change" on a continuum confuses their synergy. Our work in liberating service learning is doing projects—mostly research projects but sometimes direct action—within a social change campaign.

The main challenge in liberating service learning is determining how much we, as professors and students, should do and how much constituency members should do. How much should we interject into the research design process? How much should we do the labor of data gathering? At what point do we perhaps enhance local social change at the expense of changing the social relations of knowledge production because we know that having an airtight measure of air pollution is crucial to the local organizing effort and we worry there could be too much potential error created by involving residents in the measuring?

The community organizer standard is to never do for someone what they can do for themselves, and this is a useful standard to apply to liberating service learning. What can people do for themselves now through some educating and organizing? What do they need others to do, because of the timing of the issue and its technical requirements?

This is a question of capacity. Sometimes groups are quite capable of doing their own knowledge production, but lack the person power. In those cases they already know the secret behind the magic. I've had this experience working with Community Shares of Wisconsin. The director was trained in research, members of their board were trained in research, and they had a staff data manager trained in research. They knew the secrets behind the magic. But they didn't have the time. My graduate student and I simply joined the team, adding person power that allowed them to expand their research activities (Willis, Anders, & Stoecker, 2011). The residents involved in the community center advocacy project in southwest Madison, however, were mostly not trained in research. We were careful to involve them in every aspect of the research we did. And in both cases we made sure we wrote down everything we did so that they could take it step by step to then do it again themselves if they wanted (Stoecker, in press).

We also need to understand that, in liberating service learning, those of us from the academy are more like the community organizer than the constituency member. And along with the principle that we should never do for people what they can do for themselves, we should heed the principle that the people shall lead. This means that we don't stand out in front. When the university press photographer wants to take pictures and the university PR person wants to write a story, they want it to look and sound like the *university's* (emphasis on the *possessive*) professor and the students were the saviors of some poor helpless group of people. Bracketing for the moment that the university would avoid being associated with the ideal form of what I am arguing for, in many more covertly political forms of liberating service learning it's still possible for the university to want to take credit. Our job, just like the community organizer's job, is to make sure that the constituency leaders are front and center for the camera and the PR person, not touting the work of the professor and the students but touting the work of the constituency or, hopefully by this point, the community.

Liberating service learning fundamentally shifts the emphasis from the student to the social change. Marullo and Edwards (2000) offer principles that should guide a service learning approach with aims of social justice. In particular, they believe that "the resources of the community should be developed and expanded as a top priority (taking precedence over the enrichment or gains experienced by the volunteers)." This shift also means that we no longer develop long-term partnerships with service organizations for the purpose of supplying them with volunteers. Aside from the inequity that exists between organizations that get volunteers and those that do not, and the charity thinking such a practice reinforces, supplying a limited chosen few organizations with a steady stream of student volunteers does not fit with either form of social change. Remember that our commitment of allyship is to a constituency, not an organization. In addition, we are contributing specific skills and resources that support the development of a group's knowledge power and its achievement of social change. There are times when we actually accomplish those tasks and the group no longer needs us because they have the capacity they need. Or they may need a new capacity that we can't supply, so they then look elsewhere. The actual length of the relationship is indeterminate but it has identifiable decision points. At the end of each project we sit down to determine whether there is a next project we can contribute to.

The role of the professor is also central to this process. If we are going to contribute real skills, then we do not send students out alone to put in hours with organizations. Aside from the fact that community groups want to see the professor involved (Sandy & Holland, 2006; Tryon, Hilgendorf, & Scott, 2009), and that any professor not willing to go out with their students is a lousy role model, if we are talking about practicing a form of allyship that brings real skills and resources, then sending out single students to put in hours doing little of value is a sham. Entire classes with a professor (and partner residents) can go door to door in a community of eight thousand, support a massive community change effort, and evaluate its impacts (Hidayat, Stoecker, & Gates, 2013). They can essentially accomplish much larger, more complex projects that provide much more value to a constituency organization.

There are examples of such projects. Aside from those I have been involved with (Hidayat, Stoecker, & Gates, 2013; Stoecker & Beckwith, 1992; Willis,

Anders, & Stoecker, 2011), there are a few examples of professors and students working with constituencies toward community and social change. Beckman and Wood (in press) discuss university involvement with a group of organizations focused on food insecurity in South Bend, Indiana. Weinberg (2003) describes all the challenges of working with community-based planning in rural areas through a community development course. Henness and Jeanetta (2010) also describe a rural community visioning project. Robinson and Green's (2011b) collection provides vignettes of institutionalized service learning projects that help third-world producers access global markets, provide assessment information for volunteer recruitment, analyze people's perceptions of area amenities, provide information and communication technologies for various purposes, do environmental assessment, and engage in other educational and research activities that may work toward community. They place these vignettes in a variety of community development contexts. Dolgon and Baker (2010) have also collected examples of work that range from more traditional institutionalized service learning to forms of liberating service learning and higher education community engagement that organize constituencies while supporting their social change work.

Perhaps the most explicit example of the diagnose-prescribe-implement-evaluate model in practice is given by Calderón and Cadena (2007) concerning their work with day laborers in California. This work began with a popular education process that engaged students and workers in diagnosing the causes of the daily discrimination the workers were experiencing. Together, they identified the prescription as a matricula consular card—a form of ID card—recognized by the Mexican government and various U.S. agencies that could help the workers obtain services and defend their rights. The students and professors built coalitions with a variety of agencies to make the cards available. With a thousand workers applying for a card on the first day of the program, and five hundred fifty receiving it on the same day, the evaluation showed an early success. As the relationship continued, the students, professors, and workers continued to work on issues together. One of those involved the problem of media perceptions of day laborers, prompted by a letter to the editor of a local newspaper branding them "criminals." As everyone discussed the possible responses, with recognition that the Christmas holiday was approaching, they settled on the theme that "Jesus was a carpenter" just like the day laborers. The workers and students produced a leaflet that the students distributed while the workers walked with their tools in the local Christmas parade to applause from the sidewalk audience.

Another example of the possibilities, using more of a participatory action research process, is provided by Kellogg (1999) in a difficult to find report of a multiterm project undertaken with the St. Clair-Superior Coalition, a hybrid community organizing and development organization in Cleveland. Kellogg started with an understanding of the knowledge power challenges faced by grassroots constituencies in relation to environmental issues that "include uncertainty about what information is available or where to obtain it; lack of access to information technologies (hardware and software); less-than-necessary education and experience to understand environmental scientific data; and absence of the skills needed to process data into knowledge that is useful as the basis of participation" (p. 16). And she understood that the main fix for this condition was involving the people in the research. Her work began with supervising one of her graduate students to fulfill a request by the coalition for information on child blood toxin levels, hazardous materials sites, underground storage tanks, and a neighborhood history. That led to a request for more information, and Kellogg herself collected more history on changes in land use, surface water, water and sewer lines, and development of railroads and industry. Then the coalition asked Kellogg to bring in more students and they co-designed a class that inventoried neighborhood environmental conditions and produced a set of resource materials that the coalition could use in its outreach activities. The coalition involved a variety of residents who learned about how to do environmental testing alongside the students. The process organized a new resident-based environment committee and funding to reproduce the resource guide. A second class then worked with the coalition and the Sustainable Cleveland Partnership to provide environmental data on specific neighborhood sites and issues.

These last two examples have the hallmarks of a good community organizing process integrated with a good liberating service learning process. They built from diagnostic research to specific actions. They grew the number of people and the number of organizations participating in the process. They produced knowledge that was directly useful by the groups. Such processes build knowledge power.

When we successfully engage in social change work and challenge the distribution of benefits and power, we should expect those with power to challenge us back. More than one academic has faced the wrath of powerful opponents who want to restrict the people's knowledge power (Cronon, 2011; Gedicks, 1996). In such cases they probably won't stop at calling us communists. Those who have power most fear the possibility of people gathering enough knowledge to allow them to act with their own power. The powerful, in their continuous attempts to transform higher education into obedience training for corporations, do not want its participants questioning the very system that maintains power inequality (Tudiver, 1999). But when the powerful attack the academics, and not the organized constituency, it's also a sign that we have not fully followed the principles of allyship and community organizing. The leadership and the voice should come from the constituency, not the academic. Our work is background support work. The constituency may occasionally bring us out to speak when they need, for example, some assertion of expert knowledge. But we should do so only to enhance, not supplant, the constituency's voice.

Obviously, this says something very different about civic engagement. In contrast to what institutionalized service learning advocates would have us believe, our job should not be primarily to enhance the civic engagement of college students. Those students are far more likely to be from, and destined for, the middle and ruling classes. Trying to turn them into caring citizens before they ascend to their empowered destinies doesn't question the hierarchy of power but only their behavior as its upper occupants. My focus is not on those who may use their already assured opportunity for civic engagement for evil; it is on those who are denied the opportunity for civic engagement from the start because they are denied access to education, to money, to power. The focus of liberating service learning is to enhance the civic engagement— defined as the effective practice of power—of the oppressed, the exploited, and the excluded. And the members of those constituencies, just like the rest of us, have much to learn about becoming powerfully civically engaged and working toward community.

11

Toward a Liberating Theory of Learning

> In the first place I don't know what to do, and if I did know what to do I wouldn't tell you, because if I had to tell you today then I'd have to tell you tomorrow, and when I'm gone you'd have to get somebody else to tell you.
>
> —Myles Horton in M. Horton and P. Freire, *We Make the Road by Walking*

The cause is social change. The path is toward community. The methods are community organizing and community-based research. The meta-method is learning.

What do I mean by a *meta-method*? Learning as a meta-method transcends and provides the comprehensive framework that links all the other methods. Doing community organizing is about learning how to transform personal troubles into public issues and then act on those public issues to create social change. Doing community-based research is about learning how to gather information, transform it into knowledge, and use it to support community organizing. Doing liberating service learning is about learning how to support constituencies organizing and building knowledge to create social change.

As a meta-method, the practice of learning in liberating service learning is first, and most definitely, *not* about teaching college students course content; teaching course content is the very last thing we do in liberating service learning. Learning is also distinctly different from teaching. It is completely possible to do all the behaviors of what higher education considers teaching, and have little to no learning occur. Conversely, it is possible to have none of the accoutrements of traditional teaching and have massive amounts of learning occur. It is very important to understand that, in contrast to the language used to describe institutionalized service learning, liberating service learning is not a pedagogy. Liberating service learning is a social change strategy that employs various methods to promote learning among everyone involved in the practice.

In liberating service learning, the practice of learning is mostly about the two forms of social change—creating change around local issues and democratizing the social relations of knowledge production. And that means learning is fundamentally about the constituency members first, and then their allies, in contrast to nearly the entire literature of institutionalized service learning where learning is considered only in relation to a traditional curriculum within institutionalized education. "Teaching," in a constituency-based setting, is a contradictory practice. As we transform the social relations of knowledge production, we transform control over knowledge and our definitions of who is presumed to have knowledge and who is not. We transform notions of expertise and the power relations involved in learning.

This chapter, then, is not about teaching college students, except as a secondary consideration. It is about building the knowledge power of grassroots constituency members, and then their allies, to support social action toward social change.

Learning, Teaching, Leading: The Foundations of Popular Education

"Everyone a learner, everyone a teacher, everyone a leader" went the slogan for the Grassroots Leadership College (GLC; 2012), a premier grassroots leadership education program that transformed itself from an individual-focused personal development program to a community organizing training program engaging a wide diversity of people from white middle class neighborhood activists to radicals of various stripes, people from diverse racial/ethnic and class backgrounds, people with various disabilities, people returning from prison, and many others. As the GLC shifted its focus to fully embody its slogan, the core of its white upper middle class donor base drifted away, no longer able to use the program to enforce neoliberal hegemony of individualist failure and achievement. The GLC no longer looked like a "college." It actually never did, with a two-room office and one paid staffperson, begging and borrowing meeting space from churches and other nonprofits to hold "classes." But when it shifted fully away from credentialed experts delivering lectures to facilitated sessions where uncredentialed and thus supposedly non-expert participants learned from each other and the credentialed experts were expected to learn as well, it simply became too radical to maintain the support of its comfortable neoliberal funders.

And indeed the approach of the GLC was radical, but it was certainly not without precedent or history. Antonio Gramsci's slogan (1971, p. 350), written somewhere between 1929 and 1935 while he was a political prisoner of the Italian fascist government, was "Every teacher is always a pupil and every pupil a teacher." Today we refer to this philosophy as *popular education*. It comes from thinkers you read about in Chapter 2—Paulo Freire and Myles Horton in particular—but from an aspect of their work that has been virtually ignored even by critical and social justice service learning practitioners. That aspect is not their theories of critical consciousness but their on-the-ground methods of facilitated learning.

The epigraph for this chapter comes in the midst of a story told by the popular educator Myles Horton, who helped found and then led the Highlander Folk School. He was working with a struggling labor union at the time, and his refusal to act like an expert so enraged one union member that he pulled out a gun and demanded that Horton tell the group what to do. Horton resisted and lived to tell the story. How many credentialed experts would refuse to act the expert even at gunpoint or, more disappointingly, could resist the temptation to act the expert under any circumstances? For that is what we academics have been taught to do. When we received our degrees, we became credentialed—our knowledge and its assumed concomitant expertise was legitimized by institutionalized, and some would even say arbitrary, standards. And we train our students to believe in this system, so when students and professors venture off campus to "work with the community" they often do it with the trained arrogance of the expert who believes that credentialing is the main, or sometimes only, criterion for expertise. We can impose our knowledge on people because, by virtue of our degrees, we believe we know better and more.

Of course, imposing knowledge and then leaving keeps those people subjected to the imposed knowledge just as vulnerable and disempowered as they were before. The only way to really solve problems is for the people themselves to solve their own problems. They don't need credentialed experts to come in and fix things. They need the knowledge of the credentialed expert to add to their own local expertise to build their knowledge power (Nyden & Wiewal, 1992). As grassroots constituency members build their knowledge power, by drawing on outside knowledge and their own life experience, and then teaching each other, they increase their capacity to lead their own action. This, if you are connecting the dots, is the way toward transforming the social relations of knowledge production while working toward community.

Community organizers understand the need for an entirely different kind of education to support such a process. According to Nicholas von Hoffman, one of Saul Alinsky's organizers in the heyday of community organizing practice:

It has been amply demonstrated in adult education that lectures, discussion groups, and similar talk sessions do not lead to greater understanding on the part of the individuals involved either of themselves or the social situation that they find themselves in. Quite the contrary. We have seen time and time again that it does not matter how dramatic, how "down to earth," or how pointed the study materials are, most people still do not see how any of this affects them or how they

fit in. . . . We propose to use a new set of study materials, to wit, themselves and the circumstances they live in; and secondly, we propose to
present these study materials in such a fashion that they will actually
be able to learn. . . . We are going to send the people who attend this
class out into all the groups and organizations which they are part
of . . . in order to find like minded people who can mobilize these
different organizations and institutions. . . . In this process of coming
and going from the workshop of life back into the classroom and then
out again, they will begin to see what these abstractions which we
label power groups, in-groups, vested interests, etc., etc., really mean.
(1958, p. 2)

A full theory of popular education needs to be connected to a theory of
adult education reflecting this community organizing perspective. In 1970
Malcolm Knowles published a book, unwittingly provocatively subtitled *Andragogy vs. Pedagogy*, that quickly got the attention of the education profession. He used the term *andragogy* specifically to refer to adults. A decade later
he had expanded his stance with the new subtitle *Pedagogy to Andragogy*,
describing the two methods as on a continuum and not necessarily linked to
age as much as to situation (Knowles, 1980). Interestingly, I first learned about
andragogy from a university information technology staffperson who trained
college students to provide information technology support to faculty and
students at the University of Wisconsin. We were developing an institutionalized service learning program where students would work with nonprofit staff
to enhance their organizations' information technology capacity. After that
training, I became intrigued by the idea of andragogy. As I read, I became
especially interested in Knowles's (1980, pp. 43–44) comparison of andragogy
to pedagogy:

1. Pedagogy sees the learner as dependent, with the teacher choosing
   and designing learning; while andragogy sees the learner as moving
   toward self-directedness, with the teacher encouraging the learner
   to choose their own learning tasks and methods.
2. Pedagogy sees learners as having too little useful experience to support learning, and thus require[s] teachers and textbooks to provide
   that experience for them; while andragogy sees learners as accumulating experiences over time that can provide the basis for more
   experiential forms of teaching.
3. Pedagogy sees society as determining what should be learned, and
   standardizes teaching so that everyone learns the same; while andragogy sees people as discovering a need to learn when they are
   in situations that require they learn things, with the teacher's job

helping people discover what they need to learn and then helping them learn it.

4. Pedagogy focuses on teaching people things that are not necessarily immediately applicable; while andragogy focuses on helping learners build competencies that are immediately applicable.

Comparing these approaches makes it even more apparent just how inappropriate institutionalized service learning is for both students and constituency members. Teachers design courses, providing knowledge that is not designed for immediate application. Then they impose these courses on students, grafting on institutionalized service learning experiences that don't actually fit the course content. Learning by constituency members isn't even considered in this model. It's no wonder that institutionalized service learning hasn't even attempted to think about constituency education, as a shift to andragogy would undermine higher education practice itself. Indeed those who have taken these ideas to their logical end, such as Ivan Illich (1971), unravel the institutionalized education system.

Knowles (1980) makes some very intriguing claims for andragogy. For one thing, he links it as a practice to "groups formed primarily for the purpose of engaging in social action of some sort. . . . Many action groups engage in activities designed to increase their knowledge about the problems on which they are taking action, and often even to improve their skills as agents of change" (p. 135). Here Knowles is in step with both Paulo Freire and Antonio Gramsci, who also advocate transformative education in the context of a movement and not just by itself (Mayo, 1999, pp. 92–93).

Toward this end, Knowles advocates a "club format" for learning that can facilitate "acquisition of knowledge," "a broadening of interests," a deepening of cultural appreciation," "an understanding of social issues," and "refinement of certain skills" (1980, pp. 136–137). Then he takes yet another surprising step forward to look at community development as an even "broader and richer" (p. 149) format for andragogy and makes a distinction worthy of any popular educator: "To noneducator community development workers the end is improving communities—solving community problems—and educational activities may be one of the means for achieving this end; to adult educators using community development as a format for learning, improving communities—solving community problems—is a means to the end of helping individuals and communities learn how better to solve their problems" (p. 149). Knowles cites McClusky's (1960) description of how a community survey can support a community learning about itself, and especially about how to develop itself. Here the adult educator, in Knowles's description, sounds like a community-based researcher: "The role of the adult educator is to help the citizen-participants diagnose the skills and knowledge they need in order to carry out a systematic program of community improvement and to help them marshal the resources required to accomplish these learnings. The key spirit of the whole enterprise, however, is self-help. Of all the formats for learning, this is the one that from the very beginning has been most congruent with the principles of andragogy" (1980, p. 150).

Interestingly, Knowles was most involved in the practice of andragogy before he began to pursue advanced degrees, mostly with the YMCA rather than grassroots constituencies. Once he accepted an institutionalized higher education professorship, it was his scholarship, rather than his practice, that was prominent. So while Knowles provides us with the model of andragogy, we must turn to the popular educators themselves to inform our practice.

Popular Education and Real Participation

We live in an age drowning in the false rhetoric of participation. "Town hall meetings" are now simply formats for powerful individuals to control the definition of issues by standing at a podium and even screening questions in advance, rather than the collective group-centered problem-solving method they were originally designed to be. People are asked to participate in agendas already set by the powerful, sucking up their time without producing anything of substance in return (Whelan, 2007). They are asked to participate in planning, but without any work to develop their imagination and move outside of the boxes of their own experience that has been constrained by the social structural limits placed upon them that has enforced ignorance of local power relations and global power relations (Cooke, 2001; Mohan, 2001; Mosse, 2001). Participation has become routinized and, in having become such, been rendered impotent in comparison to organic forms of involvement (Hailey, 2001). Participation, when its process is defined by either credentialed experts or elites, becomes its own "tyranny," in the words of Cooke and Kathari (2001).

In some ways we have always known that most invitations to participate are shams, but the clearest statement of the problem was made by Sherry Arnstein (1969). Her "ladder" of participation starts on the bottom rung with what we might call hegemony—forms of participation that manipulate people to accept elites' decisions. Further up the ladder, there are limited forms of participation where elites allow people to make a few decisions from a few predetermined choices. It is only when grassroots people get to determine the agenda, the questions, and the choices that we have real participation. And even here we must be careful, because a small group within a constituency can constrain the participation of others.

In comes popular education. Popular education, much like the spirit of community organizing, shifts the ground from constituency members participating in agendas set by elites—be they government, corporate, or academic elites—to setting their own agendas. Learning is central to this process.

For Myles Horton (1973), "the motivation for decision-making, like the motivation for learning, comes through genuine involvement in an undertaking considered worthy of the effort and possible to achieve" (p. 335). For Paulo Freire (1974), "people could learn social and political responsibility only by *experiencing* that responsibility. . . . They could be helped to learn democracy through the *exercise* of democracy [emphasis in original]" (p. 32). Connected to transforming personal troubles into public issues, and taking action, popular education is about the learning needed to practice powerful democracy, and about a way of facilitating that learning. What does the method look like in practice?

The Highlander Folk School, now called the Highlander Research and Education Center, has perhaps the longest-running record of practicing the participatory process of popular education in the United States. Myles Horton provided much of Highlander's spirit and process. In many ways the process was pretty simple—you bring people together and have them talk about their problems. In talking about those problems you ask people to explore their experiences with their problems. And then you ask *them* what would help with those problems. The solutions, then, come from the people experiencing the problems (Horton, 1976). Two things happen in such a process that illustrate the process of developing a sociological imagination that transforms personal troubles into public issues. First, people realize that they are not alone. Second, they begin to realize that there is a system in place that is causing their troubles. Then—and this is the step that takes us from the sociological imagination to community organizing—people realize that they have ideas about what to do and take responsibility for doing those things. Freire (1970) then perhaps takes the analytical process a bit further with his method of problem-posing education. Problem-posing education focuses on the "why" and "how" questions, critically examining the existing explanations and justifications for social conditions, and thus uncovering and overcoming hegemony. Such a process also brings us to the model of diagnosis, prescription, implementation, and evaluation discussed in the previous chapter.

This entire process is wrapped up in Freire's (1970) famous popularization of the concept of conscientization. Roughly, the idea refers to consciousness raising, becoming critically aware of how and why society is the way it is. But it's not an armchair reflection process. Conscientization requires praxis—the cyclical integration of action and reflection. Here we get into the use of Freire in the supposedly alternative but still institutionalized service learning classroom. The professor compels students to go through a conscientization process—requiring them to critically reflect on their action in a "community." But the reflection is one-sided, and can just as easily be critical of the agency they are placed with, or the constituency members they are doing things to, or even self-critical of the student, rather than a true consciousness raising. But ultimately, the deepest most tragic problem is the disconnection of institutionalized service learning from a constituency-led social change process and the exclusion of the constituency members from a collaborative conscientization process with the students. There are only rare examples of such liberating service learning circumstances, including the project described in the previous chapter by Calderón and Cadena (2007) where students and immigrant day laborers learned and acted together to challenge dominant discriminatory perceptions of immigrant day laborers in one city.

Conscientization further shows the inadequacies of asset-based thinking. The worthy goal of asset-based community development is to get people who are oppressed, exploited and excluded to value themselves. Popular education and community organizing also support constituency members to value themselves and, additionally, to understand how they were taught to think against their own self-interests to begin with and analyze the social conditions that sustain hegemony. Unlike asset-based approaches, popular education and community organizing do not sweep the realities of oppression, exploitation, and exclusion under the rug and in fact make them visible so that constituency members can organize to challenge them.

Popular education is one of those things that is both simple and hard. It is simple because you simply bring people together and let them talk. It is hard because people can veer way off course without careful guidance and facilitation, but there is a fine line between helping people find their own solutions and constraining their discussion so it results in the facilitator's preferred analysis and solution. The process of conscientization is especially tricky. Freire (1974) distinguishes critical consciousness from magic consciousness and naïve consciousness. Magic consciousness attributes the cause of social conditions to a higher power, and compels a kind of fatalism that inhibits action. Naïve consciousness chooses its own facts and refuses new data—flat earth thinking, global warming denial, and so on. Critical consciousness continually integrates new data into a deepening analysis. Traditional pedagogy in institutionalized higher education, what Freire (1974) calls "banking education," risks reinforcing naïve consciousness by lecturing supposed truths. And if professors approach constituencies, or send their students to approach communities, with lectures that sound like static truth, they risk the same result off campus. Thus, a constituency-based participatory process is the only foundation that will lead to conscientization.

In an important sense, there are layers of participatory process. It is not enough for credentialed experts and other outsiders to design what they believe is a participatory process. They must engage with constituency members in a participatory process to design a participatory process. I can hear some of you rolling your eyes and guffawing at this apparent over-intellectualization of what should be a simple task. But wait. Designing a participatory process for a Muslim constituency without understanding the sometimes strict gender segregation practiced in such a context is doomed to failure. And that doesn't mean designing a process that excludes women. It means working with men and women in the community to figure out a way for the process to be inclusive of men and women. I have witnessed the fruits of such practice among Muslims in the Cedar-Riverside neighborhood of Minneapolis. In rural communities it means meeting with both the old guard that "has always run the town" and the unheard residents to design an inclusive process. When it comes to youth issues, it means meeting with both youth and the adults who care about them to design an inclusive process. It is, ultimately, about practicing diversity not just in the final participatory process but in the process of designing the process (Cooke, 2001; Cooke & Kathari, 2001). And, if you recall a couple of chapters back, it is about working toward community.

The Academic, Popular Education, and Working toward Community

It's easy to get the impression that academics are irrelevant in the process of popular education. But it's important to not take that perception too far. As a constituency group explores what to do, they often realize that they need information from lawyers or academics or other holders of specialized information. As the group realizes their questions, they seek out the relevant credentialed experts and bring them to the group to answer their specific questions (Open Songbook Project, 2009). Outside experts then become a resource like a book becomes a resource.

But what about those of us who want to become more than just a book that gets consulted on an occasional basis? What if we want to act out our sense of allyship more elaborately? There is not much to guide us. Only a very few academics such as Danika Brown (2001) and Herman and Shortell (1996) recognize the importance of adult constituency education as an integral part of higher education civic engagement. The field of youth participatory action research, where local youth are the constituency, is a bit better, and relies mainly on participatory action research to lead the education process (see Dolan, Christens, & Lin, 2015; Schensul & Berg, 2004).

Popular education demands much of higher education professors and students, and three things in particular. It demands first and foremost that we shift our allegiance from the powerful to the oppressed, exploited, and excluded. It is difficult indeed for those who have been invested in institutionalized service learning to give up their attachments to schools, governments, and nonprofits fully captured by the nonprofit industrial complex, or to take them to a new critical level. But practicing allyship with a constituency means working to support the process of conscientization within the constituency, and that usually also involves constituency members developing a critical consciousness of schools, governments, and nonprofits. In one unique case, two academics attempted to put popular education into a more community context in Kelowna British Columbia. Drawing on the seventeenth-century concept of the "penny university"—basically a combined coffeehouse and community intellectual space—these professors found a downtown coffeehouse willing to host a monthly meeting of a cross-section of people wanting to trade ideas on the social issues of the day (Schneider, Hanemaayer, & Nolan, 2014). And when you listen closely, you will find allies across the academy: the women's studies professor who has had a long association with a women's shelter; the math professor who has had a long association with a mosque; the leadership professor who has had a long association with an organization that trains assistance dogs for war vets; the PhD student who has been a long-time volunteer with an environmental organization. All of these people committed first to the issue and the constituency before they ever tried to get students involved through institutionalized service learning.

Second, popular education demands a shift in how we produce knowledge. We have been speaking about how to shift the social relations of knowledge production by engaging constituency members in the knowledge process. The forms of community-based research, and especially what was called participatory research (Brown & Tandon, 1983), can connect to poplar education and even to community organizing. The Highlander Folk School's Myles Horton (1976) understood this well. As he talked about what he labeled action research, it was as a community organizing process. The process starts with people defining issues at house meetings or other informal gatherings. Out of this comes a more formal group that creates "researchable questions." Horton then preferred research methods "which involve the largest number of people." For Horton, the goal was not just building knowledge but building organization: "I recall members of a Tennessee Farmers Union Cooperative doing interviews with dairy farmers by phone and personal visits and gathering for potluck supper to tabulate and analyze their findings. The farm family researchers had spent three months finding out what they wanted to know and during that period their membership almost doubled." This is much more than cogeneration of knowledge (Hilsen, 2006). It is about the nexus of knowledge, power, and action. It is about building knowledge while also building connections among people.

Third, popular education demands that we shift how to communicate knowledge. Of all the brilliant things that Paulo Freire has written, I think his best is a long essay at the end of *Education for Critical Consciousness* called "Extension or Communication" (Freire, 1974). Freire critiques, in a Brazilian context that is no less relevant to my own, the practice of Extension. In the United States, what is called Cooperative Extension is a kind of university without walls. Cooperative Extension in particular has always been about educational outreach. Growing out of the Morrill Act of 1862 that created land-grant universities and colleges, and especially the Smith-Lever Act of 1914, Cooperative Extension was originally about providing education for farmers, their wives, and their children. Many people have heard of "agricultural extension" or "4-H." The method of Extension, long before there was anything like institutionalized service learning, was to transfer the knowledge being produced in universities to farmers and their family members. But it is very much a "knowledge transfer" approach. Freire (1974) deconstructs this idea of Extension that requires an active subject, a relatively passive recipient, an act of delivery, an assumption of the superiority of that which is given away, the consequent inferiority of those who receive what is given, and the cultural invasion embodied in what is given and the way that it is given. He substitutes "communication" as an alternative approach, and imbues it with extra meaning to be sure:

> The educator's task is not that of one who sets himself or herself as a knowing Subject before a knowable object, and, having come to know it, proceeds to discourse on it to the educatees, whose role it is to file away the "communiques." Education is communication and dialogue. It is not the transference of knowledge, but the encounter of Subjects in dialogue in search of the significance of the object of knowing and thinking. (p. 126)

Freire relates his experience working with peasants who believed that they could cure their livestock of disease through prayer. He argues for the futility of imposing positivist science on those peasants because it is only through communicative dialogue that knowledge can be developed in such a situation (p. 128). The lesson: start where people are, not where you want them to be.

This is a lot to do—allyship, popular education, conscientization, community-based research, and community organizing all in one process. But neglecting any part negates the entire process. People can only gain power by organizing. They can only gain knowledge by researching (defined in the broadest sense). They can only develop critical consciousness by acting. They can only act effectively by having knowledge.

In attempting to practice this integration, I am becoming (in a stumbling manner, to be sure) a different kind of academic (my overly academic prose notwithstanding), especially in my "teaching." And that takes me further away from the problematic implementations of experiential teaching I have reviewed. It also takes me further away from the main historical reference of institutionalized service learning, John Dewey, and toward education theorists such as Knowles, Horton, Freire, and fellow travelers such as Rogers (1969), Giroux (2001), and Shor (1992). Horton (1974) also found that he had to respectfully break with Dewey. In critiquing those who would label him a Dewey disciple, he said, "I was unable to translate Dewey's ideas for academic learning into my desires to work with non-academic adults, though his teaching provided many valuable insights." Horton did not elaborate, but there are many reasons for the separation. The focus on problem posing, conscientization, community-based research, and community organizing is simply not developed in Dewey's work. Knowles, Freire, and Horton also do not propose or promote a model of experiential learning based on teachers creating experiences for pupils. They emphasize a community organizing process that creates a collective learning environment where constituency members learn from each other around a focused issue in a way that can support them acting on that issue.

In such a process, I am learning to become a learner/facilitator. As a learner, my job is to learn everything I can about constituency members' experiences and the issues they are working on. That often means that I am learning with them. When the residents of Theresa Terrace needed to know what bureaucratic challenges would be involved in converting a vacant duplex into a community center, I knew that there might be zoning, building code, and accessibility issues, but I did not know specifically what those issues might be. The residents, my students, and I had to find out together. But the skill I bring to the table is my ability to find things out—to do research—so I can facilitate the group to figure out, first, what they need to know and, second, how to know it.

This is a version of Jacques Rancière's (1991) "ignorant schoolmaster." Following nineteenth-century educator Joseph Jacotot, who discovered that he could teach what he did not know, Rancière came to the rather startling conclusion that "one can teach what one doesn't know. A poor and ignorant father can thus begin educating his children" (p. 101). Regrettably, Rancière lacked actual methods for doing so, but it is easy to link his overall philosophy to popular education.

When I have found myself working on community projects where I had little expertise, like the one described above, I have found my ignorance to perhaps be my greatest asset. Not knowing means that I must ask constituency members to teach me, and that helps balance power. It also means that I have had to learn how to ask good questions, and I have discovered that my "ignorant schoolmaster" method is focused on asking questions. The way that I employ this method is a kind of cross between a Socratic method and appreciative inquiry, attempting to emulate what I have learned about Ella Baker's (Ransby, 2003) approach to organizing what, to me, was the civil rights movement's most important organization, the Student Nonviolent Coordinating Committee. The strength of the Socratic method (Areeda, 1996) is in its ability to point out contradictions and faulty logic. An effective Socratic questioner can help others carefully assess and revise their own logic. Sadly, however, too many use this method assuming they know the answers to their questions and thus misuse the method to get the questionee to adopt their own point of view. Appreciative inquiry (Cooperrider & Srivastva, 1987), in contrast, assumes that the questioner does not know the answer and is based in an attempt to openly and gently understand the point of view of the questionee. But its gentleness is also its weakness. It shares with asset-based thinking an avoidance of exploring weakness and conflict and instead only considers strengths. The philosophy is to help the questionee feel good about themselves, and it consequently shies away from pressing on contradictions and illogic. I try to combine the "I really want to understand" approach of appreciative inquiry that doesn't assume the answers with the Socratic method's focus on developing critical understanding. I try to ask questions that support and encourage people to explore potential contradictions in their thinking. Recently I was at a neighborhood organization meeting where people wanted to create more coordination among the many separate groups and organizations operating in the neighborhood, but they were worried about having "too many people" at a meeting they were organizing toward that end. When I asked, "Can you ever have too many people?" the question sparked a lively conversation as they explored various ways to maximize the number of people involved with a structure that would produce positive results.

As much as I have tried to convince you of the importance of learning outside of the classroom, and with a constituency, I know how many of you are asking, "What about the students?" I can't do a workshop on community-based research (CBR) or service learning without the question of teaching students inserting itself. So that's what we turn to next, though probably not in the way you would prefer.

The Learning Needed for Liberating Service Learning

I've already made the argument that forced unskilled pseudo-volunteerism is not worthy of higher education and does not respect the constituencies we purport to care about off campus. If we are not providing students with anything real that they can contribute to society, nor inculcating in them a desire to make the contribution on their own rather than in response to a bureaucratic command, then we are contradicting the principles of the good society. And it is in the liberal arts disciplines where the challenges are greatest. In some ways the most depressing development in higher education is the infiltration of institutionalized service learning into the professional disciplines, forcing early career students into the same unskilled pseudo-intellectual and superficial volunteerism as the liberal arts (see, for example, Schaffer, Bonniwell, De Haan, Thomas, & Holmquist, 2014). Instead, those of us in the liberal arts should be learning how to do real community engagement from the professional disciplines.

If we actually did that, what would we learn? Perhaps most importantly we would learn to think about our curriculum as building blocks that allow students to describe themselves not in terms of majors but as complete packages of knowledges and skills. It is telling that when students complete a professional degree they can call themselves something—a nurse, an architect. When a student completes an undergraduate degree in sociology, though, we don't encourage or even necessarily allow them to call themselves a sociologist (not that anyone would know what that means anyway).

That doesn't mean we need to "professionalize" or somehow "water down" (and I don't mean at all to imply that professional programs water down anything) the liberal arts. The imagination and critical thinking that characterizes the best of the liberal arts is the energy propelling us toward a better world. And it will be even more powerful when we learn how to put it into conscious clear motion off campus.

So we need to think about the value of the liberal arts differently. A recent national study of what employers want from our students highlighted the importance of ethical judgment, intercultural skills, learning skills, critical thinking skills, complex problem-solving skills, and written and oral communication skills (Hart Research Associates, 2013). To some, this may sound like the epitome of a liberal arts education (Ray, 2013). But is it? We don't design a curriculum around these skills as much as we assume that the curriculum that we offer will "teach" these skills. What kinds of courses do we need to make sure that students have the skills we say they have? And how should we teach those skills? The "banking form" of pedagogy (Freire, 1970) still operating in too many college classrooms certainly does not teach these skills. If we instead follow the practices of andragogy and popular education in our classrooms we are halfway there. But only halfway.

The other half of the journey has to be guided by the constituencies we hope to serve, which requires designing courses around constituency-led social change campaigns, rather than force-fitting constituencies into existing content courses. This is not a simple process of creating a computer matching system where "agencies" list "needs" and professors list what learning experiences they want for students. In a neoliberal-imposed context of scarce resources, such a practice reinforces institutionalized service learning as superficial unskilled volunteerism that puts student learning in front of social change impact.

To fully serve constituencies at the highest levels of which higher education is capable, we need to begin with either training faculty or hiring skilled community workers who can spend time working with constituencies to think about their issues and organize social change campaigns. One of the possible paths comes from De Anza College, a community college in California that at least offers formal community organizing training for its students (Murphy, 2014). Too few communities have access to community organizers, and any institution that aims to serve more than the rhetoric of community engagement will provide the resources necessary for constituencies to have such access (yes, I know you've read this for the third time now). Brown (2001) is one of the few thinkers in service learning who understand the importance of the community organizer. Organizers can also help communities consider their knowledge needs and help them to mobilize the institutional resources to meet them.

Of course, there needs to be something for them to access in our colleges and universities. This is where we can learn from the European science shop model. The typical science shop exists to work with formal and informal constituency groups to develop their knowledge questions and then access higher education resources that can help them gather information around those knowledge questions (Living Knowledge, 2014). While mostly in Europe, there are a couple of examples in North America such as the Center for Urban Research and Learning in Chicago, and two Ontario, Canada sister organizations—the Trent Community Research Centre and the U-Links Centre for Community Based Research. The science shop is the best model available to date, but it is still incomplete. The main gap in the science shop model is its lack of focus on helping groups think through the strategic issues involved in connecting knowledge and action.

But establishing a science shop will not be enough. There needs to also be useful higher education resources that the science shop can offer to community groups, and this has important implications for universities and colleges, especially the liberal arts. The main change we need to make is to open up the liberal arts curriculum. Independent studies and internships are a start, but such options need much more conscious design and mentoring, again with a more skilled and theoretically informed connection between knowledge, power, and action than is currently the case. Relying on one-student-at-a-time engagement will also quickly exhaust both professors and constituency groups. So we also need to engage entire courses in single constituency-led projects. But the academic department then must be willing to create flexibility in the curriculum, and the professor must be willing to give up control over the course so that it can be custom-designed for the project. The possibility of an existing course magically fitting a constituency project is rare indeed, and thus regular courses are not good vehicles for liberating service learning. Here the liberal arts can learn from professional programs in designing studio courses and capstones. Such courses are, in the best cases, designed to allow the entire class to do a single project with a single group, leading to much greater potential impact. When the same professor is able to teach serial sections of such a course, they can support a social change effort over the longer time period that most social change campaigns need to gain momentum and begin making headway. I have had two experiences of sequenced capstone classes supporting ongoing community work, with two different constituency partners, and both with impact (Hidayat, Stoecker, & Gates, 2013; Stoecker, in press).

I have learned some lessons about attempting to pursue this path of liberating service learning in the classroom. First, I have found that the only way for me to effectively facilitate such classes is to be well versed in social change and community work in relation to that specific people and place, or have access to someone who does have that expertise as part of a team. I have also learned that I need to walk my talk. I don't send my students out to do stuff that I am unwilling to do. My new role model (in the very specific regard of walking the talk) is Pope Francis, who apparently moonlights as a priest, quite literally in the moonlight as he ventures into the streets of Rome at night to minister to people in poverty ("Is Pope Francis?," 2013) and was willing to be community laundry man even when he was rector of the seminary (Lowney, 2013). I need my students to see me rolling up my sleeves and practicing allyship with constituency members so they can see at least one option of how they can do it.

Not every academic needs to be totally committed to the constituency or their issue to make a contribution. In the popular education model, remember, experts are often brought in on a very limited basis simply to provide information, which doesn't require a long-term commitment, any special training, or even a sense of allyship. However, it does require someone in the constituency itself, a bridge person, or a committed ally who can help the group access credentialed experts for specific roles.

In other words, when we stop prioritizing the interests of our students and our higher education institutions over the interests of constituencies and our ultimate mutual interests in understanding that our liberation is bound up with each other, we can liberate service learning and all the other forms of higher education civic engagement from their academic shackles and reorient them toward real impact in the real world.

12

Toward a Liberated World?

> I asked the newspaper men why they didn't publish the facts about child labor in Pennsylvania. They said they couldn't because the mill owners had stock in the papers.
>
> —M. H. Jones, *Autobiography of Mother Jones*

It has now been two years since my students were brought up on disciplinary charges for their fully engaged allyship with food workers. Like Mother Jones, whose allyship especially with mine workers brought her great risk, hardship, and punishment at the hands of the authorities representing wealth and power well into her senior citizenhood (Jones, 1925), my students and the constituency members they ally with fight on.

It has been over four years since those and other students began sleeping in the Wisconsin state capitol, studying the state constitution and procedural rules in an attempt to stop the most intense attack on democracy in Wisconsin since the 1950s, when Joe McCarthy and his followers went on their democracy-wrecking rampage. In 2011 some individual faculty found ways to provide course credit for the students' efforts to research and learn the legislative process, the laws governing their presence in the capitol building, strategies for keeping the building open, and the history of progressivism in Wisconsin. What the students did was perhaps the most profound exemplar of action research that many of us had ever witnessed, and it far surpassed the intellectual depth and breadth found in all but a tiny number of courses.

In the time since, I've come across so many other students engaged in social change work who receive no credit, and sometimes punishment, for their efforts, all in the context of now doctrinaire institutionalized service learning with its attendant forced volunteerism and its unreflective assumption that oppressed, exploited, and excluded constituencies are deserving only of forced, unskilled, token labor from college students untrained for most of the tasks for which they are "volunteered."

But there are also glimmers of the alternative—enough glimmers that I have tried to piece together an alternative set of theories and an alternative set of practices to show how we can liberate service learning. I have difficulty imagining that any higher education institution would actually support the alternative, and I'm not even sure I'd want them to. In some ways, my best hopes are to support those already doing the hard work of real social change, to keep others awake a few nights trying to reconcile their practices with what I hope are their nobler instincts, and to challenge others in impossible situations to nonetheless ask hard questions of themselves and perhaps their institutional leaders.

I am not optimistic that my writing will make much difference. All writing, in the end, is a mass Rorschach test. Some will see in these words a cute bunny, others an evil fox (yet others, especially if you live in my neighborhood, where rabbits ravaged our gardens until the foxes moved in, will see an evil bunny or a cute fox). That is, of course, at least partly the fault of the writer, but it is a particular kind of fault that results from the writer moving outside of the reader's experience and categories. As long as the writer stays within the safe categories of, in this case, self-congratulatory institutionalized service learning, nothing will be risked and nothing will be challenged. You can critique within the categories—asking, for example, whether students are learning as much as they can—but try to critique the categories themselves and all sorts of unintended interpretations can happen.

So here are three things that I *do not* want people to take away from this book:

- *Volunteering is bad.* Absolutely false. There is no possibility of community without people voluntarily helping, supporting, nurturing each other. What is bad is pseudo-volunteering, forced volunteering, exchange volunteering. Volunteering is freely giving of one's labor without coercion or remuneration. And the creation of systems in higher education institutions to compel, coerce, or otherwise promote alienated volunteering is bad, especially when it's done in lieu of providing highly skilled resources.
- *Social services are bad.* Also false. Hungry people need food—now. Homeless people need food—now. Sick people need medical care—now. We can't wait for the revolution to address these needs. What is at issue, however, is the way we meet people's needs. The difference between meeting people's needs while disempowering them and meeting people's needs while empowering them is both subtle and profound. It's subtle because the food pantry may physically look the same under both conditions. It's profound because the difference between a food pantry where the people who come for the

food see themselves as only passive recipients and one where they see themselves as engaged in collective self-help is the difference between feeling owned and feeling ownership. Of course, how to organize services in a way that empowers people without simultaneously overburdening them and making their lives even harder is the challenge.

- *Student learning is irrelevant.* Of course not. Student learning is absolutely crucial to liberating service learning. In fact, without a deep focus on student learning, there is no quality service. The difference is that, in liberating service learning, the focus is on students learning *for* the service, rather than *from* the service. And we can't determine what students need to learn until the social change project is organized. When we start with change, and build toward community, we organize the "service" to serve the goals of the change and the community building, and decide what we all need to learn to effectively do the service that will build community and create the change. Even then, before we talk about the in-classroom method, we need to talk about curriculum—custom-designed course options such as capstones, preparatory courses in community dynamics, skills courses, and so on.

Having said all this, I also want to encourage all of us to be critical of all volunteering and all social services because, as we've discussed, most of the volunteering in higher education, and most social service provision, are deeply contradictory. Moreover, I want us all to become critical. Thinking theoretically means thinking critically—seeing the contradictions, the unintended consequences, the negative side effects. We should not simply celebrate institutionalized service learning, especially when its track record is so bad that it is becoming known in some quarters as "disservice learning" (O'Kane, 2015). We desperately need safe spaces that support "critical conversations" that allow us to examine not just our practices but our assumptions and theories about those practices so that we can improve both our practice and our thinking. That goes for what I've referred to here as liberating service learning as well. What I have outlined will not be easy, and it will not be without its own contradictions. And we need to keep our critical lens focused on our own practice regardless of what we label it and how good we think we do it.

Of course, not everyone will support this. There are legions out there who hold fast to the philosophies and practices of institutionalized service learning that I worry about so much. They will read and reject this work, developing their counter-arguments to show all the ways that this book is wrong and to justify current practices. And while I always admit to the possibility that my solution is wrong, I cannot imagine a justification for maintaining the status

quo of institutionalized service learning. If nothing else, I hope that my ob-
streperousness spurs some of the critics on to third way thinking.

As with all ideas that may sound good in theory but are challenging in
practice, there is likely a second group of people sympathetic to my concerns
and in agreement with the basic points, but convinced that any change in a
more progressive direction is patently unrealistic. These people know that their
institutional decision makers won't support anything that challenges the powerful, that their students are overwhelmingly interested in charity rather than
change, and that their academic culture equates advocacy with bias. Some of
them will say that a model starting with a sociological imagination doesn't
apply to them because they're a professor of "chemistry" or "literature" and
somehow the social conditions of the people they direct their institutionalized
service learning at are supposedly irrelevant. Others of them will say that their
administrators will never support a model that puts change first and learning last, as if somehow the only way they can do service learning is if their
administrators approve of it. So they will continue to follow the path of the
status quo, believing that it is better than nothing. But I'm not convinced that
engaging in institutionalized service learning that maintains (and, in reality,
advances) neoliberalism is better than nothing. It may be time for us to seriously consider whether we should only be doing the best, most highly skilled,
community engagement, and leave the rest for us to do as global citizen volunteers from whom less is expected rather than as supposedly educated faculty
and students.

A third group of people will read this and conclude that they are already
doing nearly all of what I am advocating or will make only minor changes in
their practice. And, of course, there are professors and students who are doing
great things, approaching the model I have presented here. In my experience,
however, they are very rare exceptions and even they have not fully achieved
the kind of constituency-based knowledge power I am referring to here. I don't
know anyone, including me, who is even close to achieving better practice. I
am throwing out the bathwater, the bathtub, the bathroom, the building con-
taining the bathroom, and the very idea that anyone could claim the land on
which the building stands. I am, however, keeping the baby and clinging with
tenacity to the primary principle of caring for it—the belief in a world where
everyone is engaged in everyone's (and everything's—remember Leopold) development of their full potential—against all who would do the baby harm
directly or indirectly through ignorance and compromise.

A (probably hypothetical) small fourth group may try to create new LSL—
"liberating service learning"—programs. I don't expect, and don't even want,
liberating service learning to become yet another acronym for yet another
program with yet another set of requirements for faculty and students inside
of higher education institutions held captive by neoliberalism and its attendant

nonprofit industrial complex. Liberating service learning is an insurgent practice. It is more easily and consistently practiced outside of formal requirements and institutionalized sanction. There are few institutionalized service learning program directors brave or free enough to openly support it. Turning it into a program—institutionalizing it—will cage it and "declaw" it in Dolgon's (2010) terms, reducing it to institutionalized service learning again.

There is a final group of students and faculty who have been feeling the same gut-churning discomfort with institutionalized service learning that I have. Hopefully they will find in these pages various ideas that resonate with what they are feeling, thinking, trying, or doing. They will compare and contrast and critique. They will reflect on their hunger for work that is more meaningful than institutionalized service learning allows. They will access their anger at the injustices around us and be better able to see our at least partial complicity in the maintenance of those injustices. They will develop allyship with constituencies, find ways of linking action to what they are learning from their higher education institution, and strategize ways of engaging in the two forms of social change. They will move beyond the limitations of these pages toward a real leap forward for real social change.

It is for this final group that I write. This is not a cookbook or a set of steps. The practice of liberating service learning is not about following recipes and steps but about pursuing a process of action and reflection in collaboration with constituency members working for social change and toward community. It is mostly, for me at least, a dramatic shift in standpoint. Rather than starting with an emphasis on student learning, tacking on some service, talking about community, and pretending about change, the liberating service learning philosophy is the complete and total inverse. It starts with change—progressive social change that reduces power and resource inequalities and allows everyone to grow to their full potential. Part of that change is working toward restoring real community. The service, then, is about the work we do toward those ends. The learning is what everyone participating needs to know to effectively work toward those ends, and what we come to know through the process of achieving those ends. That transposition stands everything on its head. Students don't come first when I take this standpoint. The curriculum does not take priority. The discipline does not exert control. The institution is not the source of direction.

This transposition of priorities is what most institutionalized educators, administrators, and students (and the double entendre is not lost on me) won't be able to wrap their heads around. They will see their mission as teaching students, producing publications, building up their institutions. And they will see institutionalized service learning as a means to those ends. The highly influential Lynton Colloquium (2014) used "crowdsourcing" to determine "critical issues in advancing community-engaged scholarship" for its 2015 colloquium and, you guessed it, all of the critical issues were about students, faculty, and administrators. The only time the word *community* appeared was in the title of their call for proposals. This is how lost institutionalized service learning and indeed any form of higher education community engagement are. That is what we are up against.

In the end, I believe we will be forced to choose—not between students and constituency or institution and community—but between working for justice and maintaining oppression, exploitation, and exclusion. Our students can learn from the standpoint I am proposing, but the purpose is not student learning. Our faculty can get publications, but the purpose is not to pad faculty resumes. Our institutions can benefit, but the purpose of the practice is not to benefit our institutions. If we ask first how can we change the world, then our next question for those of us in higher education must be how we organize our scholarship and structure our institutions so that a we which is more inclusive than just institutional actors can change the world—remember the two forms of social change. This ordering of questions is the only order that can serve the goal of justice.

It is likely that if we take this ordering seriously most institutionalized service learning, and even much community-based research, will cease. What comes next won't be anything so dramatic as a phoenix from the ashes sort of thing. There will simply be a new space—a space to think, and especially to rethink, what we are doing. We desperately need such a new space. As academic freedom gets legislated away in Wisconsin, and probably in other places as well, and faculty engaging in any kind of political introspection are attacked with official threats from right-wing power holders (Berger, 2014; Cronon, 2011), we may not be able to do any of this in the classroom. Instead, we will need to leverage new spaces to do it outside of the classroom.

One of the things that such new spaces will afford us is a chance to consider both a new practice and a new mission. I have had the chance to work on my own professional civic engagement mission statement over the past couple of years, though I must admit I have been working on it for much longer. This is my mission statement, attempting to succinctly express this new prioritization of purpose for liberating service learning, and help guide my practice:

> To build constituency power to create social change and work toward community by facilitating access to our knowledge resources, including faculty, staff, and students.

Of course, this statement requires some unpacking.

To build constituency power . . .

My overwhelming goal in all the work I do is to make sure that people struggling for justice become stronger in their struggle by my allyship and that when they are in relationship with me they can only become stronger by first determining for themselves how I can support them in becoming stronger. That means that they need to know me and what I can and cannot do and how I need to continue my own journey of liberation. Then I work with them, always toward the goal of creating a stronger collective.

> *. . . to create social change and work toward community . . .*

The focus of social change, remember, is at two levels. It is about taking on specific issues that the constituency identifies, and it is about transforming the social relations of knowledge production. I am convinced that we have to start with social change before we work toward community because it has become abundantly clear to me that community can't exist under neoliberal capitalism. So I choose constituencies and groups to work with that I see as pointing to a society in which all people can grow to their potential and can support each other in doing so.

> *. . . by facilitating access to our knowledge resources, including faculty, staff, and students.*

I am in the knowledge business. There is much that I can contribute as an ally, and sometimes that means setting up tables for the meeting or doing dishes after the event. But I also have access to vast storehouses of information in the university that can help build knowledge, methods for creating new information and building new knowledge, and strategies for amplifying voices speaking knowledge to power. So the first thing I do is try to find ways to make it easier for constituency members to access me, other faculty and academic staff around me, and students so that they can better build and speak knowledge. I am currently privileged in having a very low teaching load, and in fact part of my job description is to work "in the community." Thus, I can teach overload courses that I custom-design with constituency groups to directly support their work. I can also refer people to others on campus who I know share my values and commitment to allyship.

To some this may sound like a lot of revolutionary rhetoric, but the practical actions we take do not have to look or sound revolutionary. We only have to know that they are pointing in that direction. Supporting people in an oppressed constituency to speak up in front of their city council, and get that council to vote the right way, is pointing in that direction. Supporting people in an excluded constituency to connect with other groups to build a local movement promoting sustainability is pointing in that direction. Any time we become involved in an effort where an oppressed, exploited, or excluded constituency becomes better organized, learns how to better create and use knowledge, and acts more collectively and effectively, we are pointing in that direction.

Of course, any mission statement worth its words needs to be accompanied by a practice that is guided by a statement of practice.

Putting Liberating Service Learning into Practice

In some ways, it's actually not that difficult to take the initial steps toward liberating service learning. I try to follow a two-step process:

> **Step 1. Find constituency-led efforts with social change goals, or help them develop goals and identify knowledge projects that can help achieve the goals.**

Find constituency-led efforts . . .

Strangely enough, anyone can begin the process of moving toward liberating service learning with basic volunteering through the spirit of allyship. Allyship means that you become involved with a constituency as a human being first rather than as a professor or as a student. You act in support of that constituency not just in your day job but at your dinner table, in your friendship circles, and wherever else you can make a difference. And you approach constituency-led organizations, or service organizations that could be constituency led, not just as a professional but as an ally. So, for example, if you define yourself as heterosexual and really believe that people who are transgender should have the same rights in society as everyone else, then your task is to find groups who are acting on that value and offer your allyship (and, of course, if you already identify as transgender, you already are the constituency). At some point in that relationship, it will feel right to you or to group members to act on the liberating service learning mission statement. And this doesn't mean that you can't work with a service agency—you can as long as that agency is comfortable with organizing their constituency and supporting them to move beyond being just service recipients.

. . . with social change goals . . .

Most well-organized groups know what they want to change; the best organized among them have "cut" precise, organizable, winnable (POW!) issues to work on. Most academics, who are not used to thinking and acting in a community organizing process, will depend on a group's ability to cut issues or to access someone who can help them do this. But some of the traditional "community partners" will also not know how to do this so there may be remedial work for both because without such goals any assistance we can offer will be either in support of unrealistic and unrealizable dreams or so undirected that it won't lead anywhere of consequence except by accident.

. . . or help develop goals . . .

Here is where it gets tricky. This piece is not about developing research projects, or choosing strategies. It is about organizing the constituency to cut issues. And either the group has their own expertise or they need to have access to expertise that can help them to do that. It is possible to learn how to help groups cut an issue. But helping a group cut an issue also then invokes the responsibility of developing strategies to take on the issue, and that requires even more expertise. So the best service many of us academics can provide at this point is to invoke the last part of the liberating service learning mission statement and help the group find someone who can provide that beginning-to-end community organizing support. In the long run, connecting a group to an expert community organizer will be better than pretending that cutting an issue is easy and failing to do it right. But if a group has community organizing expertise, whether indigenous or professional, we academics can move on to filling the role of providing the knowledge power expertise that the group requests from us.

. . . and identify knowledge projects . . .

In case I'm not being redundant enough, knowledge is what we do in higher education. Not only are we expert at finding information and producing knowledge; we are also supposedly expert at helping others learn how to find information and produce knowledge. The challenge here is the "identify" part. When a group cuts an issue, a variety of knowledge issues crop up, even in deciding which issue to choose, let alone what to do to succeed with it. Those knowledge issues need to be turned into research projects of a sort—goal-directed information-gathering and knowledge-developing activities that have a clear starting point, milestones, and end point. So here again someone needs to understand the connection between knowledge and action on a particular issue.

. . . that can help achieve the goals.

This is really about two types of knowledge—substantive knowledge and strategic knowledge. It's not just about knowing how to test the water for pollution, but knowing how to understand the political context in which the group might use the testing results, and how to use the results in that political context. It's not just about a group knowing how to research the number of people being denied housing based on their race, but knowing what to do with various possible results from that research. The academic may only be able to provide substantive knowledge, and it could be up to constituency leadership or a community organizer to supply the strategic knowledge. In both cases, however, helping to achieve the goals means not just knowledge transfer (which reduces it to information transfer) but building the group's knowledge capacity overall.

Fulfilling our role as allies, in a liberating service learning framework, then shifts our attention within the process to our institutional context. And thus we get to the second step of the process.

Step 2: Find higher education resources that can support the projects and mobilize those resources to do the projects to achieve the goals.

Find higher education resources . . .

I should probably add "or create them" as most of the resources needed will require adaptation and adjustment to truly be useful. The "finding" part requires some kind of system for finding resources. I still think a campus allyship underground is the best practice—we should not be looking to an administration to support this. Universities and colleges, except in very rare cases, are just too embedded in the nonprofit industrial complex. Such an underground can function as a kind of science shop. As lead campus allies (whether professor or student, and I have had multiple cases now where my students have been the primary ally and I have been the resource they have accessed) find groups with clear goals and consequently clear knowledge projects, they can then use the underground to leverage knowledge resources.

. . . that can support the projects . . .

When we talk about leveraging knowledge resources, we are no longer talking only about classes. We are talking about everything at the college or university—meeting spaces, lab equipment, databases, libraries, technical experts, mass student labor and their apprentice expertise. And if we think about groups' knowledge needs in terms of projects, we can design knowledge development processes in such a way that we will know when we are done. I know that knowledge development is an ongoing process in academic circles. This is true in a constituency setting as well, but in a constituency setting a group also has to act, not just develop knowledge. Thus, in contrast to how we are trained in academia, in a constituency context we have to rethink our work to produce immediately usable knowledge.

. . . and mobilize those resources . . .

Here we can start by talking about classes, and sometimes only in the sense of students working with groups to access the campus knowledge resources. A group of students can serve as a mini science shop, creating a list of professors with relevant expertise for a constituency's cut issues and helping the group access them. They can access articles and books relevant to a group's issue.

Some of these knowledge projects will be focused and won't last an entire term. Others will last longer than a single term and will require an institution-based ally to span multiple courses, if students are to be involved. Some faculty and staff at the institution will be wholly involved with constituencies. Others will be involved only in very specific ways. Maybe someone only needs to consult the professor for thirty minutes about survey design. Or maybe a group needs advice on two different methods for lead paint testing. Just like most students won't get involved with the community in a relational way but only as temporary labor, so it will be for many faculty. That doesn't mean that no one needs to be an ally. In fact someone has to be an ally. But not everyone working with the group needs to do so as an ally.

. . . to do the projects . . .

The ally in the institution is very important, because it is that person's responsibility to make sure that the knowledge projects are accomplished. In liberating service learning it's not about the students. Consequently, it's not about students turning in C-level work. Students do not have a right to provide mediocre work when social justice is on the line, and professors do not have a right to let them. Professors and students also do not have a right to be late on finished products. If the city council meeting is next Monday night and the group meeting is Monday afternoon, waiting until Tuesday to turn in the report that the group was going to use at the council meeting is simply out of the question.

. . . to achieve the goals.

Ultimately, all of this is about achieving the constituency's goals—the cut issues and the transformation of the social relations of knowledge production. Consequently, it's about changing our goals for teaching and scholarship. When we work as allies with constituency groups, our teaching becomes focused on preparing the students to work most effectively with the constituency group and our scholarship becomes focused on studying how best to engage as allies. That can be about how constituency groups win on issues, how we transform the social relations of knowledge production, how we adapt particular research methods and possibly even unique research findings. But these are side effects, not the primary goals of our work. The primary goals are the constituency's goals.

Can we create an institutional structure supporting such practice? I am not certain, but I must admit I am skeptical. Too much of this practice goes against the immediate self-interest of the higher education institution—the control of the knowledge process, the limits of access only to tuition payers or grant makers. Still, the practice has implications for colleges and universities.

Institutional Implications of Liberating Service Learning

I feel uncomfortable writing this section. Because I'm not hopeful that we can change institutions, in which case liberating service learning has few to no implications for higher education institutions. In many institutions, the institutionalized service learning program is even more strangled by the neoliberal nonprofit industrial complex than is the institution itself. Too often they are funded by and named after wealthy benefactors who have a vested interest in maintaining the present system and tamping down the anger of those who suffer from it, and administered by professional administrators or faculty who lack experience with actual constituency work. Such institutionalized service learning programs are simply glorified volunteer pipelines and symbolic support systems for forced, unskilled volunteerism. In the worst examples, institutionalized service learning has become a self-congratulatory practice of neoliberal ideology used by universities and colleges as a student recruitment and grant acquisition strategy.

Shifting institutionalized service learning from such a vacuous path seems unrealistic. There are already spaces within institutions where liberating service learning can operate in the margins. Faculty with enough academic freedom in their departments can adapt some courses, particularly capstone and studio courses, to support work that is fully defined by constituency efforts. They can work informally with other students groups on social change work outside of the classroom. My main hope for higher education is that such spaces for faculty and students to work in the margins will be preserved, though that is the next battleground as other places likely follow the state of Wisconsin's lead in finding ways to curtail academic freedom. As the scenario unfolds, we might as well go for broke, in which case, here is my shopping list.

> 1. *No more chasing the Carnegie Community Engagement classification.* This is a distraction. Institutions count courses and students and reframe outcome-less activities as a way to promote themselves to students and funders. The classification encourages institutions to further silence "the community" in order to impose their own image as saviors and leaders of the "underserved." Until it measures documented outcomes involving significant power and wealth shifts, and until institutions are nominated by constituency groups, the classification is a hollow shell. Institutions also need to rein in their PR machines so that they accurately recognize and amplify the visibility of constituency leadership in community successes. Doing that will also help shift power relations.
>
> 2. *Real money for community organizing and community technical experts.* I've harped on this enough. If academics are going to be of real

value to constituency groups, the groups need to be organized enough to know what to ask academics for, how to hold them accountable, and how to put what they get from them to good use. This means that constituency groups need independent community organizers, and there are far too few trained and skilled organizers to go around. I won't believe any institution talking about social justice until they create an endowment for community organizing that the institution can't touch or influence except to ensure that the money is managed by constituency groups to organize themselves.

3. *Tenure and promotion criteria.* As I mentioned, my first venture into working with neighborhood constituencies as a young assistant professor at the University of Toledo, guided by community organizer Dave Beckwith, helped net those neighborhood groups $2 million (Stoecker & Beckwith, 1992). Soon after that my department chair "advised" me to remove myself from the joint position between my department and the Urban Affairs Center that allowed me to do the research supporting those groups and "return" to the department in order to protect my tenure. I did as I was told, I'm ashamed to say, and I've watched untenured faculty at the University of Wisconsin who put their constituency work first lose their jobs. And that's not saying anything about those two universities that's not true almost everywhere. Liberating service learning means shifting from pedagogy to andragogy, from academic-led to constituency-led research, and from institution-based to constituency-based service. The near impossibility of anything more than minor adjustments inside the institution just means that, in order to do liberating service learning, you have to do it as a professional add-on rather than as a replacement—what one colleague calls "community housework"—devalued work but now "counted" (Hubbard, 1996). Instead of an add-on policy, we need a replacement policy where a constituency policy victory that you can document your scholarly contribution to counts just as much as an academic publication. But even the American Sociological Association isn't ready for that, having rejected their own task force recommendation to endorse tenure and promotion policies more inclusive of engaged scholarship a few years back.

4. *Training for faculty and staff in community dynamics and popular education.* Anyone who is going to serve in an ally role and help constituency groups access institutional resources needs to understand community dynamics and popular education. Social justice work requires the steady mind of a surgeon, the ability to integrate multiple variables of the rocket scientist, the sensitivity of an empath, and the self-sacrifice of a mother. The best outcome we can

expect from doing it without appropriate training is nothing, and the worst outcome will be to actually make things worse. Nothing is harder than organizing constituencies for social change and toward community.

5. *Deployment of a science shop logic.* Higher education institutions should think about how to make themselves accessible to constituency groups. At UW-Madison you can't even look at the library books without a university ID (you can't get a beer on campus without one either). Science shop logic is about providing a system for people off campus to request support for knowledge issues. Until the campus makes it clear that such requests are welcome by creating such a system, it will be obvious to all that the system in place is to serve the university, not "the community." Here again is why allyship is so important. Among the jobs of the ally is accessing institution-exclusive knowledge resources that the constituency is prevented from accessing.

6. *Curricular flexibility.* Enough already on the constant admissions about how there is tension between the curriculum and the community, and how the semester timeline doesn't fit the real world. All the hand-wringing just makes us look useless and unimaginative. It's time to do something about it. Until institutions create space for faculty to actually design courses around constituency projects, real impact from our students will be the accidental exception rather than the rule. We need more year-long courses, more relaxation of requirements to sign up for summer credit if the work extends through a summer and a semester, and more opportunities to operate outside of quarter and semester restrictions altogether. We need to release faculty from disciplinary-constricted courses so they can custom-design learning around constituency-defined issues. In the liberal arts, we need to stop thinking that every disciplinary-defined course is essential when our students will not remember the vast majority of its content anyway (Arum, 2010).

7. *Expansion of classroom-based civics and issues education.* The most important message of the nearly instantly famous *A Crucible Moment* (National Task Force on Civic Learning and Democratic Engagement, 2012) is not its relevance to institutionalized service learning but its relevance to classroom education. It's time to stop exploiting poor people for our students' civic education, stop misusing experiential education theory, and stop pretending that any of it is making a difference when so many people out there can still support so many self-defeating policy positions. We've got classrooms. Let's use them for the civic education that can prepare students to do their absolute best work off campus.

Items 6 and 7, while unrealistic in an institutional context, are things that all of us can do in our own classrooms with or without institutional support, and it is to our own classrooms that I turn next.

Liberating Service Learning in the Classroom

Transforming the classroom is also challenging. We know from the research that most students would rather be involved in charity than in social change (Bickford & Reynolds, 2002; Bringle, Hatcher, & MacIntosh, 2006; Chovanec et al., 2011; Kajner et al., 2013; Liu & Kelly, 2009; Moely & Miron, 2005; Morton, 1995; Robinson, 2000a, 2000b), that is, when they can tell the difference (Moely, Furco, & Reed, 2008). With all our rhetoric about civic engagement, our practice still doesn't fit the purpose, doesn't really engage students in society, and mostly serves to support students in maintaining or improving their own socioeconomic class position. Yes, institutionalized service learning has given students a great deal of experience in serving poor people from a one-up position, but it has given them little to no experience in allying with the oppressed, exploited, and excluded to create social change. And they can't get much experience elsewhere either. It's not the sixties anymore (and hasn't been for nearly half a century). The craft of social change is lost on all but the few students who have held the activist torch through the continuing dark times of post-1960s neoliberalism.

Those of us who want to struggle against neoliberalism in our classrooms can't only spend our time pontificating on how bad things are. Yes, there are lots of students who haven't a clue about how bad things are. So let's load them up with the facts and figures and stories and videos and testimonies. There's enough material available in books and films without further imposing on people who are oppressed, exploited, and excluded to teach us live for free. Then let's move quickly into doing something about those things. And that begins with creating a process where we can all learn how people do something about those things. While us faculty are building our allyship with constituencies whose issues we care about, we can also be thinking about how students in our classes can be contributing to the two forms of social change by working with those constituencies.

As we've already seen, switching from institutionalized service learning to liberating service learning means standing the dominant institutionalized service learning teaching model on its head. It also means standing our existing teaching practice on its head:

> 1. It means designing courses for projects, not designing projects for courses. If the course professor is not allied with a constituency, they can't do liberating service learning. Well before a professor

considers any course for institutionalized service learning (including CBR), they need to have a relationship with a group and an understanding of the group's knowledge needs/issues/gaps. Then and only then can they start to design a course. Obviously this process has to happen before they offer the course.

2. It means that the professor (or whoever the teacher may be) is responsible for leading the course-based team, not irresponsible in sending students out alone. The professor maintains communication with the constituency group, and brings their own expertise into the project. If we care about providing constituency groups with the best the institution has to offer, the withholding of the professor's resources violates that principle. And if the professor lacks any of the expertise needed to fully organize the constituency, then there needs to be a community worker who can do that and guide the professor-student team as well.

3. It means real projects with a real chance for impact, not token "it's okay to fail" projects. It's okay to fail in the classroom—that's what classrooms are for. It's not okay to fail with real people who are depending on real outcomes (imagine the uproar if we said it was okay for medical students to make mistakes that killed people). That is also why the professor needs to lead the classroom-based team. Real projects with a real chance for impact are more likely to be complex and large, and that usually means that one class does one project. The project may have subparts, but they are all connected to the achievement of one precise-organizable-winnable issue by one constituency group or coalition.

4. It means that student participation in liberating service learning is an earned privilege, not a requirement. If we are going to engage students in social change, it's going to be political, and it has to be the student's choice to engage in the work. Not only is forced volunteerism wrong for all the reasons we've discussed, it's the ultimate contradiction of social change principles whose intention is to provide people with more empowerment. I will go even further and say that, far from requiring service learning, students should have to apply to do it and we should take only those who demonstrate a clear commitment and bring clear relevant understanding and skills to the task.

Many of you will say this bar is too high. Only a tiny fraction of faculty will have the academic freedom needed to even consider teaching in this way. The rest will be limited by accrediting requirements, disciplinary demands, departmental constraints, and political restrictions. Only a tiny fraction of students will even want to truly volunteer for this work out of a sense of social justice.

But examples of such practices do exist, and even if they are the exceptions then the bar is not too high. And just imagine. If we make these changes in our individual approaches to service learning, instead of reinforcing the dominant neoliberal system and the class position of the students most likely to superficially benefit from it, we will instead be accessing and supporting the students most marginalized in our universities and colleges—the activist students, the alienated students of color, the working class students, the LGBTQ students, the students with disabilities. In other words, we will be connecting with our own most oppressed, exploited, and excluded student constituencies. We can even follow their lead when those student constituencies are organizing their own social change efforts. We can be allies to our own students and admit that our higher education institutions are more a part of the problem than they are a part of the solution. We can take a lesson from De Anza College—the place that includes community organizing training among its offerings. The college administration, rather than bringing disciplinary charges against its students, responded to their organized efforts by eliminating sweatshop clothes from its bookstore and divesting from fossil fuel corporations (Murphy, 2014).

We can then take the next step and give students college credit for their social change work. What institutionalized service learning shops provide space for the activist students, their professors to gather and collectively think through the myriad intellectual and practical issues involved in social change work? What would it look like for an institutionalized service learning office to provide such support? Activism today is shunted into those campus organizations that represent the "others" on our campuses. And those "others" in the community are not represented on campus at all. What would it look like for an institutionalized service learning office to provide space for, and even help organize, community-based "others" with campus-based "others" and allies who could theorize, design, and manage social change projects together— harking back to the old settlement house model?

I'm not saying everyone should do this. Quite the contrary. Doing this kind of social change engagement takes a commitment to justice, a comfort with conflict, and a willingness to practice standards of scholarship that are often rejected in positivist-dominated higher education institutions. It takes a willingness to put the knowledge needed for social change ahead of the knowledge needed for the enforcement of disciplinary canons. If your concern is first and foremost the advancement of your discipline or the education of students, liberating service learning is not for you. Do your scholarly work and be the best researcher and/or teacher you can be. Don't try to graft onto your work a form of scholarship that provides little extra benefit for students or for constituency members. Institutionalized service learning simply doesn't offer enough to compensate for its complicity in maintaining neoliberal capitalism.

Liberating Service Learning Locally and Globally

I work in a higher education institution that pays continual lip service to something called "The Wisconsin Idea," the most often repeated and safest (because it is least meaningful) definition of which is this: "The boundaries of the university [are] the boundaries of the state" (Heinen, 2012). If we go back in history, as I learned from my colleague Gwen Drury, we find that this watered-down definition comes from a statement made by University of Wisconsin president, Charles Van Hise, in 1904. It was the institutionalized dilution of something much more important. The actual phrase "The Wisconsin Idea," it seems, was coined by Charles McCarthy in 1912 in his book of the same name. McCarthy was head of the Wisconsin Legislative Reference Library at the time, occupying a unique niche between academia and government. He had been witness to the tremendous strides that the state had made in fighting against robber baron monopoly capitalism and the corruption it had wrought across the land in his time. His book documents the long list of progressive legislation passed in Wisconsin in 1911 and underscores the principle of bringing knowledge to bear on the social issues of the time and making sure that government by the people was returned to the people. The Wisconsin Idea is, fundamentally, about building democracy that engages the people to resist oppression, exploitation, and exclusion and collectively move toward the progressive society. Thus, our work in the university should be, under the banner of The Wisconsin Idea or any other banner, engaging people in building democracy (Speck & Hoppe, 2004b, p. 30).

Building democracy doesn't mean engaging only those people who are already primed to be engaged, empowered to be engaged, and paid to be engaged. It means, most fundamentally, engaging those people who face the greatest barriers to being engaged. There is no democracy until there are no barriers to democracy for anyone. And we are going in the opposite direction. New laws that restrict voting rights and eliminate worker organizing rights, that dilute the rights of consumers to know what dangers lurk in consumer goods and to recover damages when they are harmed in the name of profit, and that limit women's control over their own bodies—such laws are expanding more rapidly today than laws removing barriers to gaining knowledge and practicing democracy. Institutionalized service learning has remained purposely oblivious to this reality.

But the question remains whether we should even try to promote liberating service learning that can further the struggle for democracy while we are comfortably ensconced inside of higher education institutions. Everything good and progressive in liberating service learning could die if we succeed in doing so. "Institutionalization" is itself part of the problem. So if we at least stop doing institutionalized service learning while supporting those few trying to do liberating service learning, we will be reducing the possibility of applauding bad practice. And while we might appear to be doing less "out there," we will actually be doing less harm, wasting less time, and redirecting fewer resources toward reinforcing the existing system.

What other choice do we have? This is not a question of whether we can and should practice liberating service learning. This is a question of whether we can and should practice democracy. And on that point I can justify no compromise. Those of us in the knowledge business have a civic mission to help build the knowledge power of those who are most oppressed, exploited, and excluded so that democracy can deepen and broaden, becoming more participatory, more diverse, more sustainable, and more resistant to dominator culture.

The risks, of course, are enormous. We are going up against enemies of democracy who now have the ability in many places to make policy without accountability and, in Wisconsin, the potential to silence anyone producing knowledge that the powerful feel threatened by. But we cannot fail. I have stood with the mothers, sisters, and neighbors of people wounded and killed by the violence that is the inevitable result of a society organized around oppression, exploitation, and exclusion. I have been gifted with the stories of those who live day to day with their only source of dignity coming from their own struggle against the system that holds them down. I have felt the pain of being confronted with the charge that my success in life comes from resources, history, and power that were taken from so many peoples of the planet. Enough is enough. It is time to act. It is time to choose. It is time to commit.

And, of course, it is difficult to figure out what to do so as to not produce new oppressions, exploitations, and exclusions. But the solution to the many and deep philosophical and strategic dilemmas involved in organizing the progressive society will not result from academics sitting around arguing about them. The solutions will come from everyone being fully involved and fully influential in the process of creating the progressive society: everyone a learner, everyone a teacher, everyone a leader.

I am still unlearning along this path. I am still stumbling. I am still embarrassing myself when I unwittingly reveal my ignorance of those whose life experiences are so different from mine. Mostly, I am still learning and trying to be conscious of the opportunities to learn that present themselves. I am getting clearer glimmers of the ways that my liberation is bound up with others'. I am still making mistakes, though they are becoming less consequential as I try to participate more as an ally in collective work than as an individual leader of others' work. My biggest challenges are still in unlearning the unreflective individualism of neoliberalism.

Thankfully, I can count among my public relationships many people who find enough value in me to guide me. Ultimately, the test of our success will be when the people out there struggling for justice find us academics worthy enough to become our allies. Then they will demand that higher education institutions change to provide the space and support for those who would practice liberating service learning, protected from the encumbrances of the neoliberal nonprofit industrial complex, so that we can become better allies to all who struggle.

Postlude

THE TWILIGHT BEFORE JUSTICE

'Twas the twilight before justice, and all through the land,
The master had silenced each woman, person, and man;
The lies had been spread 'cross the air, land, and sea,
And had blinded the people so that none could now see.

The poor were most hungry, and the sick sicker yet;
But the people now saw them defined wholly by debt;
Oppression was normal, accepted, and unseen,
And the windows to truth were all fogged and uncleaned.

Except in one little corner, of a place time forgot,
An angry young person said, "No, I will not."
"I will not accept the way that things are."
"I am convinced that we've strayed quite too far."

But how to recover the hope that was lost,
How to help everyone see fully the cost,
Of the unsustainable world they'd been forced to create,
Nearly stymied this person and sealed all our fate.

Acknowledgments: I thank Clement Clarke Moore or Henry Livingston, Jr., for format and Dr. Seuss for inspiration.

But this person kept hope up and sought out a friend,
Asking, "Please can we talk about how this might end?"
And together they talked about ways to make change,
And they then sought out others, of quite a wide range:

Of identities and colors and ages and voices,
Of backgrounds and schoolings and abilities and choices,
But they all could agree that the system was slop,
And the oppression of people was the first thing to stop.

So they kept getting together and growing their number,
And began rousing others out of their slumber,
And slowly but surely they'd gathered their forces,
And started considering whether to take courses.

"We need to know more," they said, "before we get lost,"
"And repeat the oppressions and make worse the cost,"
So they sought out the teachers and asked for the books,
But their best efforts resulted in stares and blank looks.

But eventually they found in a back corner space,
A teacher forgotten who'd left but a trace,
Who'd survived all the purges and watched for some foment,
And had patiently waited for just the right moment.

The teacher and people were not sure where to start,
Each worried the other was too far apart,
From what each other knew and what each could bring forth,
And how both could combine to create a new worth.

The teacher said, "Sorry, I know not what to do,"
"Though I know how to learn—about that I've a clue."
And the people said, "Yes, we don't want you to tell us."
"We want to learn learning; perhaps you can help us?"

So the teacher and people, who were now both together,
They started to study, teaching each other.
And the knowledge they built grew faster and faster,
And the people grew ready to throw off their master.

Out into the streets the people went with their clout,
And confronted the master and said, "You are out!"

"No more will we swallow your lies and deceit,"
"We've learned how to learn and you now face defeat!"

And the people and teacher, who now were as one,
Started a new world, aimed toward the sun,
Where all could be healthy, happy, and wise;
Where imagination and hope could soar past the skies.

References

Adam. (n.d.). *Transwhat? A guide towards allyship*. Retrieved January 14, 2015, from http://transwhat.org/allyship/.

Adams, F. (1975). *Unearthing seeds of fire: The idea of Highlander*. Winston-Salem, NC: John F. Blair.

AFL-CIO. (2013). *Constituency groups*. Retrieved January 14, 2015, from http://www.aflcio.org/About/Allied-Organizations/Constituency-Groups.

Ahn, C. E. (2007). Democratizing American philanthropy. In Incite! Women of Color Against Violence (Eds.), *The revolution will not be funded: Beyond the non-profit industrial complex* (pp. 63–76). Boston: South End Press.

Alinsky, S. (1969). *Reveille for radicals*. New York: Vintage.

Alinsky, S. (1971). *Rules for radicals*. New York: Vintage.

Alkebulan, P. (2007). *Survival pending revolution: The history of the Black Panther Party*. Tuscaloosa: University of Alabama Press.

Altschuld, J. W. (2014). *Bridging the gap between asset/capacity building and needs assessment: Concepts and practical applications*. Thousand Oaks, CA: Sage.

Anderson, T. H. (1996). *The movement and the sixties: Protest in America from Greensboro to Wounded Knee*. New York: Oxford University Press.

Andreasen, N. (2002). Civic responsibility through mutual transformation of town and gown: Service learning at Andrews University. In M. E. Kenny, L. A. K. Simon, K. Kiley-Brabeck, & R. M. Lerner (Eds.), *Learning to serve: Promoting civil society through service learning* (pp. 66–71). Norwell, MA: Kluwer Academic.

Anheier, H. K., & Salamon, L. M. (2006). The nonprofit sector in comparative perspective. In W. W. Powell & R. Steinberg (Eds.), *The nonprofit sector: A research handbook* (pp. 89–116). New Haven, CT: Yale University Press.

Areeda, P. E. (1996). The Socratic method (SM) (Lecture at Puget Sound, 1/31/90). *Harvard Law Review, 109*(5), 911–922.

Arnstein, S. R. (1969). A ladder of citizen participation. *Journal of the American Institute of Planners, 35*(4), 216–224.

Arum, R. (with Roksa, J.). (2010). *Academically adrift: Limited learning on college campuses.* Chicago: University of Chicago Press.

Ashby, R. (2008). *Rosa Parks: Freedom rider.* New York: Sterling.

Asimov, N. (2011, September 22). UC Berkeley students protest tuition hikes, cuts. *San Francisco Chronicle.* Retrieved January 14, 2015, from http://www.sfgate.com/bayarea/article/UC-Berkeley-students-protest-tuition-hikes-cuts-2308579.php.

Assembly of First Nations, Environmental Stewardship Unit. (2009). *Ethics in First Nations research.* Retrieved January 14, 2015, from http://www.afn.ca/uploads/files/rp-research_ethics_final.pdf.

Asset-Based Community Development Institute. (2009). *Welcome to ABCD.* Retrieved January 14, 2015, from http://www.abcdinstitute.org/.

Atlas, J. (2010). *Seeds of change: The story of ACORN, America's most controversial antipoverty community organizing group.* Nashville, TN: Vanderbilt University Press.

Ayers, D. F. (2005). Neoliberal ideology in community college mission statements: A critical discourse analysis. *Review of Higher Education, 28*(4), 527–549.

Bailis, L., & Ganger, T. (2006). *A framework for further research: The community impacts of service-learning.* Retrieved January 14, 2015, from the National Youth Leadership Council website: http://www.nylc.org/resources/downloads/framework-further-research.

Balliet, B. J., & Heffernan, K. (Eds.). (2000). *The practice of change: Concepts and models for service learning in women's studies.* Washington, DC: American Association for Higher Education.

Bankston, C. (2011). *The chronomyopia of higher education.* Retrieved January 14, 2015, from http://cantheseboneslive.blogspot.ca/search?q=service+learning.

Bankston, C. (2012a). *A call to national servitude.* Retrieved January 14, 2015, from http://cantheseboneslive.blogspot.ca/search?q=service+learning.

Bankston, C. (2012b). *The civic engagement doctrine.* Retrieved January 14, 2015, from http://cantheseboneslive.blogspot.ca/search?q=service+learning.

Bankston, C. (2013). *More civic engagement.* Retrieved January 14, 2015, from http://cantheseboneslive.blogspot.ca/search?q=service+learning.

Barber, B. (1991). A mandate for liberty: Requiring education-based community service. *Responsive Community, 1*(2), 46–55.

Barber, B. (1992). *An aristocracy of everyone: The politics of education and the future of America.* New York: Ballantine Books.

Barber, B. R., & Battistoni, R. (1993). A season of service: Introducing service learning into the liberal arts curriculum. *PS: Political Science and Politics, 26*(2), 235–240.

Basinger, N., & Bartholomew, K. (2006). Service-learning in nonprofit organizations: Motivations, expectations, and outcomes. *Michigan Journal of Community Service Learning, 12*(2), 15–26.

Battistoni, R. M. (1997). Service learning and democratic citizenship: Theory into practice. *Community Service Learning, 36*(3), 150–156.

Battistoni, R. M. (2002). *Civic engagement across the curriculum: A resource book for service-learning faculty in all disciplines.* Providence, RI: Campus Compact.

Beckman, M., & Wood, D. (in press). The role of community-based research in achieving community impact. In M. Beckman & J. Long (Eds.), *The teaching and practice of community-based research for community impact.* Sterling, VA: Stylus.

Beckwith, D. (1997). Community organizing: People power from the grassroots. *COMM-ORG Papers.* Retrieved January 14, 2015, from http://comm-org.wisc.edu/papers97/beckwith.htm.

Begum, S. S. (2011). *Toynbee Hall's Olympic heritage.* Retrieved January 14, 2015, from http://www.toynbeehall.org.uk/data/files/About_Toynbee_Hall/Toynbee_Olympics _Book_5th_march.pdf.

Bell, S. M., & Carlson, R. (2009). Motivations of community organizations for service learning. In R. Stoecker & E. Tryon (with A. Hilgendorf) (Eds.), *The unheard voices: Community organizations and service learning* (pp. 19–37). Philadelphia: Temple University Press.

Belmont University. (n.d.). *What is a social entrepreneur?* Retrieved July 21, 2015, from http://www.belmont.edu/se/whatis.html.

Berger, R. J. (2014). Academic freedom and its discontents: An autoethnography. *International Review of Qualitative Research, 7*(2), 258–273.

Berry, W. (2003). *The art of the commonplace: The agrarian essays of Wendell Berry* (N. Wirzba, Ed.). Berkeley, CA: Counterpoint.

Bickford, D., & Reynolds, N. (2002). Activism and service-learning: Reframing volunteerism as acts of dissent. *Pedagogy: Critical Approaches to Teaching Literature, Language, Composition, and Culture, 2*(2), 229–252.

Bierria, A. (2007). Pursuing a radical antiviolence agenda inside/outside a non-profit structure. In Incite! Women of Color Against Violence (Eds.), *The revolution will not be funded: Beyond the non-profit industrial complex* (pp. 151–163). Boston: South End Press.

Big Creek People in Action. (2014). *Service learning.* Retrieved January 14, 2015, from http://www.bigcreekpeopleinaction.org/programs.htm.

Billig, J., & Eyler, S. H. (2003). Enhancing theory-based research in service learning. In J. Billig & S. H. Eyler (Eds.), *Deconstructing service learning* (pp. 3–24). Greenwich, CT: Information Age.

Birdsall, J. T. (2005). Community voice: Community partners reflect on service learning. *Journal for Civic Commitment, 5.* Retrieved July 23, 2015, from http://ccncce .org/articles/community-voice-community-partners-reflect-on-service-learning/.

Bishop, A. (2002). *Becoming an ally* (2nd ed.). London: Zed Books.

Blouin, D. D., & Perry, E. M. (2009). Whom does service-learning really serve? Community-based organizations' perspectives on service-learning. *Teaching Sociology, 37,* 120–135.

Boettcher, J. (2011, February 14). New Belmont women's soccer coach represents a fresh start. *City Paper.* Retrieved January 14, 2015, from http://nashvillecitypaper.com/ content/sports/new-belmont-womens-soccer-coach-represents-fresh-start.

Bourdieu, P. (1986). The forms of capital. In J. Richardson (Ed.), *Handbook of theory and research for the sociology of education* (pp. 241–258). New York: Greenwood.

Boxer, M. J. (2001). *When women ask the questions: Creating women's studies in America.* Baltimore: Johns Hopkins University Press.

Boyer, E. T. (1983). *High school: A report on secondary education in America.* New York: Harper & Row.

Boyer, E. T. (1987). *College: The undergraduate experience in America.* San Francisco: Jossey-Bass.

Boyer, E. T. (1990). *Scholarship reconsidered: Priorities of the professoriate.* San Francisco: Jossey-Bass.

Boyer, E. T. (1996). The scholarship of engagement. *Bulletin of the American Academy of Arts and Sciences, 49*(7), 8–33.

Boyte, H. C. (2003). Civic education and the new American patriotism post-9/11. *Cambridge Journal of Education, 33*(1), 85–99.

Braxton, G. (1949, May 18). Letter to John McDowell. University of Minnesota, Social Welfare History Archives.

Bridger, J. C., & Alter, T. R. (2006). The engaged university, community development, and public scholarship. *Journal of Higher Education Outreach and Engagement, 11*(1), 163–178.

Bringle, R. G., & Hatcher, J. A. (2003). Reflection in service-learning: Making meaning of experience. In Campus Compact (Eds.), *Introduction to service-learning toolkit: Readings and resources for faculty* (2nd ed., pp. 83–90). Boston: Campus Compact.

Bringle, R. G., Hatcher, J. A., & MacIntosh, R. (2006). Analyzing Morton's typology of service paradigms and integrity. *Michigan Journal of Community Service Learning, 13*(1), 5–15.

Brown, D. (2000). *Learning to serve? The necessity of Marxist critique in service learning curricula.* Paper presented at the Rethinking Marxism Conference, Amherst, MA. Retrieved January 14, 2015, from http://www.redmonky.net/words/learningtoserve.html.

Brown, D. M. (2001). *Pulling it together: A method for developing service-learning and community partnerships based in critical pedagogy.* Washington, DC: Corporation for National Service, National Service Fellowship Program. Retrieved January 14, 2015, from http://www.nationalserviceresources.org/files/r2087-pulling-it-together.pdf.

Brown, L. D., & Tandon, R. (1983). Ideology and political economy in inquiry: Action research and participatory research. *Journal of Applied Behavioral Science, 19*, 277–294.

Brydon-Miller, M. (2009). Covenantal ethics and action research: Exploring a common foundation for social research. In D. Mertens & P. Ginsberg (Eds.), *Handbook of social research ethics* (pp. 243–258). Newbury Park, CA: Sage.

Brydon-Miller, M., & Stoecker, R. (2010). *Introduction: Covenantal ethics as a framework for structured ethical reflection in action research.* Paper presented at the ALARA Eighth World Congress, Melbourne, Australia. Retrieved January 14, 2015, from http://wc2010.alara.net.au/Formatted%20Papers/4.2.8.GENERIC.pdf.

Buechler, S. M. (1990). *Women's movements in the United States: Woman suffrage, equal rights, and beyond.* New Brunswick, NJ: Rutgers University Press.

Burawoy, M. (1979). *Manufacturing consent: Changes in the labor process under monopoly capitalism.* Chicago: University of Chicago Press.

Butin, D. W. (2010). *Service-learning in theory and practice: The future of community engagement in higher education.* New York: Palgrave Macmillan.

Byrne, D. (2013). *Norwich University Service Learning (NUSL) Program.* Retrieved January 14, 2015, from http://www.norwich.edu/academics/servicelearning/.

Cahill, C. (2009). Beyond "us" and "them": Community-based research as a politics of engagement. In M. L. Diener & H. Liese (Eds.), *Finding meaning in civically engaged scholarship: Personal journeys, professional experiences* (pp. 47–57). Charlotte, NC: Information Age.

Calderón, J. Z. (Ed.). (2007). *Race, poverty, and social justice: Multidisciplinary perspectives through service learning.* Sterling, VA: Stylus.

Calderón, J. Z., & Cadena, G. R. (2007). Linking critical democratic pedagogy, multiculturalism, and service learning to a project-based approach. In J. Z. Calderón (Ed.), *Race, poverty, and social justice: Multidisciplinary perspectives through service learning* (pp. 63–80). Sterling, VA: Stylus.

Callahan, S., Mayer, N., Palmer, K., & Ferlazzo, L. (1999). Rowing the boat with two oars. *COMM-ORG Papers.* Retrieved January 14, 2015, from http://comm-org.wisc.edu/papers99/callahan.htm.

Camara, D. H. (1971). *Spiral of violence*. London: Sheed & Ward.

Camara, D. H., & McDonagh, F. (2009). *Dom Helder Camara: Essential writings*. Maryknoll, NY: Orbis Books.

Campbell, J. (1995). *Understanding John Dewey: Nature and cooperative intelligence*. Peru, IL: Open Court.

Campus Compact. (2012). *Annual membership survey*. Retrieved January 14, 2015, from http://www.compact.org/about/statistics/2012-campus-compact-member-survey/.

Campus Compact. (2015). *Campus Compact statement on higher education's response to events in Baltimore and around the United States*. Retrieved May 18, 2015, from http://campaign.r20.constantcontact.com/render?ca=82dcd329-424d-492c-95c7 -585e84a4114a&c=9764b860-2144-11e3-8af2-d4ae52a82222&ch=97699a60-2144 -11e3-8af2-d4ae52a82222.

Canaan, J. E., & Shumar, W. (Eds.). (2008). *Structure and agency in the neoliberal university*. New York: Routledge.

Cannon, L. (2003). *Governor Reagan: His rise to power*. New York: Public Affairs.

Carson, C. (1995). *In struggle: SNCC and the Black awakening of the 1960s*. Cambridge, MA: Harvard University Press.

Casil, A. S. (2006). *John Dewey: The founder of American liberalism*. New York: Rosen.

Celio, C. I., Durlak, J., & Dymnicki, A. (2011). A meta-analysis of the impact of service-learning on students. *Journal of Experiential Education, 34*(2), 164–181.

Chalmers, M. (2013, February 4). Nonprofits grow in numbers despite long odds. *USA Today*. Retrieved January 14, 2015, from http://www.usatoday.com/story/news/ nation/2013/02/02/nonprofits-grow-in-numbers/1886317/.

Chamberlain, C. (2003, January). Teaching teamwork: Project-based service-learning course LINCs students with nonprofits. *Inside Illinois*. Retrieved January 14, 2015, from http://www.news.uiuc.edu/II/03/0123/linc.html.

Chandler, D., & Torbert, B. (2003). Transforming inquiry and action: Interweaving 27 flavors of action research. *Action Research, 1*, 33–52.

Chávez, A. (2005). Dolores Huerta and the United Farm Workers. In V. L. Ruíz & V. S. Korrol (Eds.), *Latina legacies: Identity, biography, and community* (pp. 240–254). New York: Oxford University Press.

Chovanec, D. M., Kajner, T., Mian, A., & Underwood, M. (2011). *Disrupting the hegemony of choice: Community service learning in activist placements*. Proceedings of the Adult Education Research Conference, Toronto, Ontario, Canada. Retrieved January 14, 2015, from http://www.adulterc.org/Proceedings/2011/papers/chovanec _etal.pdf.

Christens, B. D. (2010). Public relationship building in grassroots community organizing: Relational intervention for individual and systems change. *Journal of Community Psychology, 38*(7), 886–900.

Cnaan, R. A., & Handy, F. (2005). Towards understanding episodic volunteering. *Vrijwillige Inzet Onderzocht: Wetenschappelijk Tijdschrift voor Onderzoek naar Vrijwilligerswerk, 2*(1), 29–35. Retrieved January 14, 2015, from http://www.movisie.nl/sites/ default/files/alfresco_files/Towards%20Understanding%20Episodic%20Volunteering %20%5BMOV-516073-0.1%5D.pdf.

Coles, R. L. (1999). Race-focused service-learning courses: Issues and recommendations. *Michigan Journal of Community Service Learning, 6*(1), 97–105.

College Settlements Association. (1895). *Sixth annual report*. Retrieved January 14, 2015, from http://indiamond6.ulib.iupui.edu/cdm/ref/collection/PRO/id/56598.

Collette, W. (2004). Research for organizing. In L. Staples (Ed.), *Roots to power* (2nd ed., pp. 222–233). New York: Greenwood.

Communitarian Network. (2010). *Responsive communitarian platform.* Retrieved January 14, 2015, from http://communitariannetwork.org/about-communitarianism/responsive-communitarian-platform/.

Community Development Society. (2013). *Principles of good practice.* Retrieved January 14, 2015, from http://www.comm-dev.org/.

Cone, D., & Harris, S. (1996). Service-learning practice: Developing a theoretical framework. *Michigan Journal of Community Service Learning, 3*(1), 31–43.

Consensus Organizing Center. (n.d.a). *Consensus Organizing Center history.* Retrieved January 14, 2015, from http://consensus.sdsu.edu/history.html.

Consensus Organizing Center. (n.d.b). *Mission statement.* Retrieved January 14, 2015, from http://consensus.sdsu.edu/new-site/.

Cooke, B. (2001). The social-psychological limits to participation? In B. Cooke & U. Kathari (Eds.), *Participation: The new tyranny?* (pp. 102–121). New York: Zed Books.

Cooke, B, & Kathari, U. (2001). The case for participation as tyranny. In B. Cooke & U. Kathari (Eds.), *Participation: The new tyranny?* (pp. 1–15). New York: Zed Books.

Cooperrider, D. L., & Srivastva, S. (1987). Appreciative inquiry in organizational life. *Research in Organizational Change and Development, 1*, 129–169.

Corlett, W. (1993). *Community without unity.* Durham, NC: Duke University Press.

Corporation for National and Community Service. (n.d.). *Our history.* Retrieved January 14, 2015, from http://www.nationalservice.gov/about/who-we-are/our-history.

Coyle, E. J., Jamieson, L. H., & Oakes, W. C. (2005). EPICS: Engineering projects in community service. *International Journal of Engineering Education, 21*, 139–150. Retrieved January 14, 2015, from https://engineering.purdue.edu/EPICS/About/ovpaper.pdf.

Crabtree, R. (2008). Theoretical foundations for international service learning. *Michigan Journal of Community Service Learning, 15*(1), 18–36.

Cramer, P. F. (1998). *Deep environmental politics: The role of radical environmentalism in crafting American environmental policy.* New York: Praeger.

Cronon, W. (2011). *Abusing open records to attack academic freedom.* Retrieved January 14, 2015, from http://scholarcitizen.williamcronon.net/(2011)/03/24/open-records-attack-on-academic-freedom/.

Cruz, N. I., & Giles, D. E., Jr. (2000). Where's the community in service-learning research? *Michigan Journal of Community Service Learning, 7*(1), 28–34.

Cummings, K. (2000). John Dewey and the rebuilding of urban community: Engaging undergraduates as neighborhood organizers. *Michigan Journal of Community Service Learning, 7*(1), 97–109.

Curwood, S. E., Munger, F., Mitchell, T., Mackeigan, M., & Farrar, A. (2011). Building effective community-university partnerships: Are universities truly ready? *Michigan Journal of Community Service Learning, 17*(2), 15–26.

Daigre, E. (2000). Toward a critical service-learning pedagogy: A Freirean approach to civic literacy. *Academic Exchange Quarterly, 4*, 1–10. Retrieved January 14, 2015, from http://www.thefreelibrary.com/Toward+a+Critical+Service-Learning+Pedagogy%3A+A+Freirean+Approach+to...-a068362994.

Dalton, T. (2002). *Becoming John Dewey: Dilemmas of a philosopher and naturalist.* Bloomington: Indiana University Press.

Davis, A. (1998, September 10). Masked racism: Reflections on the prison industrial complex. *ColorLines.* Retrieved January 14, 2015, from http://colorlines.com/

archives/1998/09/masked_racism_reflections_on_the_prison_industrial_complex
.html.

Davis, A. F. (1984). *Spearheads for reform: The social settlements and the progressive movement, 1890–1914*. New Brunswick, NJ: Rutgers University Press.

Daynes, G., & Longo, N. V. (2004). Jane Addams and the origins of service-learning practice in the United States. *Michigan Journal of Community Service Learning, 11*(1), 5–13.

Deans, T. (1999). Service-learning in two keys: Paulo Freire's critical pedagogy in relation to John Dewey's pragmatism. *Michigan Journal of Community Service Learning, 6*(1), 15–29.

Deegan, M. J. (1988). *Jane Addams and the men of the Chicago School, 1892–1918*. New Brunswick, NJ: Transaction.

Defilippis, J., Fisher, R., & Shragge, E. (2010). *Contesting community: The limits and potential of local organizing*. New Brunswick, NJ: Rutgers University Press.

DeFour, M. (2013, July 24). Solidarity singers arrested in capitol rotunda. *Wisconsin State Journal*. Retrieved January 14, 2015, from http://host.madison.com/news/local/govt
-and-politics/solidarity-singers-arrested-in-capitol-rotunda/article_81d72ba7-d127
-5186-85bb-40b9104a7cbe.html.

Degelman, C., Doggett, K., & Medina, G. (2006). *Giving back: Introducing community service learning: Improving mandated community service for juvenile offenders—An action guide for youth court programs and the juvenile-justice system*. Chicago: Constitutional Rights Foundation. Retrieved January 14, 2015, from http://youthcourt.net/wp
-content/uploads/(2010)/05/GivingBack_(2006)_final.pdf.

Degener, S. C. (2001). Making sense of critical pedagogy in adult literacy education. *Review of adult learning and literacy: A project of the National Center for the Study of Adult Learning and Literacy* (Vol. 2, Chap. 2). Retrieved July 23, 2015, from http://www
.ncsall.net/index.html@id=562.html.

Deloria, V., Jr. (1969/1988). *Custer died for your sins: An Indian manifesto*. Norman: University of Oklahoma Press.

Desautels, N., Breckenridge, S., Matheson, M., Dunn, B., Wherley, R., & Wells, L. (Eds.). (2013). *Unintimidated: Wisconsin sings truth to power*. La Pointe, WI: Mad Island Communications.

Dewey, J. (1916). *Democracy and education: An introduction to the philosophy of education*. New York: Macmillan.

Dewey, J. (1930/1984). Three independent factors in morals. In J. A. Boydston (Ed.), *John Dewey, the later works, 1925–1953: Vol. 5. 1929–1930* (pp. 279–288). Carbondale: Southern Illinois University Press.

Dewey, J. (1938). *Experience and education*. New York: Kappa Delta Pi.

Dolan, T., Christens, B. D., & Lin, C. S. (2015). Combining youth organizing and youth participatory action research to strengthen student voice in education reform. *Teachers College Record, 117*(13), 153–170.

Dolgon, C. (2010). Don't celebrate, organize! A public sociology to fan the flames of discontent. *Humanity and Society, 34*(3), 233–244.

Dolgon, C., & Baker, C. (2010). *Social problems: A service learning approach*. Thousand Oaks, CA: Sage.

Douglass, F. (1857, August 3). *West India emancipation*. Speech at Canandaigua, New York. Retrieved January 14, 2015, from http://www.blackpast.org/1857-frederick-douglass
-if-there-no-struggle-there-no-progress.

Downes, D., & Rock, P. (2011). *Understanding deviance: A guide to the sociology of crime and rule-breaking* (6th ed.). Oxford, England: Oxford University Press.

Draper, A. J. (2004). Integrating project-based service-learning into an advanced environmental chemistry course. *Journal of Chemical Education, 81,* 221–224.

Dubb, S. (2007). *Linking colleges to communities: Engaging the university for community development.* Retrieved January 14, 2015, from http://www.community-wealth.org/_pdfs/news/recent-articles/07-07/report-linking.pdf.

Dunn, R., Beaudry, J. S., & Klavas, A. (2002). Survey of research on learning styles. *California Journal of Science Education, 2*(2), 75–98.

Durkheim, E. (1893/1997). *The division of labor in society.* New York: Simon & Schuster.

Eby, J. (1998). *Why service learning is bad.* Retrieved January 14, 2015, from http://www.greatlakesed.net/Resources/documents/WhyServiceLearningIsBad.pdf.

Egger, J. B. (2007, October 2). Service "learning" reduces learning. *The Examiner.* Retrieved July 18, 2015, from https://web.archive.org/web/20080229031036/http://www.examiner.com/a-966679-John_B__Egger__Service__learning__reduces_learning.html.

Egger, J. B. (2008). No service to learning: "Service-learning" reappraised. *Academic Questions, 21,* 183–194.

Eichler, M. (2007). *Consensus organizing: Building communities of mutual self interest.* Thousand Oaks, CA: Sage.

Eisler, R. (1988). *The chalice and the blade: Our history, our future.* San Francisco: Harper Collins.

Eitzen, S., Zinn, M. B., & Smith, K. E. (2012). *In conflict and order: Understanding society* (13th ed.). New York: Pearson.

Etzioni, A. (1996). *The new golden rule: Community and morality in a democratic society.* New York: Basic Books.

Etzioni, A. (2003). Communitarianism. In K. Christensen & D. Levinson (Eds.), *Encyclopedia of community: From the village to the virtual world* (Vol. 1, pp. 224–228). Thousand Oaks, CA: Sage.

Evans, S. M., & Boyte, H. (1992). *Free spaces: The sources of democratic change in America.* Chicago: University of Chicago Press.

Eyler, J., & Giles, D. E., Jr. (1999). *Where's the learning in service-learning?* San Francisco: Jossey-Bass.

Eyler, J. S., Giles, D. E., Jr., Stenson, C. M., & Gray, C. J. (2001). *At a glance: What we know about the effects of service-learning on college students, faculty, institutions, and communities, 1993–2000.* Corporation for National and Community Service, Learn and Serve, National Service-Learning Clearinghouse.

Facer, K. (2013, November 20). *Whose "public good" does engaged research serve?* [NCCPE blog]. Retrieved January 14, 2015, from http://nccpe.wordpress.com/(2013)/11/20/whose-public-good-does-engaged-research-serve/.

Ferrari, J. R., & Worrall, L. (2000). Assessments by community agencies: How "the other side" sees service-learning. *Michigan Journal of Community Service Learning, 7*(1), 35–40.

Fischer, C. S. (1982). *To dwell among friends: Personal networks in town and city.* Chicago: University of Chicago Press.

Fisher, R. (1994). *Let the people decide: Neighborhood organizing in America.* New York: Twayne.

Foucault, M. (1975). *Discipline and punish: The birth of the prison.* New York: Random House.

Foucault, M. (1980). *Power/knowledge: Selected interviews and other writings 1972–1977* (C. Gordon, Ed.). New York: Pantheon.

Fourie, F. (2006, September 3–5). *In pursuit of a South African scholarship of engagement.* Paper presented at the CHE-HEQC/JET-CHESP Conference on Community Engagement in Higher Education, Cape Town, South Africa. Retrieved January 14, 2015, from http://talloiresnetwork.tufts.edu/wp-content/uploads/InpursuitofaSouth Africanscholarshipofengagement-Fourie-CHESP.doc.

Frank, T. (2004). *What's the matter with Kansas? How conservatives won the heart of America.* New York: Henry Holt.

Freire, A. M. A., & Vittoria, P. (2007). Dialogue on Paulo Freire. *Interamerican Journal of Education for Democracy, 1*(1), 97–117. Retrieved January 14, 2015, from http://scholarworks.iu.edu/journals/index.php/ried/article/view/115/195.

Freire, P. (1970). *Pedagogy of the oppressed.* New York: Continuum.

Freire, P. (1974). *Education for critical consciousness.* New York: Continuum.

Friedland, L. (2003). *Public journalism: Past and future.* Dayton, OH: Kettering Foundation Press.

Friedman, M. (1962). *Capitalism and freedom.* Chicago: University of Chicago Press.

Fukuyama, F. (1999, October 1). *Social.capital and civil society.* Paper prepared for delivery at the IMF Conference on Second Generation Reforms, Washington, DC. Retrieved January 14, 2015, from http://www.imf.org/external/pubs/ft/seminar/1999/reforms/fukuyama.htm#II.

Furco, A. (1996). *Service-learning: A balanced approach to experiential education* (Service Learning, General, Paper 128). Retrieved July 18, 2015, from http://digitalcommons.unomaha.edu/slceslgen/128.

Gallagher, L., Planowski, E., & Tarbell, K. (n.d.). *Faculty guide to service learning.* Retrieved January 14, 2015, from the University of Colorado Denver website: http://www.ucdenver.edu/life/services/ExperientialLearning/foremployers/Documents/UC%20Denver%20Faculty%20S-L%20Guide.pdf.

Ganz, M. (2009). *Why David sometimes wins: Leadership, organization, and strategy in the California farm worker movement.* New York: Oxford University Press.

Garcia, C., Nehrling, S., Martin, A., & SeBlonka, K. (2009). Finding the best fit. In R. Stoecker & E. Tryon (with A. Hilgendorf) (Eds.), *The unheard voices: Community organizations and service learning* (pp. 38–56). Philadelphia: Temple University Press.

Garcia, R. A. (1993). Dolores Huerta: Woman, organizer, and symbol. *California History, 72*(1), 56–71.

Garoutte, L., & McCarthy-Gilmore, K. (2014). Preparing students for community-based learning using an asset-based approach. *Journal of the Scholarship of Teaching and Learning, 14*(5), 48–61.

Gaventa, J. (1993). The powerful, the powerless, and the experts: Knowledge struggles in an information age. In P. Park, M. Brydon-Miller, B. Hall, & T. Jackson (Eds.), *Voices of change: Participatory research in the United States and Canada* (pp. 21–40). Westport, CT: Bergin & Garvey.

Gecan, M. (2002). *Going public: An inside story of disrupting politics as usual.* Boston: Beacon Press.

Gedicks, A. (1996). Activist sociology: Personal reflections. *Sociological Imagination, 33*(1). Retrieved January 14, 2015, from http://comm-org.wisc.edu/si/sihome.htm.

Gee, A. (2013, December 13). Justified anger: Rev. Alex Gee says Madison is failing its African-American community. *Capital Times.* Retrieved January 14, 2015, from http://

host.madison.com/news/local/city-life/justified-anger-rev-alex-gee-says-madison-is
-failing-its/article_14f6126c-fc1c-55aa-a6a3-6c3d00a4424c.html#ixzz2yxjVlyH9.

Gee, A. (2014, December 17). Turning anger to action: Rev. Alex Gee heard from African-Americans of all ages. What did he learn? *Capital Times*. Retrieved July 23, 2015, from http://host.madison.com/ct/news/local/turning-anger-to-action-rev-alex-gee-heard -from-african/article_c46fda52-c436-5af1-93c4-735d8312adea.html.

Gehl, L. (n.d.). *Ally bill of responsibilities*. Retrieved January 14, 2015, from http://www .lynngehl.com/my-ally-bill-of-responsibilities.html.

Gell, P. L. (1888). The work of Toynbee Hall. In H. B. Adams (Ed.), *Johns Hopkins University studies in historical and political science: Vol. 7. Social science, municipal and federal government* (pp. 57–64). Baltimore: John Murphy.

Gelmon, S. B., Holland, B. A., Driscoll, A., Spring, A., & Kerrigan, S. (2001). *Assessing service-learning and civic engagement: Principles and techniques*. Providence, RI: Campus Compact.

Gender Equity Resource Center. (n.d.). *Allyship*. Retrieved January 14, 2015, from http:// geneq.berkeley.edu/allyship.

Gentry, J. W. (1990). What is experiential learning? In J. W. Gentry (Ed.), *Guide to business gaming and experiential learning* (pp. 9–20). London: Nichols/GP.

Gilbert, M., & Masucci, M. (2004). Feminist praxis in university-community partnerships: Reflections on ethical crises and turning points in Temple–North Philadelphia IT partnerships. In D. Fuller & R. Kitchin (Eds.), *Radical theory / critical praxis: Making a difference beyond the academy?* (pp. 147–158). Praxis (e)Press. Retrieved January 14, 2015, from http://www.praxis-epress.org/rtcp/contents.html.

Gilderbloom, J. I., & Mullins, R. L., Jr. (2005). *Promise and betrayal: Universities and the battle for sustainable urban neighborhoods*. Albany: State University of New York Press.

Gillis, A., & Mac Lellan, M. A. (2013). Critical service learning in community health nursing: Enhancing access to cardiac health screening. *International Journal of Nursing Education Scholarship, 10*(1), 63–72.

Giroux, H. A. (2001). *Theory and resistance in education*. London: Bergin & Garvey.

Giroux, H. A. (2013). Public intellectuals against the neoliberal university. *Truthout*. Retrieved January 14, 2015, from http://truth-out.org/opinion/item/19654-public -intellectuals-against-the-neoliberal-university.

Godar, B. (2015, May 30). Justified Anger coalition rolls out "Our Madison Plan." *Capital Times*. Retrieved July 23, 2015, from http://host.madison.com/news/ local/govt-and-politics/justified-anger-coalition-rolls-out-our-madison-plan/ article_572d3ddb-da6c-59b5-afec-e90dbe8c4322.html.

Goe, W. R., & Noonan, S. (2006). The sociology of community. In C. D. Bryant & D. L. Peck (Eds.), *21st century sociology: A reference handbook* (pp. 455–464). Thousand Oaks, CA: Sage.

Gordon, D. M., Edwards, R., & Reich, M. (1982). *Segmented work, divided workers: The historical transformation of labor in the United States*. New York: Cambridge University Press.

Gramsci, A. (1971). *Selections from the prison notebooks of Antonio Gramsci* (Q. Hoare & G. Nowell Smith, Eds. & Trans.). London: Lawrence & Wishart.

Granovetter, M. S. (1973). The strength of weak ties. *American Journal of Sociology, 78*(6), 1360–1380.

Grassroots Leadership College. (2012). Homepage. Retrieved January 14, 2015, from https:// web.archive.org/web/20120421023937/http://www.grassrootsleadershipcollege.org/.

Greder, A. (2013, May 31). Macalester alumni protest probation for 17 students in Wells Fargo sit-in. *Twin Cities.Com Pioneer Press*. Retrieved January 14, 2015, from http://www.twincities.com/ci_23355755/macalester-alumni-protest-probation-17-students-wells-fargo.

Green, A. E. (2003). Difficult stories: Service learning, race, class, and whiteness. *College Composition and Communication, 55*(2), 276–301.

Greenleaf, R. K. (2002). *Servant leadership: A journey into the nature of legitimate power and greatness* (25th anniversary ed.). New York: Paulist Press.

Greenwood, D. (2012). Doing and learning action research in the neo-liberal world of contemporary higher education. *Action Research, 10*(2), 115–132.

Griffith, E. (1984). *In her own right: The life of Elizabeth Cady Stanton*. New York: Oxford University Press.

Grimm, R., Dietz, N., Foster-Bey, J., Reingold, D., & Nesbit, R. (2006). *Volunteer growth in America: A review of trends since 1974*. Retrieved January 14, 2015, from http://www.nationalservice.gov/pdf/06_1203_volunteer_growth.pdf.

Gutting, G. (2013, Summer). Michel Foucault. *The Stanford encyclopedia of philosophy* (E. N. Zalta, Ed.). Retrieved January 14, 2015, from http://plato.stanford.edu/archives/sum(2013)/entries/foucault/>.

Hackett, R. (2013). PolicyOptions.org. Retrieved January 14, 2015, from http://policyoptions.pbworks.com/w/page/17512763/FrontPage.

Hailey, J. (2001). Beyond the formulaic: Process and practice in South Asian NGOs. In B. Cooke & U. Kathari (Eds.), *Participation: The new tyranny?* (pp. 88–101). New York: Zed Books.

Haines, H. H. (1984). Black radicalization and the funding of civil rights: 1957–1970. *Social Problems, 32*(1), 31–43.

Hall, D. D. (2011). *A reforming people: Puritanism and the transformation of public life in New England*. New York: Knopf.

Hall, K., & Spurlock, C. (2013, February 21). Paid parental leave: U.S. vs. the world. *Huffington Post*. Retrieved January 16, 2016, from http://www.huffingtonpost.com/2013/02/04/maternity-leave-paid-parental-leave-_n_2617284.html.

Hanisch, C. (1969). The personal is political. In S. Firestone & A. Koedt (Eds.), *Notes from the second year: Women's liberation*. Retrieved January 14, 2015, from http://www.carolhanisch.org/CHwritings/PersonalisPol.pdf.

Hanisch, C. (2006). *Introduction*. Retrieved January 14, 2015, from http://www.carolhanisch.org/CHwritings/PersonalisPol.pdf.

Hannah, C. L., Tinkler, B., & Miller, E. (2011). Helping teacher candidates develop a critical perspective in a foundations course: A Freirian look at how teacher candidates interpret their service-learning experience. In B. J. Porfilio & H. Hickman (Eds.), *Critical service-learning as revolutionary pedagogy: A project of student agency in action* (pp. 203–221). Charlotte, NC: Information Age.

Harker, D. (2014). Ideology, policy, and engagement: What role can service learning play in a changing democracy? In A. J. Treviño & K. M. McCormack (Eds.), *Service sociology and academic engagement in social problems* (pp. 61–82). Burlington, VT: Ashgate.

Harrison, J. L. (2011). Parsing "participation" in action research: Navigating the challenges of lay involvement in technically complex participatory science projects. *Society and Natural Resources: An International Journal, 24*(7), 702–716.

Hart Research Associates. (2013). *It takes more than a major: Employer priorities for college learning and student success*. An online survey among employers conducted on behalf of the Association of American Colleges and Universities. Retrieved January 14, 2015, from http://www.aacu.org/press_room/press_releases/(2013)/leapcompactandemploy ersurvey.cfm.

Harvard University, Institute of Politics. (2013, March 20–April 8). *Survey of young Americans' attitudes toward politics and public service* (23rd ed.). Retrieved January 14, 2015, from http://www.iop.harvard.edu/sites/default/files_new/spring_poll_13_Topline.pdf.

Hatcher, J. A., & Bringle, R. G. (1997). Reflection: Bridging the gap between service and learning. *College Teaching, 45*(4), 153–158.

Hatcher, J. A., & Erasmus, M. A. (2008). Service-learning in the United States and South Africa: A comparative analysis informed by John Dewey and Julius Nyerere. *Michigan Journal of Community Service Learning, 15*(1), 49–61.

Hayes, D., & Wynyard, R. (Eds.). (2002). *The McDonaldization of higher education.* Westport, CT: Bergin & Garvey.

Hayes, E., & Cuban, S. (1997). Border pedagogy: A critical framework for service learning. *Michigan Journal of Community Service Learning, 4*(1), 72–80.

Hedges, C. (2012, December). Why mass incarceration defines us as a society. *Smithsonian Magazine.* Retrieved July 23, 2015, from http://www.smithsonianmag.com/people -places/why-mass-incarceration-defines-us-as-a-society-135793245/?no-ist.

Heinen, N. (2012, January). Wisconsin's great idea. *Madison Magazine.* Retrieved July 26, 2015, from https://web.archive.org/web/20120314142459/http://www.madisonmagazine .com/Madison-Magazine/January-2012/Wisconsins-Great-Idea/.

Helms, S. E. (2013). Involuntary volunteering: The impact of mandated service in public schools. *Economics of Education Review, 36,* 295–310.

Henness, S., & Jeanetta, S. (2010). *RASL case study: Brookfield, Missouri.* Retrieved January 14, 2015, from http://comm-org.wisc.edu/rasl/henness2.htm.

Herman, L., & Shortell, J. W. (1996). Learning peace? Creating a class on creating community. *Michigan Journal of Community Service Learning, 3*(1), 128–138.

Hidayat, D., Stoecker, R., & Gates, H. (2013). Promoting community environmental sustainability using a project-based approach. In K. O. Korgen & J. White (Eds.), *Sociologists in action: Sociology, social change and social justice.* Thousand Oaks, CA: Pine Forge Press.

Hiemstra, R., & Sisco, B. (1990). *Individualizing instruction: Making learning personal, empowering, and successful.* San Francisco: Jossey-Bass.

Hilsen, A. I. (2006). And they shall be known by their deeds: Ethics and politics in action research. *Action Research, 4*(1), 23–36.

Hine, D. C. (1996). The greater Kent State era, 1968–1970: Legacies of student rebellions and state repression. *Peace and Change, 21*(2), 157–168.

Holland, B. (1997). Analyzing institutional commitment to service: A model of key organizational factors. *Michigan Journal of Community Service Learning, 4*(1), 30–41.

hooks, b. (2003). *Teaching community: A pedagogy of hope.* New York: Routledge.

Horton, M. (1973). Decision-making processes. In N. Shimahara (Ed.), *Educational reconstruction: Promise and challenge* (pp. 323–341). Columbus, OH: Charles E. Merrill.

Horton, M. (1974, December 2). Some rough notes. Wisconsin Historical Society Archives.

Horton, M. (1976, October 13). *Democratic involvement in decision making and action.* Prepared by Myles Horton for the Public Relations Conference, Brainerd, MN. Wisconsin Historical Society Archives.

Horton, M., & Freire, P. (1991). *We make the road by walking: Conversations on education and social change* (B. Bell, J. Gaventa, & J. Peters, Eds.). Philadelphia: Temple University Press.

Horwitt, S. (1992). *Let them call me rebel: Saul Alinsky—His life and legacy.* New York: Vintage.

Howard, J. (Ed.). (2001, Summer). *Michigan Journal of Community Service Learning: Service-learning course design workbook* (Michigan Journal of Community Service Learning companion volume).

Howard, J. (2003). Service-learning research: Foundational issues. In S. H. Billig & A. S. Waterman (Eds.), *Studying service learning: Innovations in education research methodology* (pp. 1–10). Mahwah, NJ: Erlbaum.

Hubbard, A. (1996). The activist academic and the stigma of "community housework." *Sociological Imagination, 33*(1). Retrieved January 14, 2015, from http://comm-org .wisc.edu/si/sihome.htm.

Hugh, B. (2011). *Advocacy 101: Power mapping—The key to effective advocacy.* Retrieved January 14, 2015, from the Missouri Bicycle and Pedestrian Federation website: http:// mobikefed.org/content/advocacy-101-power-mapping-key-effective-advocacy.

Hunt, A. (1999). When did the sixties happen? Searching for new directions. *Journal of Social History, 33*(1), 147–161.

Hyatt, S. B. (2008). The Obama victory, asset-based development and the re-politicization of community organizing. *North American Dialogue, 11*(2), 17–26.

Ife, J. (2010). Capacity building and community development. In S. Kenny & M. Clarke (Eds.), *Challenging capacity building: Comparative perspectives* (pp. 67–84). New York: Palgrave Macmillan.

Illich, I. (1971). *Deschooling society.* New York: Harper & Row.

Incite! Women of Color Against Violence (Eds.). (2007). *The revolution will not be funded: Beyond the non-profit industrial complex.* Boston: South End Press.

Incite! Women of Color Against Violence. (2014). *Beyond the nonprofit industrial complex.* Retrieved January 14, 2015, from http://www.incite-national.org/page/beyond-non -profit-industrial-complex.

Indigenous Action Media. (2014). *Accomplices not allies: Abolishing the ally industrial complex.* Retrieved July 30, 2015, from http://www.indigenousaction.org/accomplices-not -allies-abolishing-the-ally-industrial-complex/.

Is Pope Francis leaving Vatican at night to minister to homeless? (2013, December 2). *Huffington Post.* Retrieved January 14, 2015, from http://www.huffingtonpost .com/2013/12/02/pope-francis-homeless_n_4373884.html.

Ison, R. L. (2000). Technology: Transforming grazier experience. In R. Ison & D. Russell (Eds.), *Agricultural extension and rural development: Breaking out of traditions* (pp. 55– 75). New York: Cambridge University Press.

Jacoby, B. (1996). *Service-learning in higher education: Concepts and practices.* San Francisco: Jossey-Bass.

Jagpal, N., & Laskowski, K. (2013). *Smashing silos in philanthropy: Multi-issue advocacy and organizing for real results.* Retrieved January 14, 2015, from the National Committee for Responsive Philanthropy website: http://www.ncrp.org/files/publications/Smash ing_Silos_in_Philanthropy_Multi-Issue_Advocacy_and_Organizing_for_Real _Results.pdf.

Jagpal, N., & Schlegel, R. (2015). *Cultivating nonprofit leadership: A (missed?) philanthropic opportunity.* Retrieved July 14, 2015, from the National Committee for Responsive Philanthropy website: http://ncrp.org/paib/smashing-silos-in-philanthropy/cultivating -nonprofit-leadership.

Jelier, R. W., & Clarke, R. J. (1999). The community as a laboratory of study: Getting out of the ivory tower. *Journal of Public Affairs Education, 5*(2), 167–180.

Johnson, O. (2012, October 24). Privilege and poverty: Reconciling SUYI with the ethical problems of service. *The Spectator*, pp. 10–13. Retrieved from http://www.seattle spectator.com/2012/10/24/privilege-and-poverty-reconciling-suyi-with-the-ethical -problems-of-service/.

Johnson, T., Champagne, D., & Nagel, J. (1997). American Indian activism and transformation: Lessons from Alcatraz. In T. Johnson, J. Nagel, & D. Champagne (Eds.), *American Indian activism: Alcatraz to the longest walk* (pp. 9–44). Urbana: University of Illinois Press.

Johnson, V. (2008). Soc 285-02 Information Society. Retrieved January 14, 2015, from http://www.homepages.dsu.edu/murphym/Johnson_Soc285_Syllabus_Fall08.htm.

Johnston, F. E., Harkavy, I., Barg, F., Gerber, D., & Rulf, J. (2004). The urban nutrition initiative: Bringing academically-based community service to the University of Pennsylvania's Department of Anthropology. *Michigan Journal of Community Service Learning, 10*(3), 100–106.

Jones, M. H. (1925). *Autobiography of Mother Jones.* Chicago: Charles Kerr.

Justified anger: Let's talk about it. (2015). Retrieved July 23, 2015, from https://www.face book.com/JustifiedAngerDiscussion.

Kajner, T., Chovanec, D., Underwood, M., & Mian, A. (2013). Critical community service learning: Combining critical classroom pedagogy with activist community placements. *Michigan Journal of Community Service Learning, 19*(2), 36–48.

Kania, J., & Kramer, M. (2011). Collective impact. *Stanford Social Innovation Review, 98*. Retrieved July 30, 2015, from http://www.ssireview.org/articles/entry/collective _impact.

Keith, N. Z. (1998). Community service for community building: The school-based service corps as border crossers. *Michigan Journal of Community Service Learning, 5*(1), 86–96.

Keith, N. Z. (2005). Community service learning in the face of globalization: Rethinking theory and practice. *Michigan Journal of Community Service Learning, 11*(2), 5–24.

Keller, A. (2011). *Three Rivers Community College student service learning handbook.* Retrieved January 14, 2015, from http://www.trcc.commnet.edu/div_academics/ learninginitiatives/sl/PDF/Service%20Learning%20Student%20Handbook.pdf.

Kellogg, W. A. (1999). *Service learning and the university role in community development.* Cleveland State University, Maxine Goodman Levin College of Urban Affairs, Urban Center.

Kendall, J. C. (1990). Combining service and learning: An introduction. In J. C. Kendall (Ed.), *Combining service and learning: A resource book for community and public service* (Vol. 1, pp. 1–33). Raleigh, NC: National Society for Experiential Education.

Kenny, M. E., & Gallagher, L. A. (2002). Service learning: A history of systems. In M. E. Kenny, L. A. K. Simon, K. Kiley-Brabeck, & R. M. Lerner (Eds.), *Learning to serve: Promoting civil society through service learning* (pp. 15–30). New York: Springer.

King, T. L., & Osayande, E. (2007). The filth on philanthropy. In Incite! Women of Color Against Violence (Eds.), *The revolution will not be funded: Beyond the non-profit industrial complex* (pp. 79–89). Boston: South End Press.

Kinnevy, S. C., & Boddie, S. C. (2001). Developing community partnerships through service-learning: Universities, coalitions, and congregations. *Michigan Journal of Community Service Learning, 8*(1), 44–51.

Kliewer, B., Sandmann, L. R., Kim, J., & Omerikwa, A. (2010, June 3–6). *Toward understanding reciprocity in community-university partnerships: An analysis of theories of power.* Paper presented at the Adult Education Research Conference, Sacramento, CA.

Retrieved July 23, 2015, from http://www.adulterc.org/Proceedings/2010/proceedings/kliewer_etal.pdf.

Kliewer, B. W. (2013). Why the civic engagement movement cannot achieve democratic and justice aims. *Michigan Journal of Community Service Learning, 19*(2), 72–79.

Knight, J. (1994). *Orthodoxies in Massachusetts: Rereading American Puritanism.* Cambridge, MA: Harvard University Press.

Knowles, M. S. (1970). *Modern practice of adult education: Andragogy versus pedagogy.* Chicago: Follett / Association Press.

Knowles, M. S. (1980). *Modern practice of adult education: From pedagogy to andragogy* (revised and updated). Chicago: Follett / Association Press.

Kolb, D. A. (1984). *Experiential learning: Experience as the source of learning and development.* Englewood Cliffs, NJ: Prentice Hall.

Koliba, C. J. (2004). Service-learning and the downsizing of democracy: Learning our way out. *Michigan Journal of Community Service Learning, 10*(2), 57–68.

Konopacki, M. (2013, June 25). Mike Konopacki: Chancellor Ward, tear down that plaque. *Capital Times.* Retrieved January 14, 2015, from http://host.madison.com/news/opinion/column/mike-konopacki-chancellor-ward-tear-down-that-plaque/article_7a28e261-b897-54f1-999d-11b1cb2ae3b2.html#ixzz2fFpmdOQi.

Kretzmann, J. P., & McKnight, J. L. (1993). *Building communities from the inside out: A path toward finding and mobilizing a community's assets.* Evanston, IL: Center for Urban Affairs and Policy Research, Neighborhood Innovations Network, Northwestern University.

Kuyek, J. N. (2011). *Community organizing: A holistic approach.* Halifax, Nova Scotia, Canada: Fernwood.

La Belle, T. J., & Ward, C. R. (1996). *Ethnic studies and multiculturalism.* Albany: State University of New York Press.

Ladd, E. C. (1996). The data just don't show erosion of America's "social capital." *Public Perspective, 7*(4), 1–6. Retrieved January 14, 2015, from http://www.ropercenter.uconn.edu/public-perspective/ppscan/74/74001.pdf.

Lambert-Pennington, K., Reardon, K. M., & Robinson, K. S. (2011). Revitalizing South Memphis through an interdisciplinary community-university development partnership. *Michigan Journal of Community Service Learning, 17*(2), 59–70.

Lasch, C. (1979). *The culture of narcissism: American life in an age of diminishing expectations.* New York: Norton.

Lasch-Quinn, E. (1993). *Black neighbors: Race and the limits of reform in the American settlement house movement, 1890–1945.* Chapel Hill: University of North Carolina Press.

Learn and Serve America. (n.d.). *Inspired to serve: An online tool kit for youth-led interfaith action.* Retrieved July 30, 2015, from http://www.inspiredtoserve.org/service-learning.

Lee, B. A., Oropesa, R. S., Metch, B. J., & Guest, A. M. (1984). Testing the decline-of-community thesis: Neighborhood organizations in Seattle, 1929 and 1979. *American Journal of Sociology, 89*(5), 1161–1188.

Leeds, J. (1999). Rationales for service-learning: A critical examination. *Michigan Journal of Community Service Learning, 6*(1), 112–122.

Lehmann, C. (2011, December 2). Au revoir, noblesse oblige. *In These Times.* Retrieved January 14, 2015, from http://inthesetimes.com/article/12278/au_revoir_noblesse_oblige.

Lehmann, N. (1996, April). Kicking in groups. *The Atlantic Online.* Retrieved January 14, 2015, from http://www.theatlantic.com/past/docs/issues/96apr/kicking/kicking.htm.

Leopold, A. (1949). *A Sand County almanac.* New York: Oxford University Press.

Lewin, K. (1948). In G. W. Lewin (Ed.), *Resolving social conflicts: Selected papers on group dynamics*. New York: Harper & Row.

LGBTQ Allyship. (2013). Homepage. Retrieved January 14, 2015, from http://lgbtqally ship.org/.

Lin, C., Schmidt, C., Tryon, E., & Stoecker, R. (2009). Service learning in context: The challenge of diversity. In R. Stoecker & E. Tryon (with A. Hilgendorf) (Eds.), *The unheard voices: Community organizations and service learning* (pp. 116–135). Philadelphia: Temple University Press.

Liu, J., & Kelly, D. P. (2009). "Democracy is hard" / "democracy is messy." *Journal for Civic Commitment, 14*. Retrieved July 23, 2015, from http://ccncce.org/articles/democracy -is-harddemocracy-is-messy/.

Living Knowledge. (2014). *Science shops*. Retrieved January 14, 2015, from http://www .livingknowledge.org/livingknowledge/science-shops.

Lowney, C. (2013). When Pope Francis was put on laundry duty. *CNN*. Retrieved January 14, 2015, from http://religion.blogs.cnn.com/(2013)/11/17/when-pope-francis-was-put-on-laundry-duty/?iref=allsearch.

Loyola University Chicago. (n.d.). *Office of Experiential Learning*. Retrieved July 21, 2015, from http://www.luc.edu/experiential/.

Ludlum Foos, C. (1998). The "different voice" of service. *Michigan Journal of Community Service Learning, 5*(1), 14–21.

Lupton, R. D. (2012). *Toxic charity: How churches and charities hurt those they help, and how to reverse it*. New York: HarperOne.

Lynton Colloquium. (2014, October 21). RFP: Research on critical issues in advancing community-engaged scholarship. E-mail communication.

Macduff, N. L. (2004). *Episodic volunteering: Organizing and managing the short-term volunteer program*. Walla Walla, WA: MBA.

Maiter, S., Simich, L., Jacobson, N., & Wise, J. (2008). Reciprocity: An ethic for community-based participatory action research. *Action Research, 6*(3), 305–325.

Martin, A., SeBlonka, K., & Tryon, E. (2009). The challenge of short-term service-learning. In R. Stoecker & E. Tryon (with A. Hilgendorf) (Eds.), *The unheard voices: Community organizations and service learning* (pp. 57–72). Philadelphia: Temple University Press.

Martin, J. (2003). *The education of John Dewey: A biography*. New York: Columbia University Press.

Marullo, S., Cooke, D., Willis, J., Rollins, A., Burke, J., Bonilla, P., et al. (2003). Community-based research assessments: Some principles and practices. *Michigan Journal of Community Service Learning, 9*(3), 57–68.

Marullo, S., & Edwards, B. (2000). From charity to justice: The potential of university-community collaboration for social change. *American Behavioral Scientist, 43*, 895–912.

Marx, K. (1844/1932). *Economic and philosophic manuscripts of 1844* (M. Mulligan, Trans.). Moscow: Progress. Retrieved January 14, 2015, from https://www.marxists.org/ archive/marx/works/1844/manuscripts/preface.htm.

Marx, K. (1859). *A contribution to the critique of political economy* (S. W. Ryazanskaya, Trans.). Moscow: Progress. Retrieved January 14, 2015, from https://www.marxists .org/archive/marx/works/1859/critique-pol-economy/.

Marx, K. (1867/1999). *Capital: Vol. 1* (F. Engels, Ed., S. Moore & E. Aveling, Trans.). Retrieved January 14, 2015, from http://www.marxists.org/archive/marx/works/1867 -c1/index.htm.

Masucci, M., & Renner, A. (2001). *The evolution of critical service learning for education: Four problematics*. ERIC Clearinghouse, ED456962. Retrieved January 14, 2015, from http://eric.ed.gov/?id=ED456962.

Mayo, P. (1999). *Gramsci, Freire and adult education: Possibilities for transformative action*. New York: Zed Books.

McAdam, D. (1988). *Freedom summer*. New York: Oxford University Press.

McCabe, M. (2004). Strengthening pedagogy and praxis in cultural anthropology and service-learning: Insights from postcolonialism. *Michigan Journal of Community Service Learning*, 10(3), 16–30.

McCarthy, C. (1912). *The Wisconsin idea*. Retrieved January 14, 2015, from http://www.library.wisc.edu/etext/wireader/Contents/Idea.html.

McCarthy, K. D. (1982). *Noblesse oblige: Charity and cultural philanthropy in Chicago, 1849–1929*. Chicago: University of Chicago Press.

McClusky, H. Y. (1960). Community development. In M. S. Knowles (Ed.), *Handbook of adult education in the United States* (pp. 416–427). Washington, DC: Adult Education Association of the U.S.A.

McKnight, J. (1995). *The careless society: Community and its counterfeits*. New York: Basic Books.

Medina, E. (2011). Innovation in education: The influence of service on stereotypes. *Michigan Journal of Social Work and Social Welfare*, 2(2), 132–151. Retrieved January 14, 2015, from http://mjsw.files.wordpress.com/2011/11/medina-final-vol2iss2.pdf.

Medina, J. (2011, November 21). California's campus movements dig in their heels. *New York Times*. Retrieved January 14, 2015, from http://www.nytimes.com/2011/11/22/us/police-officers-involved-in-pepper-spraying-placed-on-leave.html.

Mehta, N. (2009). Nonprofits and lobbying: Yes, they can! *Business Law Today*, 18(4). Retrieved January 14, 2015, from http://apps.americanbar.org/buslaw/blt/2009-03-04/mehta.shtml.

Melish, J. P. (2000). *Disowning slavery: Gradual emancipation and "race" in New England, 1780–1860*. Ithaca, NY: Cornell University Press.

Merton, R. K. (1957). *Social theory and social structure*. Glencoe, IL: Free Press.

Miedzian, M. (2010, October 28). Capitalism *uber alles*: How the American working class got brainwashed. *Huffington Post*. Retrieved January 14, 2015, from http://www.huffingtonpost.com/myriam-miedzian/capitalism-uber-alles-how_1_b_775495.html.

Mieras, E. (2008). *College students, social responsibility, and settlement house work*. Paper presented at the annual meeting of the American Studies Association, Albuquerque, NM.

Mihalynuk, T. V., Seifer, S. D., & Community Campus Partnerships for Health (CCPH). (2007). Higher education service-learning in rural communities. National Service Learning Clearinghouse. Retrieved January 14, 2013, from http://www.servicelearning.org/instant_info/fact_sheets/he_facts/rural_communities.

Miller, M. (2009). A critique of John McKnight and John Kretzmann's "Community organizing in the eighties: Toward a post-Alinsky agenda." *COMM-ORG Papers*, 15. Retrieved July 30, 2015, from http://comm-org.wisc.edu/papers2009/miller.htm.

Mills, C. W. (1959). *The sociological imagination*. New York: Oxford University Press.

Minieri, J., & Getsos, P. (2007). *Tools for radical democracy: How to organize for power in your community*. San Francisco: Jossey-Bass.

Miron, D., & Moely, B. (2006). Community agency voice and benefit in service-learning. *Michigan Journal of Community Service Learning*, 12(2), 27–31.

Mitchell, T. D. (2007). Critical service learning as social justice education: A case study of the citizen scholars program. *Equity and Excellence in Education, 40*(2), 101–112.

Mitchell, T. D. (2008). Traditional vs. critical service-learning: Engaging the literature to differentiate two models. *Michigan Journal of Community Service Learning, 14*(2), 50–65.

Mitchell, T. D. (2010). Challenges and possibilities: Linking social justice and service-learning. *Michigan Journal of Community Service Learning, 17*(1), 94–97.

Mitchell, T. D., Donahue, D. M., & Young-Law, C. (2012). Service learning as a pedagogy of whiteness. *Equity and Excellence in Education, 45*(4), 612–629.

Moely, B. E., Furco, A., & Reed, J. (2008). Charity and social change: The impact of individual preferences on service-learning outcomes. *Michigan Journal of Community Service Learning, 15*(1), 37–48.

Moely, B. E., & Ilustre, V. (2011). University students' views of a public service graduation requirement. *Michigan Journal of Community Service Learning, 17*(2), 43–58.

Moely, B. E., & Miron, D. (2005). College students' preferred approaches to community service: Charity and social change paradigms. In S. Root, J. Callahan, & S. H. Billig (Eds.), *Improving service-learning practice: Research on models to enhance impacts* (pp. 61–78). Greenwich, CT: Information Age.

Mohan, G. (2001). Beyond participation: Strategies for deeper empowerment. In B. Cooke & U. Kathari (Eds.), *Participation: The new tyranny?* (pp. 153–167). New York: Zed Books.

Montague, F. C. (1888). Arnold Toynbee. In H. B. Adams (Ed.), *Johns Hopkins University studies in historical and political science: Vol. 7. Social science, municipal and federal government* (pp. 1–57). Baltimore: John Murphy.

Mooney, L. A., & Edwards, B. (2001). Experiential learning in sociology: Service learning and other community-based learning initiatives. *Teaching Sociology, 29*(2), 181–194.

Morgridge Center for Public Service. (2008). *Faculty introduction to service-learning/community-based research.* Retrieved January 14, 2015, from http://morgridge.wisc.edu/faculty/documents/S-l_cbr_faculty-intro.ppt.

Morris, A. (1981). Black southern student sit-in movement: An analysis of internal organization. *American Sociological Review, 46*(6), 744–767.

Morris Justice Project. (n.d.). *Morris Justice: A public science project.* Retrieved January 14, 2015, from http://morrisjustice.org/.

Morrow, P. C. (1978). Functionalism, conflict theory and the synthesis syndrome in sociology. *International Review of Modern Sociology, 8,* 209–225.

Morton, K. (1995). The irony of service: Charity, project and social change in service-learning. *Michigan Journal of Community Service Learning, 2*(1), 19–32.

Mosse, D. (2001). "People's knowledge," participation and patronage: Operations and representations in rural development. In B. Cooke & U. Kathari (Eds.), *Participation: The new tyranny?* (pp. 16–23). New York: Zed Books.

MoveOn.org. (n.d.). *Community power map guide.* Retrieved January 14, 2015, from http://www.moveon.org/organize/campaigns/powermap.html.

Muirhead, B., & Woolcock, G. (2008). Doing what we know we should: Engaged scholarship and community development. *Gateways: International Journal of Community Research and Engagement, 1,* 8–30. Retrieved July 17, 2015, from http://epress.lib.uts.edu.au/journals/index.php/ijcre/article/view/516.

Mulligan, M., Scanlon, C., & Welch, N. (2008). Renegotiating community life: Arts, agency, inclusion, and wellbeing. *Gateways: International Journal of Community*

Research and Engagement, 1, 48–72. Retrieved July 17, 2015, from http://epress.lib.uts
.edu.au/journals/index.php/ijcre/article/view/591/845.

Muñoz, C. (1989). *Youth, identity, power: The Chicano movement.* New York: Verso.

Murphy, B. (2014). Civic learning in community colleges. In J. N. Reich (Ed.), *Civic engagement, civic development, and higher education* (pp. 19–24). Washington, DC: Bringing Theory to Practice.

Mz. Many Names. (2008). *Attributing words.* Retrieved January 14, 2015, from http://unnecessaryevils.blogspot.com/2008/11/attributing-words.html.

National and Community Service Trust Act of 1990. Retrieved January 14, 2015, from http://www.nationalservice.gov/pdf/cncs_statute.pdf.

National Service Learning Clearinghouse. (2013). *Historical timeline.* Retrieved February 12, 2013, from http://www.servicelearning.org/what_is_service-learning/history.

National Society for Experiential Education. (2014). *Previous award winners.* Retrieved July 21, 2015, from https://nsee.memberclicks.net/previous-award-winners.

National Task Force on Civic Learning and Democratic Engagement. (2012). *A crucible moment: College learning and democracy's future.* Washington, DC: Association of American Colleges and Universities.

Neel, J. (2008). *Taking the measure of health care in America.* Retrieved January 14, 2015, from the National Public Radio website: http://www.npr.org/templates/story/story.php?storyId=92136549.

Newfield, C. (2008). *Unmaking the public university.* Cambridge, MA: Harvard University Press.

Nisbet, R. A. (1953). *The quest for community.* New York: Oxford University Press.

Northeastern University. (2013). *Experiential learning.* Retrieved July 30, 2015, from http://www.northeastern.edu/experiential-learning/service-learning/.

Northeastern University. (2014). *Experiential learning.* Retrieved July 21, 2015, from http://www.northeastern.edu/experiential-learning/index.html.

Novack, G. (1975). *Pragmatism versus Marxism: An appraisal of John Dewey's philosophy.* New York: Pathfinder Press.

Nyden, P., & Wiewal, W. (1992). Collaborative research: Harnessing the tensions between researcher and practitioner. *American Sociologist, 23*(4), 43–55.

Oden, R. S., & Casey, T. A. (2007). Advancing service learning as a transformative method for social justice work. In J. Z. Calderón (Ed.), *Race, poverty, and social justice: Multidisciplinary perspectives through service learning* (pp. 1–22). Sterling, VA: Stylus.

O'Kane, T. (2015). *Nesting in the city: Birds, children and a city park as teachers of environmental literacy.* Unpublished doctoral dissertation, University of Wisconsin, Madison.

Open Songbook Project. (2009). *Democracy now: Utah Phillips talks about Myles Horton and the Highlander Folk School.* Retrieved January 14, 2015, from https://www.youtube.com/watch?v=jbEWfWuqOTY.

Palmer, N. (2012). Hegemony: The haves and "soon to haves." *Sociology in Focus.* Retrieved January 14, 2015, from http://www.sociologyinfocus.com/2012/02/08/hegemony-the-haves-and-soon-to-haves/#more-1345.

Parker-Gwin, R., & Mabry, J. B. (1998). Service learning as pedagogy and civic education: Comparing outcomes for three models. *Teaching Sociology, 26*(4), 276–291.

Patel, V. S. (2011). Moving toward an inclusive model of allyship for racial justice. *Vermont Connection, 32*, 78–88. Retrieved January 14, 2015, from http://www.uvm.edu/~vtconn/v32/Volume_32_Full.pdf#page=78.

Pawlowski, D. R. (2007). *Tutorial 1: Introduction to service-learning (community-based learning/CBL) and its connection to Jesuit ideals.* Retrieved January 14, 2015, from https://www.creighton.edu/fileadmin/user/AEA/ServiceLearning/docs/what_is_slfinal.ppt.

Paxton, P. (1999). Is social capital declining in the United States? A multiple indicator assessment. *American Journal of Sociology, 105,* 88–127.

People's Grocery. (n.d.). *Allyship program.* Retrieved January 14, 2015, from http://www.peoplesgrocery.org/allyship_program.

Perlstein, D. (1990). Teaching freedom: SNCC and the creation of the Mississippi Freedom Schools. *History of Education Quarterly, 30*(3), 297–324.

Petersen-Smith, K., & Bean, B. (2014). *Fighting racism and the limits of "ally-ship."* Retrieved July 30, 2015, from http://socialistworker.org/2015/05/14/fighting-racism-and-the-limits-of-allyship.

Peterson, T. H., Dolan, T., & Hanft, S. (2010). Partnering with youth organizers to prevent violence: An analysis of relationships, power, and change. *Progress in Community Health Partnerships: Research, Education, and Action, 4*(3), 235–242.

Piaget, J. (1970/1983). Piaget's theory. In W. Kessen (Ed.), *Handbook of child psychology: Vol. 1. History, theory, and methods* (pp. 103–126). New York: Wiley.

Piketty, T. (2014). *Capital in the twenty-first century* (A. Goldhammer, Trans.). Cambridge, MA: Harvard University Press.

Piven, F. F., & Cloward, R. (1993). *Regulating the poor: The functions of public welfare* (2nd ed.). New York: Vintage.

Polanyi, M., & Cockburn, L. (2003). Opportunities and pitfalls of community-based research: A case study. *Michigan Journal of Community Service Learning, 9*(3), 16–25.

Porfilio, B. J., & Hickman, H. (2011). Introduction. In B. J. Porfilio & H. Hickman (Eds.), *Critical service-learning as revolutionary pedagogy: A project of student agency and action* (pp. ix–xx). Charlotte, NC: Information Age.

Porpora, D. (1999). Action research: The highest stage of service learning? In J. Ostrow, G. Hesser, & S. Enos (Eds.), *Cultivating the sociological imagination: Concepts and models for service-learning in sociology* (pp. 121–123). Washington, DC: American Association for Higher Education.

Porter, J. R., Summers, M., Toton, S., & Aisenstein, H. (2008). Service-learning with a food stamp enrollment campaign: Community and student benefits. *Michigan Journal of Community Service Learning, 14*(2), 66–75.

Pritchard, I. A. (2001). Community service and service-learning in America: The state of the art. In A. Furco & S. H. Billig (Eds.), *Service learning: The essence of the pedagogy* (pp. 3–22). Charlotte, NC: Information Age.

Putnam, R. D. (1995). Bowling alone: America's declining social capital. *Journal of Democracy, 6,* 65–78.

Putnam, R. D. (2000). *Bowling alone: The collapse and revival of American community.* New York: Simon & Schuster.

Rahman, M. A. (1991). The theoretical standpoint of PAR. In O. Fals-Borda & M. A. Rahman (Eds.), *Action and knowledge: Breaking the monopoly with participatory action research* (pp. 13–23). New York: Apex Press.

Rakoff, J. S. (2015, May 21). Mass incarceration: The silence of the judges. *New York Review of Books.* Retrieved July 23, 2015, from http://www.nybooks.com/articles/archives/2015/may/21/mass-incarceration-silence-judges/.

Rancière, J. (1991). *The ignorant schoolmaster: Five lessons in intellectual emancipation.* Stanford, CA: Stanford University Press.

Ransby, B. (2003). *Ella Baker and the Black freedom movement: A radical democratic vision.* Chapel Hill: University of North Carolina Press.

Ray, E. J. (2013, July 24). The value of a liberal arts education in today's global marketplace. *Huffington Post.* Retrieved January 14, 2015, from http://www.huffingtonpost.com/edward-j-ray/the-value-of-a-liberal-arts-education_b_3647765.html.

Reardon, K. (1999). Promoting community development through empowerment planning: The East St. Louis Action Research Project. In W. D. Keating & N. Krumholz (Eds.), *Rebuilding urban neighborhoods* (124–139). Newbury Park, CA: Sage.

Reeb, R. N., & Folger, S. F. (2013). Community outcomes in service learning: Research and practice from a systems theory perspective. In P. H. Clayton, R. G. Bringle, & J. A. Hatcher (Eds.), *Research on service learning: Conceptual frameworks and assessment: Communities, institutions, and partnerships* (pp. 389–418). Sterling, VA: Stylus.

Reeves, R. (2002). *President Nixon: Alone in the White House.* New York: Simon & Schuster.

Reinke, S. J. (2003). Making a difference: Does service-learning promote civic engagement in MPA students? *Journal of Public Affairs Education, 9,* 129–157.

Rhoads, R. A. (1997). *Community service and higher learning: Explorations of the caring self.* Albany: State University of New York Press.

Rhoads, R. A. (1998). Critical multiculturalism and service learning. In R. A. Rhoads & J. P. F. Howard (Eds.), *Academic service learning: A pedagogy of action and reflection* (pp. 39–46). San Francisco: Jossey-Bass.

Rice, K., & Pollack, S. (2000). Developing a critical pedagogy of service learning: Preparing self-reflective, culturally aware, and responsive community participants. In C. R. O'Grady (Ed.), *Integrating service learning and multicultural education in colleges and universities* (pp. 115–134). Mahwah, NJ: Erlbaum.

Rimmerman, C. A. (2011). *Service-learning and the liberal arts: How and why it works.* New York: Lexington Books.

Ritzer, G. (1993). *The McDonaldization of society: An investigation into the changing character of contemporary social life.* Thousand Oaks, CA: Pine Forge Press.

Robinson, J. W., & Green, G. P. (2011a). Developing communities. In J. W. Robinson & G. P. Green (Eds.), *Introduction to community development: Theory, practice, and service-learning* (pp. 1–10). Thousand Oaks, CA: Sage.

Robinson, J. W., & Green, G. P. (Eds.). (2011b). *Introduction to community development: Theory, practice, and service-learning.* Thousand Oaks, CA: Sage.

Robinson, T. (2000a). Dare the school build a new social order? *Michigan Journal of Community Service Learning, 7*(1), 142–157.

Robinson, T. (2000b). Service-learning as justice advocacy: Can political scientists do politics? *PS: Political Science and Politics, 33,* 605–612.

Rockefeller, S. C. (1991). *John Dewey: Religious faith and democratic humanism.* New York: Columbia University Press.

Rodgers, C. (2002). Defining reflection: Another look at John Dewey and reflective thinking. *Teachers College Record, 104*(4), 842–866.

Rodin, J. (2007). *The university and urban revival: Out of the ivory tower and into the streets.* Philadelphia: University of Pennsylvania Press.

Rogers, C. R. (1969). *Freedom to learn.* Columbus, OH: Charles E. Merrill.

Rogers, C. R. (1983). *Freedom to learn for the 80's.* Columbus, OH: Charles E. Merrill.

Rogers, M. B. (1990). *Cold anger: A story of faith and power politics.* Denton: University of North Texas Press.

Rosas, M. (2010). *College student activism: An exploration of learning outcomes.* Unpublished doctoral dissertation, University of Iowa. Retrieved July 20, 2015, from http://ir.uiowa.edu/cgi/viewcontent.cgi?article=1774&context=etd.

Rosenberger, C. (2000). Beyond empathy: Developing critical consciousness through service learning. In C. R. O'Grady (Ed.), *Integrating service learning and multicultural education in colleges and universities* (pp. 23–43). Mahwah, NJ: Erlbaum.

Ross, F. (1989). *Conquering Goliath: Cesar Chavez at the beginning.* Keene, CA: United Farm Workers.

Ross, J. A. (2014). *Evaluation of community-campus partnerships in the post-Katrina Lower 9th Ward recovery.* Unpublished doctoral dissertation, University of Wisconsin, Madison.

Rossi, P. H., Lipsey, M. W., & Freeman, H. E. (2004). *Evaluation: A systematic approach* (7th ed.). Thousand Oaks, CA: Sage.

Rothman, J. (1995). *Strategies of community intervention: Macro practice.* Itasca, IL: Peacock.

Russell, D., & Ison, R. L. (2000). The research-development relationship in rural communities: An opportunity for contextual science. In R. Ison & D. Russell (Eds.), *Agricultural extension and rural development: Breaking out of traditions* (pp. 10–31). New York: Cambridge University Press.

Ryan, W. (1976). *Blaming the victim.* New York: Random House.

Salant, P., & Laumatia, L. (2011). Better together: Coeur d'Alene Reservation Communities and the University of Idaho. *Journal of Higher Education Outreach and Engagement, 15*(3), 101–112. Retrieved January 14, 2015, from http://openjournals.libs.uga.edu/index.php/jheoe/article/view/577/464.

Saltmarsh, J. (1996). Education for critical citizenship: John Dewey's contribution to the pedagogy of service learning. *Michigan Journal of Community Service Learning, 3*(1), 13–21.

Sandy, M. (2013). Tracing the liberal arts traditions. *Humanity and Society, 37*(4), 306–326.

Sandy, M., & Holland, B. A. (2006). Different worlds and common ground: Community partner perspectives on campus-community partnerships. *Michigan Journal of Community Service Learning, 13*(1), 30–43.

Schaffer, M., Bonniwell, D., De Haan, J., Thomas, G., & Holmquist, J. (2014, June 13). *Reducing health disparities through community engagement.* Paper presented at the Upper Midwest Civic Engagement Summit, University of Wisconsin, Stout.

Schensul, J. J., & Berg, M. (2004). Youth participatory action research: A transformative approach to service-learning. *Michigan Journal of Community Service Learning, 10*(3), 76–88.

Schmidt, A., & Robby, M. (2002). What's the value of service-learning to the community? *Michigan Journal of Community Service Learning, 9*(1), 27–33.

Schneider, C. J., Hanemaayer, A., & Nolan, K. (2014). Public teaching as service sociology. In A. J. Treviño & K. M. McCormack (Eds.), *Service sociology and academic engagement in social problems* (pp. 177–190). Burlington, VT: Ashgate.

Schneider, P. (2013a, December 1). Q&A: Lingran Kong works to light a passion for workers rights at UW-Madison. *Capital Times.* Retrieved January 14, 2015, from http://host.madison.com/ct/news/local/writers/pat_schneider/q-a-lingran-kong-works-to-light-a-passion-for/article_de42a38c-5790-11e3-9e9c-0019bb2963f4.html.

Schneider, P. (2013b, November 20). Men's expedition into homelessness in Madison sets off lively discussion on social media. *Capital Times.* Retrieved January 14, 2015, from

http://host.madison.com/ct/news/local/writers/pat_schneider/men-s-expedition-into
-homelessness-in-madison-sets-off-lively/article_b3331dd0-5181-11e3-890c-001a4b
cf887a.html.

Schor, J. (1993). *The overworked American: The unexpected decline of leisure* (7th ed.). New York: Basic Books.

Scientific American. (n.d.). Citizen science. Retrieved January 14, 2015, from http://www.scientificamerican.com/citizen-science/.

Sciulli, D. (2011). *Etzioni's critical functionalism: Communitarian origins and principles.* Boston: Brill.

Seider, S., Huguley, J. P., & Novick, S. (2013). College students, diversity, and community service learning. *Teachers College Record.* Retrieved January 14, 2015, from http://www.tcrecord.org/Content.asp?ContentId=16880.

Seifer, S. D., Shore, N., Drew, E., Bajorunaite, R., Wong, K., & Moy, L. (2009, November). *Understanding community-based processes for research ethics review.* Oral presentation at the 137th Annual Meeting and Exposition of the American Public Health Association, Philadelphia, PA. Retrieved January 14, 2015, from http://depts.washington.edu/ccph/pdf_files/p-ethics-apha1109.pdf.

Sen, R. (2003). *Stir it up: Lessons in community organizing and advocacy.* San Francisco: Jossey-Bass.

Shabazz, D. R., & Cooks, L. M. (2014). The pedagogy of community service-learning discourse: From deficit to asset mapping in the Re-envisioning Media Project. *Journal of Community Engagement and Scholarship, 7*(1). Retrieved July 30, 2015, from http://jces.ua.edu/the-pedagogy-of-community-service-learning-discourse-from-deficit-to-asset-mapping-in-the-re-envisioning-media-project/.

Shor, I. (1992). *Empowering education: Critical teaching for social change.* Chicago: University of Chicago Press.

Sigmon, R. (1979). Service learning: Three principles. *Synergist 9-11.* Retrieved January 14, 2015, from http://critical.tamucc.edu/~wiki/uploads/AWebb/sl3p.pdf.

Silka, L., Cleghorn, G., Grullon, M., & Tellez, T. (2008). Creating community-based participatory research in a diverse community: A case study. *Journal of Empirical Research on Human Research Ethics, 3,* 5–16.

Silvertown, J. (2009). A new dawn for citizen science. *Trends in Ecology and Evolution, 24*(9), 467–471.

Simmel, G. (1905/1956). The metropolis and mental life. In K. Wolff (Ed. & Trans.), *The sociology of Georg Simmel* (pp. 409–424). New York: Free Press.

Simmons, V. C., & Toole, P. (2003). *Service-Learning Diversity/Equity project report executive summary.* Retrieved July 18, 2015, from https://web.archive.org/web/20061001223259/http://www.nylc.org/objects/inaction/initiatives/DiveristyEquity/summer03articles/1EDExSummary2003.pdf.

Simonaitis, P. (2010, October 12). MUSG service amendment shot down. *Marquette Tribune.* Retrieved January 14, 2015, from http://marquettetribune.org/(2010)/10/12/news/musg-mg1-tw2-dac3-service-amendment-shot-down/.

Skelton, G. (2004, August 5). Forcing community service by college students would be mistake. *Los Angeles Times.* Retrieved January 14, 2015, from http://articles.latimes.com/(2004)/aug/05/local/me-cap5.

Slayton, B. (1986). *Back of the yards: The making of a local democracy.* Chicago: University of Chicago Press.

Smith, A. (1776). *An inquiry into the nature and causes of the wealth of nations.* London: W. Strahan and T. Cadell.

Smith, L. T. (2012). *Decolonizing methodologies: Research and indigenous peoples.* London: Zed Books.

Snyder, Z. K., & Karlen, J. C. (2014). The power of place: Community partnerships and student experiences. In A. J. Treviño & K. M. McCormack (Eds.), *Service sociology and academic engagement in social problems* (pp. 91–102). Burlington, VT: Ashgate.

Social Sciences and Humanities Research Council. (2009–2011). *SSHRC's knowledge mobilization strategy.* Retrieved January 14, 2015, from http://www.sshrc-crsh.gc.ca/about-au_sujet/publications/KMbPI_FinalE.pdf.

Social Sciences and Humanities Research Council. (2013). *Community-university research alliances.* Retrieved January 14, 2015, from http://www.sshrc-crsh.gc.ca/funding-financement/programs-programmes/cura-aruc-eng.aspx.

Speck, B. W., & Hoppe, S. (2004a). Introduction. In B. W. Speck & S. Hoppe (Eds.), *Service-learning: History, theory, and issues* (pp. vii–xi) Westfield, CT: Praeger.

Speck, B. W., & Hoppe, S. (Eds.). (2004b). *Service-learning: History, theory, and issues.* Westfield, CT: Praeger.

Squires, G. D. (Ed.). (2003). *Organizing access to capital: Advocacy and the democratization of financial institutions.* Philadelphia: Temple University Press.

Stall, S., & Stoecker, R. (1998). Community organizing or organizing community? Gender and the crafts of empowerment. *Gender and Society, 12,* 729–756.

Staples, L. (2004). *Roots to power: A manual for grassroots organizing.* New York: Praeger.

Stein, M. (1960). *The eclipse of community: An interpretation of American studies.* New York: Harper & Row.

Stengel, B. (2007). Dewey's pragmatic poet: Reconstructing Jane Addams's philosophical impact. *Education and Culture, 23*(2), 27–62.

Stevans, L. (2009). The effect of endogenous right-to-work laws on business and economic conditions in the United States: A multivariate approach. *Review of Law and Economics, 5*(1), 595–614.

Stevens, Ch. (2003). Unrecognized roots of service-learning in African American social thought and action, 1890–1930. *Michigan Journal of Community Service Learning, 9*(2), 25–34.

Stoecker, R. (1992). Who takes out the garbage? Social reproduction as a neglected dimension of social movement research. In G. Miller & J. A. Holstein (Eds.), *Perspectives on social problems* (Vol. 3). Greenwich, CT: JAI Press.

Stoecker, R. (1994). *Defending community: The struggle for alternative redevelopment in Cedar-Riverside.* Philadelphia: Temple University Press.

Stoecker, R. (1998). Capital against community. *Research in Community Sociology, 8,* 15–41.

Stoecker, R. (2003a). Community-based research: From practice to theory and back again. *Michigan Journal of Community Service Learning, 10*(2), 35–46.

Stoecker, R. (2003b). Understanding the development-organizing dialectic. *Journal of Urban Affairs, 25,* 493–512.

Stoecker, R. (2004). The mystery of the missing social capital and the ghost of social structure: Why community development can't win. In R. Silverman (Ed.), *Community-based organizations in contemporary urban society: The intersection of social capital and local context* (pp. 53–66). Detroit, MI: Wayne State University Press.

Stoecker, R. (2009). Are we talking the walk of community-based research? *Action Research, 7,* 385–404.

Stoecker, R. (2012). Community-based research and the two forms of social change. *Journal of Rural Social Sciences, 27*(2), 83–98.

Stoecker, R. (2013). *Research methods for community change* (2nd ed.). Thousand Oaks, CA: Sage.

Stoecker, R. (in press). The fundamental lesson. In C. Dolgon, T. Mitchell, & T. K. Eatman (Eds.), *Cambridge handbook on service learning and community engagement*. New York: Cambridge University Press.

Stoecker, R., Beckman, M., & Min, B. H. (2010). Evaluating the community impact of higher education civic engagement. In H. E. Fitzgerald, D. L. Zimmerman, C. Burack, & S. Seifer (Eds.), *Handbook of engaged scholarship: The contemporary landscape: Vol. 2. Community-campus partnerships* (pp. 177–196). East Lansing: Michigan State University Press.

Stoecker, R., & Beckwith, D. (1992). Advancing Toledo's neighborhood movement through participatory action research: Integrating activist and academic approaches. *Clinical Sociology Review, 10*, 198–213.

Stoecker, R., Loving, K., Reddy, M., & Bollig, N. (2010). Can community-based research guide service-learning? *Journal of Community Practice, 18*, 280–296.

Stoecker, R., & Schmidt, C. (2008). *Geographic disparities in access to service learning.* Paper presented at the annual meeting of the Rural Sociological Society, Manchester, NH.

Stoecker, R., & Tryon, E. (2009a). Unheard voices: Community organizations and service learning. In R. Stoecker & E. Tryon (with A. Hilgendorf) (Eds.), *The unheard voices: Community organizations and service learning* (pp. 1–18). Philadelphia: Temple University Press.

Stoecker, R., & Tryon, E. (with Hilgendorf, A.) (Eds.). (2009b). *The unheard voices: Community organizations and service learning.* Philadelphia: Temple University Press.

Stokamer, S. (2013). Pedagogical catalysts of civic competence: The development of a critical epistemological model for community-based learning. *Journal of Higher Education Outreach and Engagement, 17*(1), 113–122.

Strand, K., Marullo, S., Cutforth, N., Stoecker, R., & Donohue, P. (2003). *Community-based research and higher education: Principles and practices.* San Francisco: Jossey-Bass.

Stukas, A. A., Snyder, M., & Clary, E. G. (1999). The effects of "mandatory volunteerism" on intentions to volunteer. *Psychological Science, 10*(1), 59–64.

Summers, G. F. (1986). Rural community development. *Annual Review of Sociology, 12*, 341–371.

Swaminathan, R. (2007). Educating for the "real world": The hidden curriculum of community service-learning. *Equity and Excellence in Education, 40*(2), 134–143.

Swanson, D. (2010). *Should service learning be mandatory for college students?* Retrieved January 14, 2015, from http://daleswanson.blogspot.ca/(2010)/12/should-service-learning-be-mandatory.html.

Sylvester, D. (2009). Service-learning for political engagement program. *Journal for Civic Commitment, 14.* Retrieved July 23, 2015, from http://ccncce.org/articles/service-learning-for-political-engagement-program/.

Taylor, V. (1989). Social movement continuity: The women's movement in abeyance. *American Sociological Review, 54*, 761–775.

Teller. (2012, March). Teller reveals his secrets. *Smithsonian Magazine.* Retrieved January 14, 2015, from http://www.smithsonianmag.com/arts-culture/teller-reveals-his-secrets-100744801/?no-ist.

Tennessee Guerilla Women. (2010). *Backlash grows: Students protest Belmont's anti-gay discrimination.* Retrieved January 6, 2015, from http://guerillawomentn.blogspot .com/2010/12/backlash-grows-students-protest.html.

Till, J. (2013). *Icons of Toynbee Hall: Samuel Barnett.* Retrieved January 14, 2015, from http://www.toynbeehall.org.uk/data/files/About_Toynbee_Hall/Barnett_low_res.pdf.

Tilley-Lubbs, G. A. (2009). Good intentions pave the way to hierarchy: A retrospective autoethnographic approach. *Michigan Journal of Community Service Learning, 16*(1), 59–68.

Tinkler, B. (2010). Reaching for a radical community-based research model. *Journal of Community Engagement and Scholarship, 3*(2), 5–19.

Tocqueville, A. de. (1840/1988). *Democracy in America* (J. P. Mayer, Ed., G. Lawrence, Trans.). New York: Harper & Row.

Toennies, F. (1887/1963). *Community and society.* New York: Harper & Row.

Torre, M., Stoudt, B., Bartley, P., Bracy, F., Downs, A., Greene, C., et al. (2014, July 12). *Keynote: Morris Justice Project.* Presentation at the "What Went Wrong": Reflecting and Learning from Community-Engaged Research Conference, Minneapolis, MN.

Treviño, A. J., & McCormack, K. M. (2014). Introduction: What is service sociology? In A. J. Treviño & K. M. McCormack (Eds.), *Service sociology and academic engagement in social problems* (pp. 1–24). Burlington, VT: Ashgate.

Tryon, E., Hilgendorf, A., & Scott, I. (2009). The heart of partnership: Communication and relationship. In R. Stoecker & E. Tryon (with A. Hilgendorf) (Eds.), *The unheard voices: Community organizations and service learning* (pp. 96–115). Philadelphia: Temple University Press.

Tucker, R. E. (1999). Biting the pragmatist bullet: Why service learning can do without epistemology. *Michigan Journal of Community Service Learning, 6*(1), 5–14.

Tudiver, N. (1999). *Universities for sale: Resisting corporate control over Canadian higher education.* Toronto, Ontario, Canada: Lorimer.

UK Social Centres Network. (n.d.). *What's this place?* Retrieved January 14, 2015, from http://socialcentrestories.files.wordpress.com/(2008)/06/whats-this-place_lo-res.pdf.

Ullman, O. (1986, May 25). Reagan wooing youth vote for GOP. *The Inquirer.* Retrieved January 14, 2015, from http://articles.philly.com/(1986)-05-25/news/26050928_1 _young-voters-reagan-presidency-youth-vote.

UMKC Service-Learning. (2013a). *Community service-students.* Retrieved January 14, 2015, from http://www.umkc.edu/servicelearning/comservice.asp.

UMKC Service-Learning. (2013b). *Faculty and staff give back to Kansas City.* Retrieved January 14, 2015, from http://www.umkc.edu/servicelearning/FacStaffService.aspx.

University Neighborhood Partners. (2013). *How we work in partnership.* Retrieved January 14, 2015, from the University of Utah website: http://partners.utah.edu/who-are-we/ how-we-work-in-partnership/.

University of British Columbia. (2012a, July 9). "Aboriginal Community as Teacher" program wins national award. *Medicine Matters.* Retrieved July 21, 2015, from http:// blogs.ubc.ca/medicinematters/2012/07/09/aboriginal-community-as-teacher-program -wins-national-award/.

University of British Columbia. (2012b). *University of British Columbia—The Aboriginal community as teacher.* Retrieved July 21, 2015, from the J. W. McConnell Family Foundation website: http://www.mcconnellfoundation.ca/en/resources/multimedia/video/ university-of-british-columbia-the-aboriginal-community-as-teach.

University of Central Florida, Office of Experiential Learning. (n.d.). *Service-learning.* Retrieved July 21, 2015, from http://www.explearning.ucf.edu/categories/143.

University of Nebraska–Kearney. (2015). *Service-learning as pedagogy.* Retrieved July 21, 2015, from http://www.unk.edu/offices/service-learning/.

University of Washington. (2015). *Center for Experiential Learning and Diversity.* Retrieved July 21, 2015, from http://expd.uw.edu/.

U.S. Census. (2013). *Poverty.* Retrieved January 14, 2015, from http://www.census.gov/hhes/www/poverty/about/overview/.

van de Sande, A., & Schwartz, K. (2011). *Research for social justice: A community-based approach.* Black Point, Nova Scotia, Canada: Fernwood.

Vancouver Citizens Committee. (2014). *The citizen's handbook.* Retrieved January 14, 2015, from http://www.citizenshandbook.org/.

Vassar Miscellany Weekly. (1916, October 13). Should the College Settlements Association have a place in the college community? Retrieved January 14, 2015, from http://news paperarchives.vassar.edu/cgi-bin/imageserver/imageserver.pl?oid=miscellany19161013 -01&key=&getpdf=true.

Verjee, B. (2012). Critical race feminism: A transformative vision for service-learning engagement. *Journal of Community Engagement and Scholarship, 5*(1). Retrieved January 14, 2015, from http://jces.ua.edu/critical-race-feminism-a-transformative-vision-for -service-learning-engagement/.

Vernon, A., & Foster, L. (2002). Community agency perspectives in higher education service-learning and volunteerism. In S. Billig & A. Furco (Eds.), *Service-learning through a multidisciplinary lens: Advances in service-learning research* (pp. 53–175). Charlotte, NC: Information Age.

Vernon, A., & Ward, K. (1999). Campus and community partnerships: Assessing impacts and strengthening connections. *Michigan Journal of Community Service Learning, 6*(1), 32–37.

Vidal, A., Nye, N., Walker, C., Manjarrez, C., & Romanik, C. (2002). *Lessons from the Community Outreach Partnership Center program.* Washington, DC: U.S. Department of Housing and Urban Development, Office of Policy Development and Research. www.cpn.org/topics/youth/highered/pdfs/COPC_Program.pdf.

von Hoffman, N. (1958, February 9). Professional correspondence. Industrial Areas Foundation Records, Special Collections and University Archives, University of Illinois at Chicago.

Wade, R. C. (2000). From a distance: Service-learning and social justice. In C. R. O'Grady (Ed.), *Integrating service learning and multicultural education in colleges and universities* (pp. 93–111). Mahwah, NJ: Erlbaum.

Walker, T. (2000). A feminist challenge to community service: A call to politicize service-learning. In B. J. Balliet & K. Heffernan (Eds.), *The practice of change: Concepts and models for service-learning in women's studies* (pp. 25–45). Washington, DC: American Association for Higher Education.

Warren, J. L. (2012). Does service-learning increase student learning? A meta-analysis. *Michigan Journal of Community Service Learning, 18*(2), 56–61.

Warren, M. (2001). *Dry bones rattling: Community building to revitalize American democracy.* Princeton, NJ: Princeton University Press.

Washburn, J. (2005). *University Inc.: The corporate corruption of higher education.* New York: Basic Books.

Weah, W., Simmons, V. C., & Hall, M. (2000). Service-learning and multicultural/ multiethnic perspectives: From diversity to equity. *Phi Delta Kappan*, 673–675.

Weber, M. (1904/1949). Objectivity in social science. In E. A. Shils & H. A. Finch (Eds. & Trans.), *The methodology of the social sciences* (pp. 49–112). Glencoe, IL: Free Press.

Weinberg, A. S. (2003). Negotiating community-based research: A case study of the "Life's Work" project. *Michigan Journal of Community Service Learning, 9*(3), 26–35.

Westbrook, R. (1993). *John Dewey and American democracy.* Ithaca, NY: Cornell University Press.

Western Michigan University. (2014). *Service learning.* Retrieved January 14, 2015, from http://www.wmich.edu/sustainablebusiness/service-learning.

Westheimer, J., & Kahne, J. (2004). Educating the "good" citizen. *PS: Political Science and Politics, 37*, 241–247.

Whelan, J. (2007). Six reasons not to engage: Compromise, confrontation and the commons. *COMM-ORG Papers.* Retrieved July 14, 2015, from http://comm-org.wisc.edu/papers2007/whelan.htm.

Williams, D. R., & Ehrlich, T. (2000). Participants in, not spectators to, democracy: The discourse on civic responsibility in higher education essay review. *Michigan Journal of Community Service Learning, 7*(1), 158–164.

Williams, M. R. (2002). Consortia and institutional partnerships for community development. *New Directions for Higher Education, 120*, 29–36.

Williams, R. L., & Ferber, A. L. (2008). Facilitating smart-girl: Feminist pedagogy in service learning in action. *Feminist Teacher, 19*(1), 47–67.

Willis, C., Anders, C., & Stoecker, R. (2011). When the community leads. In L. Hossfeld, G. Nyden, & P. Nyden (Eds.), *Public sociology: Research, action, and change.* Thousand Oaks, CA: Pine Forge Press.

Witkop, L. (2005). *Enhancing education: The benefits of service learning.* Retrieved January 14, 2015, from http://www.back2college.com/servicelearning.htm.

Wolfe, D. E., & Byrne, E. T. (1975, April 9–11). Research on experiential learning: Enhancing the process. In R. H. Buskirk (Ed.), *Simulation games and experiential learning in action: Proceedings of the second national ABSEL conference, Bloomington, Indiana* (pp. 325–336). Austin: University of Texas, Bureau of Business Research.

Wolfe, T. (1976, August 23). The me decade. *New York Magazine.* Retrieved January 14, 2015, from http://nymag.com/news/features/45938/.

Wolfe, T. (n.d.). *About Tom Wolfe.* Retrieved January 14, 2015, from http://www.tomwolfe.com/bio.html.

Woods, J. (2014). 12 ways to be a white ally to Black people. *The Root.* Retrieved July 30, 2015, from http://www.theroot.com/articles/culture/2014/08/ferguson_how_white_people_can_be_allies.html.

Woolf, S. H. (2008). The meaning of translational research and why it matters. *JAMA, 299*(2), 211–213.

Wright, E. O. (1985). *Classes.* London: Verso.

Yeh, T. L. (2010). Service-learning and persistence of low-income, first-generation college students: An exploratory study. *Michigan Journal of Community Service Learning, 16*(2), 50–65.

Yin, J. S. (1998). The community development industry system: A case study of politics and institutions in Cleveland, 1967–1997. *Journal of Urban Affairs, 20*(2), 137–157.

Zald, M. N., & Ash, R. (1966). Social movement organizations: Growth, decay and change. *Social Forces, 44*(3), 327–341.

Index

Randy Stoecker is Professor in the Department of Community and Environmental Sociology at the University of Wisconsin, with a joint appointment in the University of Wisconsin–Extension Center for Community and Economic Development. He is the co-editor (with Elizabeth A. Tryon and Amy Hilgendorf) of *The Unheard Voices: Community Organization and Service Learning* (Temple).